Glasgow

Books by Maurice Lindsay

The Lowlands of Scotland: Glasgow and the North
The Lowlands of Scotland: Edinburgh and the South
The Scottish Renaissance
Robert Burns: the Man: his Work: the Legend
Clyde Waters
By Yon Bonnie Banks
The Discovery of Scotland
Environment: a Basic Human Right
The Eye is Delighted
Portrait of Glasgow
Robin Philipson
History of Scottish Literature
Lowland Scottish Villages
Francis George Scott and the Scottish Renaissance
The Buildings of Edinburgh (with Anthony F. Kersting)
Thank You For Having Me: A Personal Memoir
Unknown Scotland (with Dennis Hardley)
The Castles of Scotland
Count All Men Mortal: The Story of the Scottish Provident
Victorian and Edwardian Glasgow
Edinburgh: Past and Present (with David Bruce)
Glasgow
An Illustrated Guide to Glasgow 1837
The Burns Encyclopedia

POETRY
Collected Poems 1940–90
Walking Without An Overcoat
On the Face of It: Collected Poems Volume Two
News of the World
Comings and Goings
Worlds Apart

ANTHOLOGIES
Poetry Scotland 1–4 (4 with Hugh MacDiarmid)
No Scottish Twilight (with Fred Urquhart)
Modern Scottish Poetry: an Anthology of the Scottish Renaissance 1925–1985)
John Davidson: Selected Poems: with a preface by T.S. Eliot and an introduction by
    Hugh MacDiarmid
A Book of Scottish Verse
Scottish Poetry 1–4 (with George Bruce and Edwin Morgan)
Scottish Poetry 7–9 (with Alexander Scott and Roderick Watson)
Scotland: An Anthology
As I Remember: Ten Scottish Writers Recall How for Them Writing Began (Ed.)
Scottish Comic Verse

(With Joyce Lindsay)
The Scottish Dog
A Pleasure of Gardens
The Scottish Quotation Book
The Music Quotation Book
The Theatre and Opera-Lover's Quotation Book
The Burns Quotation Book
A Mini-Guide to Scottish Gardens

Glasgow

Fabric of a City

MAURICE LINDSAY

ROBERT HALE · LONDON

© *Maurice Lindsay 2001*
First published in Great Britain 2001

ISBN 0 7090 6518 3 (hardback)
ISBN 0 7090 6973 1 (paperback)

Robert Hale Limited
Clerkenwell House
Clerkenwell Green
London EC1R 0HT

2 4 6 8 10 9 7 5 3 1

Typeset by
Derek Doyle & Associates, Liverpool.
Printed by
Kyodo Printing Co. Pte Ltd, Singapore

'That Glasgow on the base of commerce rose
A noble fabric, all the World knows.'

Anon: *Glasgow Museum*, or *Weekly Instructor*, 1773

Contents

Acknowledgements

I should like to thank the following for permission to quote from copyright works under their control:

Mrs Lois Godfrey for a quotation from Naomi Mitchison's *The Bull Calves*; Charlie Allan for a quotation from John R. Allan's *A Farmer's Boy* (now reissued by Mercat Press); Professor Blake for permission to quote from his father, George Blake's *Heart of Scotland*; Stewart Conn and Bloodaxe Books for his poem 'Family Visit'; Edwin Morgan and Carcanet Press for lines from his poem 'Glasgow Green', from his *Collected Poems*; Billy Connolly, *The Sunday Times* and Tickety-Boo for his quotation on living in Glasgow; the MacDiarmid Estate and Carcanet Press for a poem by Hugh MacDiarmid and a prose quotation; Dr Ronald Mavor for a passage from James Bridie's autobiography *One Way of Living* and 'The West End Perk'; Tom Leonard for his poem 'The Good Thief'; The University of Glasgow for a quotation from Sir Compton Mackenzie's rectorial address; *The Observer* and Edward Mace for his quotation; Faber & Faber for permission to quote a few lines of verse by W.H. Auden and Chatto & Windus for a passage from Edwin Muir's autobiography.

Every effort has been made to trace the copyright-holders of works by authors no longer with us. Where I have been unsuccessful in doing so, I offer my apologies.

Thanks are due to the Mitchell Library, particularly the staff of the Glasgow Room, for assistance in many ways.

I should also like to thank both Joyce, my wife, and Mrs Joan Cunningham for coping with my arthriticky handwriting – and my wife in particular for checking the text and word-processing the final copy. Finally, I am deeply indebted to Mrs Fran Walker for proofreading and preparing the index.

Preface

W HAT EXACTLY IS the fabric of a city? Its buildings, streets and parks, certainly, but also the occupations that give rise to them; the character of its people and their pastimes and diversions, together with their social customs and the reactions of observing travellers to all these things. I have tried to weave these diversities into an impression of Glasgow and the forces that formed it that will, I hope, increase the reader's pleasure in the place.

Old houses opposite the Barony Church. The crow-stepped gable was a Scottish tradition

Economics influence place, dictating the buildings needed for earning a living, the degree of prosperity achieved influencing the quality of lifestyle enjoyed. I have therefore considered Glasgow's physical development and successive industrial phases together. The following section deals with Glasgow's people. Their pastimes and the views of visitors to Glasgow – 'as ithers see us', so to say – make up the remaining sections.

I am myself a Glaswegian. As a small boy I used to say the syllables of Glasgow over and over again, as a kind of proprietary mantra, experiencing what was to prove an early and continuing fascination with the place to which I belonged – a fascination which I hope this book reflects.

An author must, to some extent, depend on what previous writers have recorded and specialists sought to analyse and explain. I have quoted at length from early eye-witness writers in order to give period 'flavour', and I have identified my sources in my text. Since I myself have been an eye-witness for a considerable stretch of the twentieth century, I have recorded my own reactions, making this, quite openly, a very personal account of my native city, a gallimaufry perhaps. Readers wishing to investigate this or that particular aspect of the city should find the Select Bibliography on p.275 useful.

Some of the material in this book has been subsumed from my own earlier studies *Glasgow* (1989) and *Portrait of Glasgow* (1972 and 1981).

Let Glasgow Flourish

I

Here is the tree whose low bough Mungo tore
to flourish light in darkened monastery.
Here is the robin that, when wounded sore,
Mungo restored to flight and liberty.
Here is the Roman bell that Mungo brought
to toll throughout his city, so that those,
forgetting living's brevity, be taught
to pray for the departed soul's repose.
Here is the jewel an adulterous Queen
gave to a knight who had betrayed his King.

As the knight slept beside the trinket's gleam
his passing monarch saw the pretty thing;
seized it and threw it deep into the Clyde
to gulp a snatch-jawed salmon's swallowing.

Back to his palace went the King. Inside,
he saw his anxious throne-mate following.
He questioned her: *Show me the ring I gave you.*
'No, no,' she gasped. *Show it, on pain of death.*
'Unkind,' she flustered. *Weeping will not save you.*
With that, she rushed to Mungo, out of breath
blurting her story, begging him relent
and save her. Mungo, filled with saintly pity
at seeing her distressfully repent,
fleshed out the motto of his future city.

He scanned Clyde waters, east, west, north and south,
till down the river to his trailing hand
a salmon swam, the gold ring in its mouth,
and he retrieved the guilty marriage-band.

Thus legend has it. Had it not been so,
how ever could the legend-maker know?

13

II

About this Glasgow of yours, the man said;
*what are its people like? What sort of place
is it really?* Statues of the famous dead
frowned on George Square as I answered. 'See that face?
Yon woman there? And the two behind again?
Each of them feels a different Glasgow. No
sense of place is the same for any two men,
let alone thousands. All I can do is show
the Glasgow I have explored through eighty years.
Whoever you speak to, where you see, or go
down the labyrinths of history, there appears
another Glasgow; one that I couldn't know,
angles of vision imagining the mind
as varied as the range of humankind.'

Maurice Lindsay

The High Street *c.* 1840 with a market in progress

Illustrations

Illustration Credits

1   The Place

A SENSE OF PLACE and a sense of history are among the most valu-
able assets with which an individual can be gifted. It is often said
that there is no such thing as objective history; only a catalogue of
dates and happenings that professional historians interpret subjective-
ly in accordance with their politics or predilections. Much the same is
true of place; more than individual buildings, squares or open spaces,
yet presenting different associations and therefore a different meaning
to everyone. Glasgow was my first experience of the sense of place.

There have been settlements at Glasgow since the earliest times.
Stone Age remains were found on the Clyde, the river that flows
through Glasgow's heart and on which the life-blood of its prosperity
once depended. Canoes were unearthed in crannogs, prehistoric
canoe-like dwellings, in St Enoch's Square in 1780, Stockwell Street
in 1824 and the former Victoria Dock in 1875. We know, too, that
when the Romans occupied the Clyde Valley, the natives were then a
Druidian tribe called the Damoni, but it is virtually impossible to
trace the physical anatomy of Glasgow further back than the Middle
Ages.

The present city lies roughly in an area inside the Antonine Wall,
built by the Romans as an outpost to hold back the fierce northern
Caledonians. A Roman ford crossed the Clyde near the site of the Old
Glasgow Bridge. Just before the 1914–18 War, a Roman fort was exca-
vated at Balmuildy, near the then northern boundary of the modern
city, and one of the only two stone forts in the Antonine Wall. The
settlement in the Clyde Valley must surely have seemed a cold outpost
to its soldiers, used to the warmth of Italian sunshine. On the route to
the wall from the south, there is no evidence that the Romans ever had

a settlement in Glasgow, though Tacitus in his account of his march into Scotland in AD 81 first refers to the Clyde as 'Clota'.

If legend is to be believed, St Ninian, who arrived in Cathures, as Glasgow was once known, from early Rome in the fifth century, established a wooden cathedral more or less on the site of the present one. A century or so after Ninian's death, the King of Lothian's erring daughter produced a child by a princely lover to whom she was not married. The boy, Kentigern or Mungo, as he became popularly known, grew up in Fife, in the care of a holy man, Fergus, who extracted the strange promise from his protégé that upon his own death, his body would be drawn westward by two untamed bulls and buried where the animals first rested. The bulls stopped at the Molendinar Burn, near Ninian's burial place by this cathedral. There Fergus was duly buried; and there Mungo set up his own religious community, calling it Glaschu, thought by some to mean 'the church within the enclosed space', by others, 'the dear green place'.

Though King Rhydderch of Strathclyde gave Mungo his protection, an invading pagan king forced Glasgow's future patron saint temporarily to flee to Wales, where he founded the monastery of St Asaph: but King Rhydderch won the Battle of Arderyd in 573 and called Mungo back. After an interlude in Dumfriesshire, the future patron saint eventually returned to Glaschu, the village by the ford over the Clyde, where he died in 590. Dumbarton, lower down the Clyde, with its own ford at Dumbuck, was then the capital of Strathclyde, an honour it retained until Scotland, more or less as we know it, came together under David I, who, in 1110, persuaded the Pope to appoint the former royal tutor, John Achaius, Bishop of Glasgow.

Achaius built the next cathedral over Mungo's tomb. Consecrated in 1136, it burnt down in 1197. One of his successors, Bishop Jocelin, built a third cathedral on the site. This was consecrated in 1197, part of the lower church and some of the lower wall of the nave perhaps being incorporated into the present edifice, finished in 1258 under Bishop William de Bondington. In its hey-day it was the second largest Gothic church in Scotland, exceeded only by the Cathedral of St Andrews, which John Knox's reformers wantonly destroyed. Glasgow narrowly escaped a similar fate after the lead was stripped from its roof and its altar and statues were destroyed. Fortunately, someone persuaded the leaders of the Members of the Trades' House to intervene, and the cathedral was saved. It was turned into three churches, the lower church in 1595 going to the Barony congregation,

The cathedral, the Royal Infirmary with (*right foreground*) Glasgow's oldest house, Provand's Lordship (1457) and (*left foreground*) Ian Begg's Museum of Religion built 1990–3 in mock castle style

the nave in 1648 becoming the Outer High Church and High Kirk, and the choir being the Inner High. The cathedral's unity was not restored until 1833.

The west front was flanked by two towers, which were removed between 1846 and 1848. Money was raised to replace them, but this undertaking was never carried out.

Nearby stood the Bishop's Palace and Prebendary Mansions. The palace building, a ruin by the end of the seventeenth century, disappeared to make way for Robert Adam's Royal Infirmary in 1792, itself removed to make way for a larger Victorian building. The present edifice near the site of the palace houses a Museum of Religion and is the work of the architect Ian Begg. Only one of the houses that originally occupied Drygate, Rottenrow, Kirk Street and Castle Street, each one with its garden and orchard, survives: the restored but gardenless Provand's Lordship, the manse of the Prebendary of Barlanark, who also bore the title Laird of Provan.

While the cathedral and Provand's Lordship are the only medieval Glasgow buildings to survive, Crookston Castle, at the junction of the Levern with the White Cart, is pre-Reformation in origin. Ruined Cathcart Castle – until 1980 another period survivor – was shockingly demolished for no good reason in 1995.

The college of Glasgow, showing its two quadrangles, with the High Street in the foreground and the gardens behind

Side view of the University of Glasgow, Gilmorehill

Though Glasgow University, established by a Papal Bull of Pope Nicholas V, was founded by Bishop William Turnbull in 1451 on a site in Rottenrow, it was later to move to a site south of the cathedral. This courtyard building, of considerable distinction, was unfortunately destroyed when the ground was sold to a railway company, the decline of that part of the city prompting removal to the present site on Gilmorehill in 1870. At this time, the City Improvement Trust also demolished the surrounding old domestic buildings.

Two great fires in 1652 and 1678 destroyed much of the housing built in the seventeenth century. The last survival, reputedly dating from 1678, was demolished in 1975 along with St Enoch's Railway Station, to become the entrance to a car park.

Trongate *c.* 1790

Churches were plentiful during the seventeenth century, that era of fierce religious disputation when the threat of Episcopacy loomed larger than the return of Roman Catholicism. The Trongate, named after the tron or weighing machine put up in towns at the end of the fifteenth century, had originally been St Theresa's Gate, named after Mungo's mother, and was destroyed by fire in 1793. A little to the west was the Sang School. On the west side of Castle Street stood St Nicholas Hospital, built in 1460 but taken down in 1808. When it was built, Glasgow Green, still tree-covered, was known as the Bishop's Forest. Isolated across the river stood that necessary adjunct of medieval life, the Leper Hospital.

In the late twentieth century – although we have not quite annihilated distance, we have at least tamed it by air travel – it is not always easy for us to appreciate the difficulties of communication when the horse was the fastest mode of transport. Part of Glasgow's subsequent development as a major urban centre resulted from the building in 1345 of the five-arched stone bridge by Bishop Rae and Lady Lochow (who paid for one arch) over the Stockwell shallows. It replaced the wooden structure described by the poet Blind Harry in his poem 'Wallace' as 'Glasgow's brygg that biggit [built] was of tree.' So well, however, was this stone biggin constructed that, with minor alterations and restorations, it lasted until 1847.

Glasgow's Tolbooth, as it would have been seen by many early visitors to Glasgow

Hutchesons' Hall 1802–5, built by David Hamilton (1768–1843) to commemorate
the Hutcheson brothers. The first floor was designed by John Baird. The building
presently houses the National Trust for Scotland Glasgow headquarters

Three seventeenth-century towers of former public buildings have survived. The five-storey Tolbooth or Town House, put up in the 1620s, was partly rebuilt and gothicized in 1814 by David Hamilton. Except for its elegant, seven-storey steeple, it was pulled down in 1921. Campbell of Blythswood's Merchants' House, in the Bridgegait, was erected in 1629. Built round a courtyard, which included a hospital and a guildhall, all except the steeple was demolished in 1817, leaving the steeple towering above the former fish market, now converted to accommodate craftsfolk and small businesses.

The third survival is the Tron kirk tower. First rebuilt on the site of the Collegiate Church of St Mary and St Anne in 1592, it was rebuilt again by Robert Adam after the drunken members of the Hell Fire Club set it alight in 1793. At one time the Tron was housed in the tower, but it was taken out in 1853, when the present arches were constructed.

The original Hutchesons' Hospital, founded in 1641 by two merchant benefactors, George and Thomas Hutcheson of Lambhill, stood on the north side of the Tron, but was demolished in 1805 when Hutcheson Street was connected to the Trongate. David Hamilton built its replacement, Hutchesons' Hall in Ingram Street, in 1802. Only the statue of the two brothers, carved by James Colquhan in 1649, survives from the previous building.

Glasgow had embarked upon its trading future well before the arrival of tobacco and cotton, using Ayrshire ports to discharge cargoes for onward transmission on pack horses. In 1670, the new harbour of Newport, from 1774 called Port Glasgow, was used, pack horses or small horse-drawn vessels being employed to convey the imported goods to Glasgow.

In 1656, Cromwell's Commissioner for Customs and Excise, Thomas Tucker, recorded that all but the college students were

> traders and dealers: some from Ireland with small smiddy coals in open boats from four to ten tonnes, from whence they bring hoopes, ringes, barrel-staves – all needed for the craft of coopering – meale, oates and butter: some [for] France with pladding, coales and herring, for which they return salt, pepper, rosins [raisins] and prunes – some to Norway for timber and every ane theyr neighbours the Highlanders, who come hither from the isles and western parts.

Tucker saw Newark, though not yet with its harbour of Newport, as the place where 'all vessels doe ride, unlode, and send theyr goods up river to Glasgow in small boates'; Greenock where 'small open boates trade in fish with the Western Isles and Ireland' to which 'fish and cattell' were also carried; and Bute, where the islanders 'were all countrymen and cowherds, who feede cattell and spinne and make some woollen clothe ... to be dyed, and dressed at Glasgow, where they bring ... whatever they have occasion of for theyr expence and provision.' Irvine was then a small port easily clogged with sand, maintaining a small trade to France, Norway and Ireland with herring and other goods brought on horseback from Glasgow, 'for the purchasing of timber, wine and other commodityes to supply their occasions with'.

Though Glasgow grew as an important trading centre in the seventeenth century, it was during the eighteenth century that it really flourished in the expanding city. Thus, when John Ray, the Essex-born minister and naturalist rode into Glasgow in 1662, he still found it to be 'fair, large, and well built, crosswise, somewhat like unto Oxford, the streets very broad and pleasant'. He thought the College 'a pretty stone building ... not inferior to Wadham or All Soul's in Oxford,' and of the Cathedral, noted that 'they have now divided it'.

Another English clergyman, John Browne, surveying the Glasgow prospect in 1669, was even more enthusiastic, finding delightful its 'very fair bridge, supported with eight arches' that crossed 'the river Glotta or Cluyd, pleasantness of sight, sweetness of air and delightfulness of its gardens and orchards enriched with the most delicious fruits, surpasseth all other places in this tract'.

At the close of the twentieth century, and with the re-establishment of a Scottish Parliament (albeit one devolved from Westminster), it is perhaps difficult for us to appreciate the value those concerned with trade perceived in the Union of 1707, contrasting with the more emotional opposition to the ending of the 'auld sang' that others, not so concerned, clearly felt. In 1695, the Scots had passed an Act giving powers to a company trading with Africa and the Indies to extend their operations. Advised by William Paterson, later the founder of the Bank of England, this company decided to establish a trading colony at Darien, in Panama. The first ship arrived there from Leith on 4 November 1698 and established the fort of New Caledonia: but sickness, caused by the unhealthy climate, lack of provisions and the hostility of the natives, said to have been whipped up by the Scots' English rivals, led to disaster and the departure of the survivors in June 1699. A second expedition of four frigates sailed from Rothesay Bay in the summer of 1699, but after an initial victory over the Spaniards, settled in Tubacanti, on the Isthmus of Panama. They, too, suffered defeat and decimation by the same climatic conditions that wrought havoc on the builders of the Panama Canal many generations later. New Caledonia was abandoned. Fewer than fifty of the settlers got back to Scotland in 1700. The economic climate was thus favourable to some kind of union with England, though with the hindsight of two-and-a-half centuries, we may think it a pity that Andrew Fletcher of Saltoun's idea of Federal Union rather than Incorporating Union did not prevail.

Everyone knows that the two Jacobite risings of 1715 and 1745 originated in Scotland. Though Glasgow's defences in the 1715 affair were never put to the test, in September 1745 the magistrates received a letter from Prince Charles Edward Stuart demanding the sum of £15,000 sterling, a huge amount in these days. On grounds of poverty, Glasgow got away with paying only £5,000 and £5,000 worth of goods. Volunteers to oppose the Jacobites included men from Glasgow, but they were defeated at the Battle of Falkirk.

When Charles, on his retreat north, entered Glasgow again on 25 December 1746, he demanded 6,000 coats, 12,000 linen shirts, 6,000 pairs of hose and a similar quantity of shoes and blue bonnets – and got them. He himself occupied Shawfield House, at the foot of Glassford Street, the most elegant mansion in the city and owned by John Glassford. Here he was waited upon by Clementina Walkinshaw, daughter of John Walkinshaw of Barrowfield. She became his mistress, joined him in France and bore him a daughter, later legitimized as Duchess of Albany. On the way south, the prince held a review on Glasgow Green, his troops marching to Fleshers Haugh to the skirl of the pipes – an occasion upon which, we are told, the Glasgow people 'looked coldly'. The prince closed most of the shops to teach the city a lesson, and was only persuaded from sacking it by Cameron of Lochiel.

There were local troubles too. In 1725 there was a riot over the imposition of a malt tax of three pence on every barrel of beer. A mob attacked Shawfield, which stood on what is now Glassford Street and which was then the home of the Glaswegian MP Daniel Campbell, who had voted for the tax. A detachment of soldiers, under one Captain Bushnell, failed to quell the riots and there was a number of fatalities. General Wade then arrived in Glasgow, accompanied by Duncan Forbes of Culloden. The provost and a number of the city fathers were arrested and taken to Edinburgh, but freed after a day's imprisonment. Others arrested were given prison sentences and whipped through the streets. The magistrates sought to arrest Bushnell, but were prevented from doing so by the government, Campbell claimed. The latter received more than £6,000 indemnity, with which he bought an estate on Islay. Glaswegians had to pay a further £3,000 as expenses, so that the Shawfield affair rankled long in local memories.

After the Jacobites were defeated at Culloden, the provost of Glasgow tried to extort £14,000 from the government by way of indemnity. In 1749, parliament made a grant of £10,000 with which the city had to be content.

Even after the Union, the Glasgow merchants found that they were being obstructed by the merchants of Whitehaven, Liverpool and Bristol. In any case, after the French war broke out, many of the southern ports closed altogether. By the 1730s, the shorter Atlantic crossing enabled ships to avoid the English Channel. Before long, sugar from the West Indies and tobacco from America came into Glasgow in increasing quantities, for export to England, France and the Low Countries. By 1775, more than half the tobacco imported into these islands passed through Glasgow. The tobacco lords, with their scarlet coats and gold-topped canes, proudly walked the plainstanes, or crown of the street. But tobacco wealth was concentrated in relatively few hands.

Andrew Cochrane, himself a tobacco lord, ship-owner and partner of the Glasgow Arms Bank, claimed that the expansion of Glasgow was due to the business awareness of four men, Alexander Spiers of Elderslie, James Ritchie of Busby, William Cunninghame of Lainshaw and John Glassford of Dougalston. Spiers (1714–52) owned a seventh of all that came into the Clyde and a twelfth of what Europe imported. He and his family donated generously to charities to be administered by the Merchants' House, where his portrait now hangs. Glassford, who, according to Smollett in *Humphry Clinker*, once owned 'twenty-five ships with their cargoes, and traded for about half-a-million sterling a year', speculated unwisely, was a noted gambler and supported the revolutionaries in the American War of Independence – which, in fact, brought to an end Glasgow's tobacco trade. The only tobacco lord not to be much affected by the ensuing economic crash was said to be William Cunninghame (d.1789), who quickly bought up all the existing stocks of tobacco before it became a scarce commodity. With his resulting fortune, he acquired the estate of Lainshaw, in Ayrshire. His mansion, built in Glasgow's Royal Exchange Square in

The corner of George Street and High Street, 1897. The tightly packed houses are
already on the way to becoming slums

1788, was enlarged in 1827 by David Hamilton to become Glasgow's
Royal Exchange, and further enlarged in 1886 by David Thomson. It
is now an art gallery.

Apart from Cunninghame's mansion, encased by Hamilton, other
buildings survive from the period including some in Candleriggs.
Spreull's Land, particularly interesting because it features in Thomas
Hamilton's Glasgow novel *The Youth and Manhood of Cyril Thornton*,
was demolished as recently as 1978. I visited it shortly before its
destruction and had no difficulty in envisaging it once as the home in
which David Spreull entertained in its gracious rooms. The Spreulls
were, in fact, a family of successful merchants and traders, one of whose
members, James Spreull (d.1824), played an important role in the
improvement of the navigable potential of the Clyde.

Tobacco merchant Lord Provost Patrick Colquhoun was responsible
for setting up Glasgow's Chamber of Commerce, the first in the United
Kingdom, with an initial membership of 216, including about a third

The Merchants' House, George Square, built in 1874–7 by John Burnet, senior
(1814–1901) with later stained-glass additions

from the neighbouring towns of Greenock, Port Glasgow and Paisley. It met at first in the Tontine Hotel, but in 1877 moved into the newly constructed Merchants' House in George Square.

The first Merchants' House was built in the Bridgegait in 1659 and did duty for over 150 years, a popular venue for gatherings of all kinds. By 1817, however, the Bridgegait had become full of what a contemporary called 'the residences of the inferior classes', so the building was sold for £7,500, though the steeple was not included in the transaction. The second Merchants' House opened in Hutcheson Street in 1849. This site, however, was required by the city in 1863, whereupon the merchants moved to their third and present home in George Square.*

II

The famous novelist, Daniel Defoe came to Glasgow in 1706 as a spy for Queen Anne's minister Robert Harley, to promote the Union. Defoe was then known as 'Alexander Goldsmith'. Under his own name he made four journeys to Glasgow between 1724 and 1726, when he found 'The four principal streets ... the finest for breadth and the finest built that I have ever seen in one city together.' His impressions were first published in his *Travels Through Great Britain* in 1724, later updated.

Probably the most famous building in eighteenth-century Glasgow was Allan Dreghorn's Town Hall, built between 1737 and 1748 and influenced in style by the piazzas of Inigo Jones and Isaac de Caux in London's Covent Garden. It was bought by Pat Colquhoun, a future provost of Glasgow, and remodelled internally to become the Tontine Hotel, which was linked to a coffee house equipped with so many newspapers and periodicals that it was considered to be the most elegant in Europe. It survived until about 1868, when it was absorbed into shop accommodation.

Dreghorn, who was originally an iron and steel merchant, is also credited with the beautiful St Andrew's Church of 1739 in St Andrew's Square, still with us and recently restored as an Arts venue.

St Enoch's Square, begun in 1782 as a residential area, but gradually converted to include shops, has none of its original buildings left; but George Square, at the heart of Glasgow, laid out in 1781 and

* The Junior Chamber was established in 1937 for members under forty years of age.

Royal Crescent and Fitzroy Place *c*. 1890

named after George III, retains the building of 1787 that is now a small hotel.

By the time of the American War of Independence, which broke out in 1775 and lasted until 1783, Glasgow's trading had greatly increased. According to John Gibson, author of a 1777 history of the city, it included the manufacture of hardware, nails, shovels, threads and tapes, leathercraft, glass and, most important of all, cotton textiles.

Time and again, Glasgow has survived and expanded as a result of the versatility of its inhabitants. Almost at the height of the tobacco trade – in 1771, 47 million pounds (in weight) of tobacco was imported – its population in 1765 was 28,000. By 1791, it had risen to 67,000. By 1830, it was 200,000.

John Gibson declared: 'Let but a spirit of manufacturing be diffused among the people, and we will never want manufacturers for should a change of fashion which operates powerfully upon manufacturers, banish any particular branch, the people possessed of this spirit will immediately turn their attention to others.' From tobacco, Glasgow turned to cotton.

Writing in 1805, a generation after Gibson, David Macpherson, author of *Annals of Commerce*, recorded that:

Before America became independent of Great Britain, the foreign commerce of Glasgow was chiefly with that country ... But the enterprising spirit of the merchants ... found new channels of commerce sufficient to employ their capital and industry. They have also turned their attention more than formerly to manufacturers, whereby the city has become the centre and fostering parent of a prodigious number of manufacturing establishments.

He listed thirty printfields in the environs of Glasgow, 'several iron-works for making cannon and other articles of cast iron' and 'works for window glass, brittle glass and ornamental glass', as well as 'sugar baking, and brewing', noting that 'the manufacturers requiring fire have the vast advantage of coals close to the city'.

All this activity was made possible largely because of the discovery of James Watt (1736–1819), the son of a Greenock ship chandler, who, while repairing a Newcomen steam engine, realized that if the steam was condensed in a separate vessel which could be kept cold, the efficiency of the engine would be greatly increased and fuel consumption reduced. By producing the first expansion steam engine, Watt made it possible for locally constructed machinery to be used – machinery that previously would have had to be imported from England, Holland or France. The first Watt steam engine is said to have been installed in a cotton mill at Springfield, on the Clyde.

James Manson, who worked on the staff of the *Glasgow Herald* (founded in 1783 as the *Advertiser*, becoming the *Glasgow Herald and Advertiser* in 1802, and still surviving, though without the 'Glasgow' in its title) in 1863 published a poem, 'Let Glasgow Flourish'. Writing, no doubt, with a touch of irony, he exclaimed:

> Long, long ago, both cowl and sword
> Which slaves obey'd and fools ador'd,
> Are dust; now merchants fill the land,
> And truth and honour, hand in hand
> Walk through the streets, no juxtering guide
> Entraps you with a heartless smile;
> All fraud is fled ...

In the same year, an even more prosaic poet, James Nicolson, a Freemason at Govan Workhouse and an upholder of the temperance movement, wished:

That drunkeries all were abolished, and plotted in their stead,
The reading-room and school-room and shops for the sale of bread.

In 1827, parliament had appointed a commission, later known as the Board of Trustees for Manufacturers, to administer a fund for the encouragement of industry, particularly the linen industry. (The board eventually became the 'foundation stone' of the British Linen Bank.) Housewives were encouraged to grow lint (flax) and hemp.

Linen seems to have been brought to Glasgow by William Wilson, a Scots Guardsman who returned from service in Germany in 1700 with a blue and white chequered handkerchief, which he eventually successfully copied. Though he had no capital to enable him to exploit his discovery, others profited from it. The first cambric and printfields were set up in Pollokshaws in 1742. Legislation subsequently gave the new industry protection by banning the importation of French cambrics.

Other related developments soon followed. In 1732, a Glaswegian imported not only two inkle looms from Holland, but also a skilled Dutch workman, thus breaking that country's monopoly in tape-making. The invention of the spinning jenny and the spinning frame, by James Hargreaves and Richard Arkwright respectively, led an English firm to set up a cotton mill at Rothesay, on the island of Bute, in 1778. Two years later, James Monteith discovered how to weave an imitation Indian muslin entirely of cotton. All his six sons became cotton manufacturers. By the end of the century, Glasgow had gone over wholeheartedly to cotton-making, leaving the manufacture of linen to firms in Forfarshire and Fife.

The most famous of these cotton manufacturers was undoubtedly David Dale (1739–1806), who, with Monteith and others, invited Arkwright to Glasgow in 1783 and showed him the site of New Lanark by the Clyde. There Dale set up what became in Scotland the largest cotton-mill and in which, for a time, Arkwright was a partner.

Conditions in Dale's New Lanark mill, later taken over by his son-in-law Robert Owen, were undoubtedly much better than those in most of Glasgow's steam-weaving factories, where 8,400 pieces of cloth were produced every week on 2,800 looms; or in the city's fifty-two cotton mills housing 511,200 spindles on which over a million yards of material, valued at £5 million, were produced.

The earliest power mills in Glasgow had spun cotton for home-bred handloom weavers to make into cloth. Early in the nineteenth century, however, factories began producing their own cloth, leading to distress among the handloom weavers. Wages fell from £2.10s a week to 10s as the factories took over. After the Napoleonic Wars broke out in 1797, rum from the West Indies was replaced by whisky and gin as the poor man's tipple. There was sporadic trouble among the oppressed, culminating in desultory rioting in April 1819. Two Bonniemuir weavers, Andrew Hardie (an ancestor of Keir Hardie, founder of the Labour Party) and John Baird, were hanged and beheaded at Stirling, a fate also suffered by James Wilson in front of 20,000 spectators on Glasgow Green. Fifteen others were transported for life. In 1825, the right to strike was first recognized and four years later the Catholic Emancipation Act was passed, followed by the Reform Bill in 1832, when 70,000 people rejoiced on Glasgow Green.

The cotton industry reached its peak in 1860, when some sixty cotton mills lacquered the sky with sooty chimneys and 20,000 people, three quarters of them women, operated a similar number of looms.

Then things went wrong. The failure of the Western Bank in 1857 resulted in four of the textile firms being unable to pay their debts. Trouble in America, culminating in the Civil War that divided the country, led to the cutting-off of cotton supplies from the Confederacy in the early 1860s. As always happens, many of Glasgow's best overseas customers had begun to copy the materials they imported. Glasgow's stocks had to be sold off cheaply; the ladies of fashion no longer sought materials now so generally available. As Glasgow's quality cloth trade shrank, mills in Lancashire with markets in Africa, India and the Far East, and the ability to produce more cheaply, gradually took over.

III

Fortunately, Glasgow's resilience once again came to the fore. Charles Tennant (1768–1838) – Burns's 'Wabster Willie' – founded the St Rollox chemical works in 1800, manufacturing a bleaching agent so successful that his became the largest concern of its kind in Europe. However, the chimney of his factory, 'Tennant's Stalk' – at 436 feet high, the tallest in Europe – deposited by-products on the surrounding area which badly fouled the environment.

A dyestuff manufacturer, Charles Macintosh (1766–1843) discovered how to dissolve rubber for use in making waterproof fabrics. From 1834 his operations were based in Glasgow, though his factory later moved to Manchester and eventually became the Dunlop Rubber Company.

Since 1754, iron smelted with charcoal had been produced at the Lorn Furnaces on Loch Etive, using ore shipped from England. The Carron Works, founded in 1760, smelted with Scottish and English ores. One of its travellers, Thomas Edington, in 1786 went into partnership with William Cadell to promote the Clyde Ironworks and, with other partners, similar works at Dalnotter and elsewhere. Their products, however, proved too expensive to export, until in 1828 the manager of the Glasgow Gas Works discovered how to use hot instead of cold air in the blast furnace. The contribution of the hot-blast furnace and blackband ironstone resulted in pig iron, cutting coal consumption by 50 per cent. Cheap Highland and Irish labour, together with the further discovery that gasses from the furnaces could be used to heat the blast, allowed the ironmasters to stay competitive.

Unpleasant and overcrowded as the living conditions were of many of Glasgow's growing army of workmen, the construction of housing for the better-off continued to grow.

Pollok House, built 1747–52 by William Adam for Sir John Maxwell, the second baronet. Finished by his son but added to in the nineteenth century. The Burrell Art Collection has been housed in a gallery in the grounds since 1983. The house is now with the National Trust for Scotland

Among former great country homes that once surrounded Glasgow, only Pollok House still remains, managed by Glasgow City Council and the National Trust for Scotland on behalf of Glaswegians and those who visit the city. A gallery to house the art collection that the shipowner Sir William Burrell bequeathed to the city is housed in the grounds. Many such 'country' estates were swallowed up in the city's steady nineteenth-century expansion.

A Glendevon man who had come to Glasgow in 1790, William Harley (1770–1829) was a successful manufacturer of turkey-red gingham and later an equally successful dairyman and provider of water. He bought Sauchiehall House (hence Sauchiehall Street) on the Blythswood Estate in 1802, anglicizing the name to Willowbank House. On the estate, he laid out a public pleasure-garden and Glasgow's first hot and cold public baths, to reach which he had to provide access roads, eventually including the future Bath Street, West Nile Street, St Vincent Street and Sauchiehall Street. He also established a successful bakery but, like many, suffered ruin at the end of the Napoleonic Wars. Harley's successor, William Hamilton Garden, a property speculator, employed the architect John Brash (d.1848), who first developed the 'Blythswood' style of house.

With the better-off eager to get away from the fumes of the growing number of factory chimneys, the westward move had begun. The Blythswood 'new town' style was described by Andrew Graeme and David Walker in their definitive *Architecture of Glasgow* as comprising 'a fairly short terrace two or three storeys high, generally with centrepiece and end pavilions given considerable emphasis ... The facing is, of course, all ashlar which recent cleaning has revealed a lovely soft biscuit colour underneath the Victorian grime.'

Commercial pressures on the Blythswood 'new town' began as early as 1840 and the area is now given over almost entirely to offices; but at least 'Harley's Hill', as Blythswood Square was first called, is now a conservation area and so is protected.

The showpiece of the square is still the Royal Scottish Automobile Club, which occupies the whole of the east side. Its central entrance is the work of James Miller (1899–1947). Here the unity of window groupings, the balancing pavilions and the astragals (the little bars in small square windows used before plate glass was invented) have all been preserved. Its future is presently uncertain.

Where conservation of the interiors of listed buildings is impossible, even with what some architects pejoratively call, 'gutting and stuffing', the next best solution is the retention of the façade with redevelopment behind it. This is what has happened to the houses on the South Side of the Square. Charles Rennie Mackintosh (1868–1928) put an Art Nouveau door on Number 5, once the Lady Artists' Club. Number 7 was the scene of Madeleine Smith's alleged poisoning of her lover, L'Angelier (with a cup of cocoa), for which she was tried and released under a 'Not Proven' verdict in 1857. She married twice, became a Bloomsbury hostess and died in America at the age of ninety-two.

The Glasgow tenement possibly evolved out of the Edinburgh 'lands', where a building usually of four or more storeys on a narrow space comprised a number of flats – in Glasgow approached through a common entrance known as a close. The Blythswood development extended northwards up Garnethill, on the other side of Sauchiehall Street, with such flats intended for people unable to afford 'whole' houses in Blythswood Square. The centrepiece of Garnethill is now Charles Rennie Mackintosh's Glasgow School of Art, considered by many to be his masterpiece, which was built as a result of an imaginative commission from the director, Fra Newberry. In recent years some of the surrounding tenements have been restored. One flat, time-warped almost since the turn of the century, is now in the care of the National Trust for Scotland.

There was also expansion on the south side of the Clyde, where in 1780 the village of Bridge-end or Gorbals lay surrounded by agricultural land, divided into 'crofts' and owned, for the most part, by Glasgow Corporation, the Trades' House and Hutchesons' Hospital. When Glasgow extended its official boundaries to take in Gorbals, James and David Laurie bought up forty-seven acres of the croft lands and set out to develop the area 'according to one plan or design ... for houses of a superior description'. The architect Peter Nicholson (1765–1844) was engaged to design the two terraces of Carlton Place, and Italian craftsmen were brought in to decorate the interiors. Nicholson left them unfinished and John Baird (1798–1859) took over.

These impressive three-storey terraces with basements, each of forty bays, pavilions with porches and coupled columns and a double porch for a centrepiece, have suffered some damage, including the addition of a mansard roof; but Laurieston House, intended by the brothers for their own use, has been restored and conserved by Philip Coulter and Partners. The two terraces are divided by the end of South Portland Street, which Laurie lined up with Buchanan Street, across the river.

Main Street, Gorbals, 1868, not then the slum it later became

Abbotsford Place, four-storey terraces with Ionic and Corinthian porches fronting a broad street, gives some indication of the unrealized scale of the development that the Laurie brothers originally envisaged. Encroaching industry defeated their plans. The link intended to join up with Buchanan Street was never built and although Abbotsford Place was, for a time, a residential street chosen by Glasgow doctors, the favoured expansion of the city was to the west. Monteith Row, built between 1818 and 1845, and which once looked out on to Glasgow Green, features in one of the best novels set in Glasgow, Guy McCrone's *Wax Fruit*. The Row has now mostly gone.

Part of the trouble was that in 1837 Dixon set up Dixon's Blazes, whose foundry fire lit up the sky with an orange glow. In these days before mandatory planning, nothing could be done to stop Dixon from driving a track across Laurieston down to the quay at Windmillcroft. Brickworks and coalfields on the outskirts of the district and the growth of numerous small backyard industries eventually drove out the wealthier residents. The big houses were divided and subdivided, and

George Square c. 1840 with Sir Walter Scott's statue on the column in 1837, the first of its kind in Scotland. The square's original buildings are still mostly hotels

from 1830, tenements were built, ultimately becoming so overcrowded that within a half-century the Gorbals had become one of the most notorious slums in Europe, Irish, Jews, Indians and Pakistanis and other indigent incomers cramming the buildings. The old Gorbals was mostly demolished to be replaced with highrise flats (themselves since demolished) in the post-Second World War years.

A word should be said about the Trades' House in Glassford Street. From the eleventh century onwards, a system of guilds of craftsmen and merchants flourished. From the fifteenth to the eighteenth centuries, the government of the Burgh of Glasgow was largely controlled by the merchant guilds, with the trade guilds occupying an important, if subordinate, position. By the beginning of the nineteenth century, these old craft associations had lost their influence, and their powers were finally removed by parliament in 1846. In many other towns they were simply wound up, but in Glasgow they were maintained as charitable and public bodies, and indeed still function in this role.

The fourteen remaining incorporations meet in what might be

described as 'Glasgow's Guildhall', the Trades' House in Glassford Street, which was built between 1791 and 1794 by Robert Adam. Later architects, including in 1888 James Sellars (1843–1899), the designer of Glasgow's famous St Andrew's Halls (destroyed by fire in 1962), John Keppie in 1916 and Walter Underwood in 1955, have added to, restored or internally embellished the original Adam building. Its banqueting hall, panelled in Spanish mahogany, has on the north and south sides a series of panels carrying the names of all the Deacon Convenors since 1604, beginning with Duncan Semphill, a sea captain. The hall's other adornments include a fine Adam fireplace and a nineteenth-century frieze showing the crafts at work – tailors, hammermen, wrights, coopers, fleshers, masons, gardeners, barbers, skinners, bankers, weavers, maltmen and cordiners.

Towards the end of the eighteenth century, Glasgow was celebrated at length in verse by Dumfries-born John Mayne (1759–1836), much influenced by Fergusson and Burns, whose birthday he shared. When he wrote this poem, Mayne was an apprentice to the printer Andrew Foulis the younger, a member of the family who established a short-lived Academy of Fine Art in the city, and whose publishing house produced books that included splendid editions of the *Iliad* and the *Odyssey*, and a Folio *Paradise Lost* in 1770, as well as humbler editions of classical and modern authors. Mayne invited his readers to:

> Look thro' the town; – the houses here
> Like royal palaces appear
> A' things the face o' gladness wear,
> The market's thrang –
> Bus'ness is brisk – and a's asteer
> The streets alang.

Equally eloquent in sentiment was his Stirling-born contemporary Robert Galloway who, in 1788, rhapsodized 'Glasgow Reviewed and Contrasted':

> Fair Glasgow, now step forth and make your claim,
> For, 'mongst the first of cities stands your name;
> Sing forth your beauties hitherto untold,
> Your outside painted, and your inside gold.

Your spacious streets so regular in form,
Your stately fabrics, fit to stand a storm;
Your state to paint, night hardly gives me time,
But for to try't will scarce be deemed a crime:
Her form is oval, spreading with her wings,
Or, as a balance, when it equal hings.
Five crosses she contains, which make her vie
With most of modern towns beneath the sky;
Saint Mungo's kirk stands high from East to West,
And of a' Scotland's choirs it looks the best;
Two stately spires it has, in one a bell,
For bulk and costly wark it does excel;
Three places here for worship, in repair
And many a decent prelate has been there ...

The College next, I think, commands respect,
The place of learning we must ne'er neglect:
Two stately squares it shows with halls all round;
Where youths are taught in learning most profound,
To fill the Pulpit, or the Bench, or Bar,
To make them councillors for peace or war,
Here come the Nation's hopes from ev'ry quarter,
And do their cash and time for education barter.'

Hardly great poetry, but a sincere and interesting tribute nonetheless –
and no such thing as free education in those days!

A tribute to the value young Glaswegians put upon education was
recorded by Alexander Carlyle (1722–1805), known as 'Jupiter
Carlyle' because of his impressive appearance and demeanour (and
also, perhaps, a reference to the fact that the artist Gavin Hamilton
used him as a model for the King of the Gods). He was for almost sixty
years minister of Inveresk Parish in Musselburgh. His lively autobiography was left in manuscript and only published in 1860. He came to
Glasgow University in 1743, after attending Edinburgh University,
and observed: 'One difference I remarked between this university and
that of Edinburgh, where I had been bred, which was, that although at
that time there appeared to be a marked superiority in the best scholars and most diligent students of Edinburgh, yet in Glasgow, learning
seemed to be an object of more importance, and the habit of applica-
tion was much more general.'

IV

Apart from sailing, riding on horseback or jolting in a badly sprung family coach, public travel to another town or city was by stagecoach, an uncomfortable experience on the rough pre-tarmacadam roads, often resulting in accidents to the wheels. Passengers had to endure delays at the often unsatisfactory staging inns *en route*, and those seated outside faced exposure to the elements.

Prior to the establishment of a national system of mail coaches towards the end of the eighteenth century, the mail was carried by mounted postboys. In 1678, the magistrates signed a contract with an Edinburgh coach-owner, one William Hume, for the provision of 'ane sufficient strong coach to run betwixt Edinburgh and Glasgow, to be drawn by sax able horses, to leave Edinburgh ilk Monday morning and return again (God willing) ilk Saturday night'. Like modern air travellers, the passengers were restricted in the matter of accompanying luggage, being allowed only 'a cloak bag to receive their clothes, linen and sic like'. The burghers of Glasgow were to have travel preference. The cost of the journey was £43.16s Scots (about £3.50 today) in summer,

Trongate and Argyle Street in the 1820s

£5.8s (40p) in winter; bad weather no doubt extended the travelling time. Mr Hume was to have payment of 200 merks for a period of five years.

In 1784, the beginnings of a national system of mail coaches was established, with government-backing by one Mr Palmer, offering a quicker and safer means of delivery. The Royal Arms were printed in gold on the doors. The guard wore scarlet livery and sat on a high seat above the back of the coach. The coach set out for London at the foot of Nelson Street, near the Trongate. Seats had to be pre-booked no fewer than eight days in advance. Though comfort was hardly improved, at least the service was more reliably regular.

Peter Mackenzie, editor of *The Reformer's Gazette*, recorded in his *Reminiscences of Glasgow* (1865) that in its early days

> the London Mail Coach ... arrived pretty regularly in Glasgow, at or about five o'clock of the morning, containing of course the usual post boys, with some eight or ten passengers ... four inside and six outside ... This was absolutely all the direct conveyance between London and Glasgow at that time, occupying three long days and two nights journey! And truly it was frequently ludicrous to see some of these weary mail coach passengers as they arrived at their long journey's end, with their faces besmeared, and almost as black as ink, from want of being cleaned, shaven or shorn; and their legs benumbed with cold, or nearly paralysed with heat, according to the seasons; and yawning and sneezing, and rubbing their eyes, as if they had just awakened from a long, dreamy and comfortless slumber, but still mustering strength sufficient anxiously to enquire from all loving friends, so long away, and what news?

A wagon-way had been constructed from Monkland to Kirkintilloch, leading from the old Monkton collieries to the Forth and Clyde Canal. In 1826, locomotives supplanted horses on this line, and there is some evidence that passengers may have also been carried over the ten-mile stretch of the main track. In 1828, the Ballochney Railway added three branches to the Monkland to Kirkintilloch line, the result being a dramatic fall in coal prices, first in Edinburgh and later in Glasgow.

The real beginning of railroad travel in Scotland, however, was on 27 September 1831, when the Glasgow and Garnkirk Railway, which had opened for mineral traffic in 1827, first carried passengers at 7 miles an hour along its eight-mile length from St Rollox Station. It used steam locomotives from the beginning. Most of those early railways – though, curiously, not the Glasgow and Garnkirk – were phenomenally successful, the benefits they conferred leading not only to an upsurge in the mineral values of the areas they served but, naturally, also to a substantial rise in the value of the owning company's shares.

In 1830, the Pollok and Govan Railway Company and the Rutherglen Railway Company were formed, the former with capital of £66,000, the latter with £20,000. These were small enterprises.

The second major Glasgow railway was also originally associated with coalfields. In 1837, the line to Paisley, Kilmarnock and Ayr, designed to serve the Ayrshire coalfields, was authorized, and opened in 1840. In 1869, the Glasgow and South Western Railway Company secured the unfinished Ardrossan Canal and later built their link from Port Eglinton to Paisley along its bed.

Thereafter railway development was not tied so closely to coalfields. The Glasgow to Greenock line was authorized in 1837 and was opened for passenger traffic in 1841. The Edinburgh and Glasgow Railway Company, with capital of £900,000 and a loan of £300,000, linked Glasgow to Edinburgh in 1842, the tunnel between Queen Street and Cowlairs, where a locomotive works was established, costing £40,000.

Since 1832, a railway line to connect Scotland and England had been talked of and some survey work had been carried out; but throughout the 1830s a dispute raged about the route to be followed. The route to connect Edinburgh with London through Berwick-upon-Tweed and Newcastle was obvious enough. The row that ensued was over the Glasgow to London link. Should the line go over Beattock Summit, with all the engineering and subsequent operating difficulties this would entail? Or should it traverse the flatter Ayrshire coalfields to the west? A Royal Commission was formed to investigate the proposals during the years of railway mania, which came to a peak about 1845. It had actually favoured the Nithsdale route in preference to that via Beattock; yet in 1845, a parliamentary decision was given in favour of the Caledonian Railway Company's Beattock route. It opened in February 1848, two years after the North British Railway Company's east-coast route had first crossed the border at Berwick.

Construction of the rival Nithsdale route was authorized in 1846, and the Glasgow, Paisley, Kilmarnock and Ayr Railway was, after an amalgamation, soon to become the Glasgow and South Western

Railway Company, the third of the three big companies that dominated railway operation out of Glasgow throughout the nineteenth century.

To the north, the Scottish Central Railway ran up to Perth in 1840, its owners amalgamating eventually with the Caledonian Railway. Travel from Glasgow was further extended to Inverness and Nairn in 1855 – eventually to Thurso along the track of the Highland Railway – and from 1852, to Elgin and Lossiemouth along the track of the Great North of Scotland Railway.

C.A. Oakley (1901–93) has pointed out that Glasgow had become the second city of the British Empire some forty years before the direct rail link with London was established. Even so, Glasgow Corporation was at first reluctant to allow the new means of travel to penetrate to the heart of the city. Both the Glasgow, Paisley, Kilmarnock and Ayr and the Glasgow, Paisley and Greenock companies had to be content with a station on the south side of the river; yet the owners of the

Engines being built in the North British Locomotive works at Springburn. Locomotive building began at Springburn in the 1840s from where engines were exported throughout the Empire

Glasgow and Edinburgh line were able to build their terminal at Queen Street in the 1840s (reconstructed in 1878–80), while Buchanan Street Station, the terminal for the companies running to the north, went up in 1849. Although in passenger-carrying terms the London link was by far the most important, the Glasgow and South Western Railway Company's station was kept out at Bridge Street. The St Enoch Station and Hotel were not completed until 1880. It was 1879 before the Caledonian Company could bring their trains into Central Station, having previously used Buchanan Street Station or an inconvenient station at the junction of Cathcart Street and Pollokshaws Road. Both new stations necessitated the construction of separate railway bridges over the Clyde.

Both Buchanan Street and St Enoch's stations have now been demolished and redeveloped. The levelling of the arches on which the agreeably Gothic St Enoch's Station Hotel stood has removed a familiar Victorian Glasgow landmark, though James Miller's subway station of 1896 has survived as a tourist office. Queen Street Station, the work of James Carswell, though modernized internally, still carries its two great fanlights, one of them now somewhat obscured by redevelopment on the north side of George Square.

It was from Queen Street Station that the first Sunday train ran from Glasgow, setting out for Edinburgh on 13 March 1842, 'filled with peaceful and respectable persons, gliding quietly away on its mission,' as a contemporary journalist sympathetically put it. Such a smooth departure must have disappointed the Presbytery of Glasgow, who had denounced the running of Sunday trains as:

> a flagrant violation of the law of God as expressed in the Fourth Commandment, a grievous outrage on the religious feelings of the people of Scotland, a powerful temptation to the careless and indifferent to abandon the public ordinances of Grace, and most disastrous to the quiet of the rural parishes along the line of the railway, by the introduction into them every Sabbath, of many of the profligate and dissipated who inhabit the cities of Glasgow and Edinburgh.

In Edinburgh, a threatening battery of ministers, presumably unaware of the inclusion of their city in their Glasgow brethren's condemnation, lined the platforms and informed the detraining passengers that they had bought tickets to Hell, a claim which does not seem to have deterred many of them from making their way towards Prince's Street.

Janet Hamilton (1795–1873) was a remarkable Lanarkshire woman (married in Glasgow by J.G. Lockhart's minister father), fifth in descent from John Whitelaw, a Covenanter executed at the Old Tolbooth of Edinburgh for his part in the Battle of Bothwell Brig, herself unable to write until she was fifty and the mother of ten children. She celebrated the inaugural journey in 'The Sunday Rail', which rises to this indignant smoke-plume of a climax:

> Now range up the carriages, feed up the fires!
> To the rail, to the rail, now the pent-up desires
> Of the pale toiling million find gracious reply,
> On the pinions of steam they shall fly, they shall fly,
> To beauties of nature and art to explore,
> To ramble the woodlands and roam by the shore,
> The city spark here with his smart smirking lass,
> All peg-topped and crinolined, squat on the grass,
> While with quips and with cranks and soft-wreathèd smiles,
> Each nymph with her swain the dull Sabbath beguiles.
>
> Here mater and paterfamilias will come
> With their rollicking brood from their close city home,
> How they scramble and scream, how they scamper and run,
> While pa and mamma are enjoying the fun!
> And the urchins bawl out, 'Oh, how funny and jolly,
> Dear ma, it is thus to keep Sabbath-day holy.'
>
> Now for pipe and cigar and the snug pocket-flask,
> What's the rail on a Sunday without them, we ask?
> What the sweet-scented heather and rich clover-blooms,
> To the breath of the weed as it smoulders and fumes?
> So in courting and sporting, in drinking and smoking,
> Walking and talking, in laughter and joking,
> They while the dull hours of the Sabbath away.
> What a Sabbath it is! Who is Lord of the Day!

The effect of the arrival of the railways upon the fabric of central Glasgow must have been somewhat similar to that made by the construction of urban motorways in the mid twentieth century. For one thing, it settled the already declining fortunes of Laurieston, the Laurie brothers' housing development south of the river; for another, it cut broad swathes through medieval and pre-Industrial Revolution

Glasgow. Much of what went had become an overcrowded health hazard. The City Improvement Act of 1866 gave the Corporation powers to acquire, compulsorily in some cases, land and houses, to widen streets and to build new houses for 'mechanics, labourers and other persons of the poorer and working-classes for let or sale'.

Unfortunately, much that could have been conserved, using other means to solve the social problems, was thoughtlessly swept away. Up to a point it is fair to compare the way mid-nineteenth-century Glaswegians treated the heart of the city with what, say, contemporary Copenhageners or Hamburgians did to theirs. Our Glasgow forebears do not emerge with much credit on the environmental side, however admirable their social promptings.

The area on which they concentrated was the old city. The Trust, through which the Corporation operated, cleared and rebuilt the High Street, the Saltmarket, Kirk Street and Calton, some of their replacement tenements, indeed, still being in use. They also covered in the Molendinar Burn and laid out Alexandra Park.

Their most disastrous decision was to demolish the medieval university in order to make way for High Street Goods Station. This had first been mooted in 1845, when a move to Woodside had been proposed, but a powerful faction of magistrates and professors at that time took the view that a university should remain at the heart of a place and, by its influence, try to revivify it. In Glasgow, however, money has always talked loudly, and short-term economic gains have usually seemed more attractive than long-term environmental advantages. By the 1860s, when a second railway bid came in, the idealists had lost the battle.

With the artificially clear view of hindsight, it is easy to lament the destruction of the city's medieval core; but the pressures of the moment were real and urgent – just as, indeed, they were in the late 1940s, when the Corporation responded to the post-war clamour for housing stock at all costs by establishing huge colonies like Drumchapel and Easterhouse, without providing many of the amenities necessity sooner or later demands.

Alcoholism, one of the poor man's few, if temporary, reliefs, had long been a Glasgow problem (some would say, still is). The Home-Drummond Act of 1828 was followed by the Forbes Mackenzie Act of 1854, limiting drinking hours from 8 a.m. to 11 p.m. and prohibiting the sale of alcohol within six miles of a tollhouse, an early attempt to discourage the 'one for the road' custom.

The Trust itself prohibited the sale of alcohol in its new developments, a prohibition carried forward by the Corporation into its municipal housing estates, with which the city was eventually fringed, and this prohibition was strictly maintained until after the 1939–45 War.

Further controls were imposed by the provision of various conditions for licensing the sale of drink, culminating in the Act of 1903. The Act was the outcome of the report of an 1899 Royal Commission, setting up licensing courts in burghs with a population of 4,000 or more. This established the present system of control, allowing electors in 'dry areas', should they so wish, to vote for 'no change' under the Scottish Temperance Act of 1913, but thereby establishing a 'not in my back yard' method of transferring the problem of drunkenness to some other neighbourhood. So draconian were these anti-drink laws that in the changed circumstances of the mid twentieth century, they were found damaging to the Scottish tourist industry, leading in 1978 to reforms that liberalized the situation.

Poverty, which heavy drinking increases, is surely only one aspect of the problem, though the novelist George Blake once opined that: 'The living conditions almost anywhere in the industrial belt of Scotland are quite enough to drive any man to drink.' Cold, gloomy northern winters no doubt encouraged the Scots habit of absorbing a 'pint and a chaser' – a whisky quickly followed by a pint of beer (or, if preferred, in the reverse order!). Many Glaswegians would no doubt echo Sir Compton Mackenzie's view that 'Beer does not taste like itself unless it is chasing a dram of neat whisky down the gullet, preferably two drams.'

The poet Edwin Muir vividly recalled his acquaintance with the Glasgow slums of the 1930s:

I walked to and fro from my work each day through a slum, for there was no way of getting from the south side of Glasgow to the city except through the slums. These journeys filled me with a sense of degradation: the crumbling houses, the twisted faces, the obscene words casually heard in passing, the ancient haunting stench of pollution and decay, the arrogant women, the mean men, the terrible children, daunted me, and at last filled me with an immense, blind dejection.

In what the novelist Lewis Grassic Gibbon (James Leslie Mitchell) called 'that strange, deplorable city which has neither sweetness nor

75 High Street, 1868. The clotheslines were a common sight in the early closes

pride, the vomit of a cataleptic commercialism,' slum violence has become habitual. In their realist novel of Glasgow life, *No Mean City* (1938), assembled by H. Kingsley Long from an ill-ordered manuscript by Alexander MacArthur (1901–47), slum violence was thus defined:

> Battles and sex are the only free diversions in slum life. Couple them with drink, which costs money, and you have three principal outlets for that escape complex which is forever working in the tenement dweller's subconscious mind ... The slums as a whole do not realise that they are living an abnormal life in abnormal conditions. They are fatalistic and the world outside the tenements is scarcely more real to them than the fantastic fairy-tale world of the pictures.
>
> Fighting is truly one of the amusements of the tenements. Nearly all the young people join in, if not as fighters themselves, at least as spectators and cheering supporters.

The provision of what is sometimes called (though not by me) 'working-class' houses accelerated after the Housing (Scotland) Act 1919 was passed, making it mandatory for Local Authorities to build enough accommodation to house their own populations. More than 50,000 such houses were built between 1919 and 1929 by Glasgow.

'Ordinary' housing schemes were built for better-off workers – in Knightswood and Scotstoun, among other areas, in the west; Riddrie and Shettleston in the east; and Mosspark and Carnwadric in the south. The designs were uniform, usually low-rise and sometimes with small gardens. Then followed 'intermediate' houses for those only able to pay subsidized rents. From about 1923, concentration was on the rehabilitation of the slum-dwellers from Anderston, Cowcaddens, Townhead and Calton. Some of these new estates, like the Blackhill scheme, became notorious; not surprising when the underprivileged and deprived were decanted *en masse* into one concentrated area. The Trust gave way to managing Corporation departments. By the end of that century, these in turn had their roles taken over by local housing associations.

The architecture of the between-the-wars council houses, though internally a huge improvement on the accommodation the tenants had left, was drab in shape and grey in colour: semi-detached houses, each of two flats, resembling nothing so much as a man with a hat pulled over his ears. After the 1939–45 War, colonies of high-rise flats, misadapted from Le Corbusier's use of them for suitable childless occupants as part of an ensemble, created new problems. Perhaps the most notorious in this respect were the massive Gorbals blocks by the distinguished architects Sir Basil Spence and Sir Robert Matthew, presumably responding to official briefing. Their buildings have since been demolished.

During the nineties, refurbishment greatly improved many a dismal block of municipal flats. New blocks frequently show a pleasing variety of design invention. Another improvement has been the replacement of flat roofs with pitched ones.

Glasgow's boundaries were extended several times during all this expansion. Govanhill, Crosshill, Pollokshields East, Pollokshields, Hillhead and Maryhill were incorporated into Glasgow in 1891, along with the districts of Mount Florida, Langside, Shawlands, Kelvinside, Possilpark and Springburn. Other burghs came in 1912, including Govan, Partick and Pollokshaws and the districts of Shettleston, Tollcross, Cathcart, Dawsholm, Temple and North Knightswood.

While rail and steamer travel were mostly the concern of the well-to-do, in the city itself the horse-drawn omnibuses, which first appeared on the street in 1834, carried a broader cross-section of the public. Working men of the poorer sort still preferred to walk to factory or foundry, for low-cost workers' tickets were not introduced until about 1894. The middle classes relied for transport upon their own carriages throughout Victorian times, a status-symbol provoking the same sort of snobbery as the motor car was to inspire a hundred years later.

Robert Frame, a member of the staff of the *Reformer's Gazette*, began running buses at 2d for the single journey between Barrowfield Toll, Bridgeton and Gusset-House, Anderston, on 1 January 1845. Before long, the magistrates had to lay down safety regulations to curb dangerous speeding by no fewer than four rivals, though Frame held his own until the famine of 1846, which raised the price of corn from 16s to 35s a boll (six bushels), bankrupting Frame and his rivals.

After eighteen busless months, Forsyth, Craig and Mirchell again tried running services. The 'father' of Glasgow's street transport system, however, was Andrew Menzies (1822–73), who took over many of the city's omnibus services early in the 1850s. His buses were painted in the Menzies tartan, those of his rival, Duncan MacGregor, in the tartan of Rob Roy. Gentlemen travelled on the exposed top deck, leaving ladies the shelter of the straw-flooded lower deck. Journeys in these vehicles can hardly have been pleasant experiences, especially in wet or steamy weather.

Cross-river ferries, vehicular and passenger, were established, and from 1884, a fleet of small boats, known as Cluthas, provided a fifteen-minute service. They were taken off in 1903, rendered superfluous by the electrification of the tramcars and the opening of the subway in 1896.

It is impossible to exaggerate the importance of the arrival of piped water to Glasgow. At the end of the eighteenth century, water still came from the thirty public wells, or from the reservoir of William Harley near West Nile Street, from which it was fetched in barrels by water-carriers and sold from pony-carts at a halfpenny a stoup. There were also wells in the gardens of the mansions in Buchanan Street, Queen Street and Miller Street.

The Glasgow Water Company, formed in 1806, pumped water from the Clyde at Dalmarnock, which, after being filtered, was then pumped to the city centre and the new suburbs. A similar operation was set up in 1808 at Anderston by the Cranstonhill Company, though within a decade it had also to move to Dalmarnock because of the increasing industrial pollution in the Clyde. The companies competed until 1858, when they amalgamated, though it was several decades later before piped water came to the houses of the less well-off.

When pure piped water did reach the city from Loch Katrine in 1859 (with an extension carrying water from Loch Arklet following in 1885), the initial scheme was officially inaugurated by the Queen herself. James Nicholson, in *Kilwuddie and Other Poems* (1863), thus celebrated the benefits:

Thou comest to a city where men untimely die,
Where hearts in grief are swelling, and cheeks are seldom dry.
A city where merchant princes to Mammon basely kneel,
While those that drag the idol's car are crushed beneath the wheel.

Throughout her mighty system of tunnel, tube and main,
The healthful current is pulsing, pulsing through every vein;
In the fever den, in the attic, in cellars under the street,
The poor have long been waiting to quaff the waters sweet.

The full benefits did not immediately become apparent, because the establishment of the water closet resulted in a substantial increase in the quantity of water used. Untreated sewage was at first flushed straight into the Clyde, the first treatment plant not being established until 1894, at Dalmarnock.

It was the less sweet waters of the Clyde, however, that were to carry Glasgow's fame still further abroad. During the late 1770s John Golborne of Chester devised a scheme for improving the situation. He made his first report to the City on the possibilities of deepening the sandy-banked Clyde in 1781. Work began on his recommendation, projecting walls to assist the scouring effects of the river. After a damaging flood in 1795, Glasgow turned to John Rennie (1761–1821), Golborne having died in 1783. Rennie was conducted on his original inspection by James Spreull, a member of a well-known merchant family. In 1798 Spreull was to succeed John Bennet as the second River Superintendent. It was, however, the great Thomas Telford (1757–1834) a colleague of Rennie's and then engaged on the construction of the Caledonian Canal, who, in 1806, came up with the solution, namely, that the extension of the parallel 'carried on by Mr Spreull' be continued through both banks of the river, thus joining up Golborne's groynes and canalizing the channel. His other recommendations included deepening the river upstream from Dumbuck by adjusting the west end of the Lang Dyke, as the south side sand-retaining wall was (and still is) known.

Eventually, this led to the vast expansion of the Glasgow Harbour. In 1806, less than four hundred yards of quay space was available, much of it on the north side of the Broomielaw. At much expense and after the passing of several Improvement Acts of Parliament, new quays were built on both the north and south side of the river. Deepening was to be carried out until it was 'at least nine feet deep at neap tides in every port between the Bridge of Glasgow and the Castle of Dumbarton'.

In 1809, responsibility for the river passed to a River Improvement Trust and the work of deepening continued, using increasingly effective plough-like dredging apparatus. (The first steam-powered bucket dredger was introduced in 1824.) From 1810 vessels could be registered in the city, a decided improvement in the recognition of mercantile status.

The passing of the Clyde Navigation Act in 1858, established the Clyde Navigation Trust (chaired by the lord provost of Glasgow) to take over from the former body. Between 1842 and 1871, the breadth of the channel was widened. Deepening continued into the twentieth century, highlighting, so far as spectators were concerned, the magnificent passage down-river of the Cunard Liner *Aquitania* on 10th May, 1914 and the even more admired passage of the *Queen Mary* (delayed on the stocks in building because of the depression) from the yard of John Brown on 25th March 1936).

Additional berthage was added to the Harbour at Windmillcroft (later Kingston Dock), Lancefield, Springfield, Mearnskirk and Finnieston, Yorkhill and the south quays of Queen's Dock, used by cargo ships. Plantation Dock and Prince's Dock were to be added before Glasgow Harbour reached its zenith. Great liners from most parts of the world sailed to and from Glasgow and were a familiar sight in the city's midst after the 1914–1918 War.

Following the report of the Rochdale Committee in 1962, having as its main recommendation that 'all ports within one river or estuary should be managed by a single authority', the Clyde Navigation Trust gave place to the Clyde Port Authority operating within a National Port Authority.

In the years that have followed, as John F. Riddell poetically puts it:

> New trades, new methods of cargo handling, and the prodigious growth in ships' size have all wrought many changes in the River Clyde. Rivalled in effect only by those resulted by the introduction of the steam boat more than a century and a half before, these developments have reduced the Port of Glasgow, once bustling over many miles with ships and trade, to the merest shadow of its former glory. Long rows of quays and ships lie deserted, and reaches of the river now drift for days untroubled by the turn of the screw. Apart from a few isolated areas still actually handling Scotland's trade, Glasgow Harbour has become enveloped in a peace unknown for nearly two-hundred years. Like a faithful servant resting after a long and arduous life, the river which made the city, and which was made by the city, lies asleep.

The development of container traffic has decreased the time taken to load and unload cargoes and also rendered unnecessary the number of ports required to handle this trade. The development of air travel has reduced and, in Glasgow's case, totally wiped out the passenger liner service traffic. Cruise ships depart mostly from Southern ports (though a few do call in at the Tail of the Bank, on the Clyde, off Greenock), so liners are no longer to be seen in the heart of Glasgow.

Meadowside Quay now serves the granary of that name, but nearly all the other docks that made up Glasgow's harbour are gone, grassed over or lying derelict. Only the King George V dock and the adjacent riverside quay still handle non-container cargo traffic, local container traffic being handled at Greenock. Rothesay Dock no longer handles coal but has been used to put together units for the North Sea oil industry. Hunterston, on the Ayrshire coast, has handled the iron ore trade since its establishment in the 1970s.

On Monday, 10 August 1812, the *Glasgow Herald* understood that 'a beautiful and commodious boat has just been finished, constructed to go by wind-power and steam, for carrying passengers on the Clyde between Glasgow, Port Glasgow, Greenock and Gourock. On Thursday it arrived at the Broomielaw in three hours and a half from Port Glasgow.' That boat was the *Comet*, probably launched from the yard of John Wood on 14 July 1812.

James Pagan, the author of *Glasgow Past and Present* (1884), wrote: 'There has been much said about the Clyde, and the improvements which have been made upon it ... I shall only state that I sailed in the "fly-boat" from the Broomielaw to Greenock and taken twelve hours to perform the feat; and also in the *Comet* of 1812, and managed the task in six hours, although lying on the bank at Erskine for a couple of hours.'

The transformation of travel on the Clyde was due to the ingenuity of the remarkable Henry Bell (1767–1830), a Linlithgow man who began life as a mill-wright and mechanical engineer, but settled in Helensburgh where he ran a hotel. Under his guidance, John Wood, a

A coal-carrying puffer passing a shipyard in 1949, just before the decline of ship-building on the Clyde

Port-Glasgow shipbuilder, constructed the 43 foot long ship the *Comet* (named after a recent appearance of one in the sky), with a boiler by John Napier and Son and a steam engine by John Robertson of Glasgow. Paddle propelled, she inaugurated a service between Helensburgh, Port Glasgow and Glasgow, extending her range to Oban and Fort William; but in December 1820, she was wrecked in a storm on Craignish Point, her engines not being powerful enough to pull her clear. A second *Comet* also came to disaster, but between 1812 and 1816 about twenty paddle-steamers were built on Clydeside, some of them reaching a speed of 8 miles per hour. Soon, these little vessels were regularly sailing to Liverpool and Northern Ireland. Another celebrated historian of the city, Andrew McGeorge, in his *Old Glasgow* (1886), tells us that Bell had to regulate the time of sailing, even though the ship had only a draught of four feet, so as to avoid low water. On being asked by a lady passenger what happened if she grounded, Mr Bell replied: 'Oh, the men just stepped over the side and pushed her across the shoal.' The popular saying 'The Clyde made Glasgow and Glasgow made the Clyde' should perhaps be adapted to end 'and Henry Bell made the Clyde', for, thanks to his invention, Glasgow became a great port, the first foreign trading ship sailing into the City in 1818.

Shipping at the Broomielaw in the 1820s

Jamaica Street (Old) Bridge. A very early paddle-steamer amidst the
predominating sail

Sailing ships had been built on the Clyde long before the coming of
steam. Indeed, Barclay, Curle began building sailing ships at Stobcross
in 1818, but in 1874 were constructing combined passenger and cargo
ships at Whiteinch, surviving there until 1967. Early steamboats could
not carry enough coal for long voyages to be sustained, so clipper sailing ships continued to be built until the 1890s.

The Clyde came fully into its own when steel was substituted for
wood in hull construction. The making of iron was facilitated by the
ready availability of coal from Glasgow's surroundings. Coal had been
mined in Glasgow itself from medieval times – under Glasgow Green
and in Kelvinside, Jordanhill and in the south side of the city – resulting in subsidence beneath property in the mid twentieth century and
the need to resort to costly underpinning.

The earliest recorded figure for coal production is for the year 1854,
when just under 7½ million tons was produced, about one-third of
which went to sustain the iron industry. By the early 1870s the coal
industry was no longer able to rely on the iron industry to absorb the
major part of its output, and firms from both East and West had also to
face up to foreign competition, principally from Germany.

One of the challenges to coal came from the discovery of shale oil by James 'Paraffin' Young (1811–93), though from 1870 onwards the distilling of paraffin from shale was superseded when it became a by-product from the refining of petrol, produced from imported crude oil.

The main competitor to iron was in fact steel, the production of which began in Scotland in 1857. Steel proved more malleable and stronger than brittle cast iron. Though Scottish pig-iron was found to be unsuitable for steelmaking, the invention of the Bessemer Converter proved more successful. By 1900, there were 115 open-hearth furnaces in and around Glasgow, producing about 617,000 tons of steel in various forms. Shipbuilding, and indeed heavy engineering generally, had all the necessary ingredients to hand.

The first steel ship was produced by Denny of Dumbarton in the 1870s, for the Union Ship Company of New Zealand. The first steel Cunarder, the *Servia*, which won the blue ribband for speed across the Atlantic, came from Clydebank in 1880.

John Elder, using Watt's ideas, developed the first compound (as opposed to single-action) engine in 1854, reducing coal consumption by up to 40 per cent and thus affecting sailing distance. He followed this invention four years later with another improvement, the condenser, obviating the need to use sea water, which was damaging to boilers. Coal consumption was reduced still further with the perfection of the triple expansion engine in 1886 and the quadruple a decade later.

Screw steamers had long since replaced paddle steamers, except for rivers or shallow estuarial work. The invention of the turbine engine by the Honourable C.A. Parsons resulted in the turbine method of propulsion, called by Lord Kelvin, 'the greatest advance in steam-engine practice since the days of Watt'. In 1901, the Clyde pleasure steamer *King Edward*, the first Clyde turbine steamer, was launched by Denny of Dumbarton, reaching a smooth-sailing top speed of 20½ knots. She survived in service until 1951. Her engines are now to be seen in Glasgow's Kelvingrove Art Gallery.

Famous Clyde yards came into being: Fairfield of Govan in 1870; John Brown in 1899 at Clydebank; and in 1906 Yarrows, particularly associated with the construction of naval vessels.

Shipbuilding on the Clyde probably suggests to most people the Cunard liners *Queen Mary* and the two *Queen Elizabeths*, built at Clydebank; but ships of every shape and size were launched from Clyde yards. By Victorian times, yachting had become the favourite hobby of many wealthy Glaswegians. A correspondent of 1902 observed in the *Herald*:

It has become so much a matter of habit to look on yachting as our most picturesque and health-giving pastime, and, with the exception of cricket, our most pure and wholesome sport, that it would be very little of an exaggeration to say that the individual aspect of it is very seldom remarked.

In recent years Mr G.L. Watson, the leading Glasgow yacht designer, has received from wealthy British and Continental men, and from American millionaires, orders, including a couple of steam yachts, the tonnage of which ran in the aggregate to between 3,000 and 4,000 tons, and which cost about £250,000. Even on the Clyde, where the placing of large orders for shipping is an everyday commonplace, the building of yachts like these cannot be despised.

By 1914, when the First World War broke out, the Clyde was building half the world's tonnage, using a workforce, including the ancillary finishing trades, of almost 100,000.

The first major development in shipbuilding that did not come out of the Clyde was the building of the Copenhagen oil-fired diesel ship *Selandia* in 1912. Benefit of hindsight suggests that this event marked the beginning of the end of the Clyde's supremacy in shipbuilding and the start of the long years of decline in the post-war period.

In 1888, Bass Kennedy, described by Hamish Whyte in his excellent anthology *Mungo's Tongues* as 'a kind of poet laureate of the Govan area', wrote:

> Ho, mates, go lay the keel-blocks down,
>   And bring along the keel,
> For we must build an iron ship,
>   And that right off the reel!
> And that right off the reel, my boys!
>   With no faults to conceal.
> Her frame's of treble B-shell
>   Of Siemens-Martin's steel ...
>
> Lay face to face and butt to butt,
>   And swing your hammers free.
> See that no idle hands surround
>   This virgin of the sea;
> This virgin of the sea, my boys!
>   For know when she's afar,
> The sailor's life is centred in
>   Her weakest plate and bar.

Even more vivid in its detail is 'Twin-Screw Set – 1902' by William
J.F. Hutcheson (1883–1951), a civil engineer who served his apprenticeship in the Fairfield yard.

Week after week I watched the darlings growing
Like two strange children in an orphan home,
Aft from the thrust block to the stop-valve throw-in,
Up from the bedplate to the L.P. dome.
One afternoon we swept the pit logs cleanly,
Set down a line of wedges, steel on wood,
Then laid the bedplate as you would a pin lay,
And saw the thing was good.

We squared it up and lined the eight great bearings;
Bedded the crankshaft down, and set up well
The eight box columns, and with plumbline fairings
Brought crosshead slides dead true and parallel.
We dropped connecting rods into their places
And bedded down the great big bottom ends;
Chipped oil grooves in the smooth whitemetal faces,
And felt they were our friends.

We faired the cylinders central and level,
Marked in the fitted bolts and screwed them tight;
Set the condenser, faced-up by 'The Devil',
One inch cast iron, and considered light.
We lined the pumps behind the L.P. columns,
And steam reverser, a new patent stunt;
Set starting gear and other what-d'ye-call-'ems
Upon the engine front.

The piston rods to pistons were adjusted,
The thrust shoes on their collars brought to bear;
Fixed lubricators with their dripper worsted,
Put balanced valves on the eccentric gear;
Connected pumps and tubed the big condenser,
Packed well its ferrules; and later the exhaust
Pipe pattern tried to place, so its ends were
Cast true and nothing lost.

We set the valves; the bearing leads were taken,
The cleating fixed, and platforms laid in place;

Handrails and footplates put, and not a shake in
The whole arrangement from the top to base.
Survey them there, each one of them a beauty,
Five thousand H.P. on point six cut-off;
Designed for honest cross-Atlantic duty,
And each one looks a toff.

Take note of them; the crankshaft fourteen inches,
The L.P. cylinders are sixty-seven;
Stroke forty-eight, high-bred like all the princes,
An inspiration from the hosts of heaven.
The thrust is seven, all valve travels ditto,
The crosshead pin's diameter's the same;
Connecting rods at middle are a bit o'
That figure's sacred name.

The great propellers, shining like a sovereign,
Are seventeen feet diameter, three blades;
Seventy square feet of bronze on each shaft hovering
To push her through the currents and the trades.
They take their steam full bore about two-twenty,
The furnaces one hundred feet below
The funnel tops; and, fed with coal aplenty,
What care they if it blow!

The Broomielaw c. 1840 – showing the steady growth of Glasgow as a port

Such was the spirit that made 'Clyde-built' synonymous with excellence in shipping circles for many a generation.

Less romantically, in 1804, the city chamberlain, Dr John Strang, published Glasgow and Its Clubs, in which he proudly recounted his city's achievements near the beginning of the century – the century that was to see the Clyde's rise as the major ship-building river of Europe.

> Glasgow unites within itself a portion of the cotton-spinning and weaving manufactures of Manchester, the printed calicos of Lancashire, the shawls and the stuff of Norwich and the masselines of France, the silk-throwing of Macclesfield, the flax-spinning of Ireland, the carpets of Kidderminster, the iron and engineering works of Wolverhampton and Birmingham, the pottery and glassmaking of Staffordshire and Newcastle, the shipbuilding of London, the coal trade of Tyne and Wear and all the handicrafts connected with, or dependent on, the full development of these. Glasgow also has its distilleries, breweries, chemical works, tan-works, dye-works, bleachfields and paper manufacturers, besides a vast number of staple and fancy handloom fabrics which may be strictly said to belong to that locality.

One of these was the Paisley shawl, woven on handlooms, the design using the cone-like cornucopia fertility symbol, a fashion at its height between 1830 and 1880. Its production soon afterwards moved to the Clydebank area.

Another was carpet-making, brought to Scotland by James Templeton, a shawl manufacturer who first set up business in Paisley, then moved to premises in Glasgow. He decided, however, to commission premises especially. He had William Leiper build his highly eclectic carpet factory in 1889. Known as the Doge's Palace, being Venetian in style – or rather, 'Paduan Gothic' – it has been described as 'one of the most extravagant polychromatic brick buildings in Britain, broadcasting an international outlook and cosmopolitan taste,' with elaborately inventive detail.

A dispute between the architect and the engineer during construction about the tying-in of the façade led to a near total collapse. It was twice extended by George Boswell (1879–1952) and in 1984 converted into the Templeton Business Centre. Frank Wordsall calls it 'the world's finest example of decorative brickwork – a strange distinction in a stone city, and for an architect who never before or after worked in that material'.

Glasgow Stock Exchange, 1954, built by Sir John James Burnet 1857–1938 in
Venetian Gothic inspired by Ruskin in 1874. In 1971 it was completely rebuilt by new
owners behind the original façade

Venice had already provided inspiration for the London Scot William Young (1843–1900), who won the competition to design Glasgow's City Chambers, 1883/8. Three tiers of classical columns support a pediment with two small towers, and also a large central tower topped by a cupola, the front elevation flanked by two smaller turrets. The carving around the entrance is mostly by George Lawson. An imposing marble staircase leads up to the banqueting hall, where the decoration includes work by the 'Glasgow Boys' Henry, Lavery, Roche and Walton. At right angles to the City Chambers, Robert Mathieson's 1875/6 General Post Office (replacing the Adam Assembly Rooms that once stood on this site) is also Italianate in style. Later extended down Ingram Street, its profile was altered when the end bays were raised in the 1980s.

Babcock and Wilcox started making boilers at Renfrew in 1893, while in pottery, the Verrefield Company, the Glasgow Pottery Company and the Britannia Pottery Company excelled. The triumphant Doulton Fountain of 1890 (from the Exhibition of 1888) still survives, on Glasgow Green to celebrate the city's pottery-making skills. In it Sir Henry Doulton celebrated in red terracotta allegorical figures dominated by the representation of Queen Victoria.

All this activity produced wealth. It was fortunate that, to gratify expensive tastes, a number of highly talented local architects emerged to lavish their skills on the development of the burgeoning city.

V

Tobacco merchant Andrew Buchanan founded the street that still bears his name, on ground he had bought to the west of his father's house in Argyle Street. He was in the business of feuing, the Scots word for leasing land for housing, for houses before he lost his fortune as a result of the American Revolution; but shops began to appear as early as 1820, the arcade linking Buchanan Street and Argyle Street, once housing a variety of shops but now given over to jewellers, having been built for the Incorporation of Wrights in 1828.

Even the Blythswood New Town could not satisfy the expansion needs of Glasgow's increasing population of successful men of business, so the move to the west began.

The estates of Kelvingrove (which once boasted a 1782 mansion house by Robert Adam) and Woodlands (which had a Gothic hilltop

Charing Cross and the 'leaning fountain', formerly known as Cameron Memorial Fountain. Note the early electric trams – converted horse-drawn vehicles which were in service between 1900 and 1923

house) were bought in 1852 by the Corporation to form Kelvingrove Park, sometimes called the West End Park, laid out by Sir Joseph Paxton in 1854. Part of the higher ground was to be used for high-class housing terraces. Charles Wilson was appointed to design the lay-out. Now an Outstanding Conservation Area, it is one of the city's most impressive architectural developments.

The first terrace, Woodside Crescent, is the work of Edinburgh architect George Smith (1793–1877). Now shorn of its two lower-end houses because of the ringroad construction, it curves through a right-angle and turns into Woodside Place across the intervening garden. Early in the 1840s, John Baird built a mansion on the ground to the west, extending it to become Claremont Terrace in 1847. Lyndoch Crescent, also the work of Smith, went up in 1845.

The one-time 'sylvan charms' of Sauchiehall Street, west of Charing Cross, also steadily changed as a series of terraces was built along it, the first being Newton Place, also by George Smith. Other terraces soon followed: on the south side, Newton Terrace (1844/5), opposite its namesake; Sandyford Place, though in a rather more imposing manner; and there was Clifton Place, remodelled in 1970. Classical precedent

Charing Cross in 1949, showing the turreted Charing Cross Mansions by Sir J.J. Burnet. The 'Coronation' type tramcar came into service in 1936

was abandoned by Alexander Taylor (d.c. 1845), who built in the decade 1839–49. Mention should be made of the spectacular French Renaissance-like convex Charing Cross Mansions, built in 1889–91 by Sir J.J. Burnet (1857–1938) and J.A. Campbell (1860–1909), with its tower, Baroque-style clock and sculpture by William Birnie Rhind (1853–1933).

Still further out, the new straight road running westwards *en route* to Loch Lomond and the Western Highlands, the Great Western Road (planned in the mid 1830s), was also soon fringed with imposing terraces. The first to go up was Kirklee Terrace (originally High Windsor), begun in 1845 by the young Charles Wilson (1810–63). Kew Terrace by John Thomas Rochead (1814–78) soon stood opposite it. Rochead then added Buckinghame Terrace, followed by the attractive Venice-inspired Grosvenor Terrace in 1855, which, with its 'enormous number of identical semicircular-headed windows on each floor and very

70

little masonry,' looks, as Walker and Gomme put it, 'almost as if a design for cast iron has been adopted for stone'.

Even more distinguished is Great Western Terrace by Alexander 'Greek' Thomson (1812–75), a long terrace with pillared porches and two higher pavilions set in six bays from both ends.

Thomson, properly regarded as the city's most celebrated Glasgow architect after Charles Rennie Mackintosh, prompts a diversion to consider some of those remarkable architects who, in Victorian times, were to give Glasgow its distinctive quality, even by European standards.

Although the builders of the great medieval cathedrals must have possessed considerable architectural skill, their names have not come down to us. Until the eighteenth century, builders and master masons

Great Western Terrace by Alexander 'Greek' Thomson, built 1870–4 during
Glasgow's westward expansion

did their own designing, notably the Mylne family in Scotland. Virtually the earliest identifiable architect to work in Glasgow was Allan Dreghorn (1706–64), originally an iron merchant, by 1741 a baillie and said to be the first person in the city to keep a four-wheel carriage. He worked with the Edinburgh architect James Craig (1744–95) on the Town Hall, demolished in 1911, and on Dreghorn Mansions in Clyde Street, incorporated into a warehouse in 1857 and pulled down in 1980. Only his St Andrew's Church, in St Andrew's Square, survives.

The 'father' of Glasgow architecture, however, is usually said to be David Hamilton (1768–1843), who seems as a young man to have had some contact with the Adam family. Hamilton apparently started life as a carpenter or mason, but soon became a favourite designer of country houses for the wealthy. His pre-Victorian achievements included Dunlop House, the massive Hamilton Palace (demolished in 1926), Lennox Castle and Castle Toward in Argyll. Much of his work in Glasgow has been demolished, but his 1802 masterpiece survives – Hutchesons' Hall in Ingram Street (containing a magnificent hall, remodelled by John Baird II in 1876, but converted in 1982 by Jack Notman to become the West of Scotland headquarters of the National Trust for Scotland). So, too, does his Nelson Monument on Glasgow Green and the former Royal Exchange in the delightful Royal Exchange Square, which he and John Smith are said to have completed to an original plan by Archibald Elliott the younger, and which is now an art gallery.

Both Wilson and Rochead were Hamilton's pupils. Wilson's surviving masterpieces include the 1857/8 Queen's Rooms in La Belle Place (presently a cult church); the former Western Club in Buchanan Street, now offices; and the Royal Faculty of Procurators building in 62 West George Street, which Walker and Gomme justly describe as the 'finest surviving example of the Venetian Renaissance craze which swept the Western world from Warsaw to Portland, Oregon, in the mid-1850s'.

Rochead's Grosvenor Terrace, badly damaged by fire in 1978, but with urgent popular support faithfully restored, has already been mentioned. He was also responsible for the Bank of Scotland building on the west side of George Square, now a pub/restaurant, and North Park House, Hillhead, built for John Bell, who ran the extremely successful pottery at Port Dundas and was also an art collector. It now forms the core of BBC Scotland's Broadcasting House.

John Baird I also played an influential role in the development of

Victorian Glasgow. His was the tobacco warehouse, 41–5 James Watt Street, put up in 1854, but now a store. Some might say that his masterpiece was the cast-iron Gardiner's Warehouse, 30–4 Jamaica Street, and still in use. It made architectural history, being the first commercial building in which the Crystal Palace's prefabricated structure was used. His, too, is the Argyle Arcade (already mentioned), the earliest of its kind in Scotland. Numbers 120–34 Queen Street, once MacDonald's sewed muslin warehouses, were taken down in the 1860s. Number 64 Buchanan Street, with its iron mullioned windows, survives at the time of writing, as do 189–99 Bath Street, built in 1833.

Other architects whose monuments remain include Alexander Kirkland (c. 1824–92), responsible for the noble St Vincent Crescent; John Baird II (1816–93), who went into partnership with James Thomson (though after a disagreement, Baird was replaced by Alexander's brother, George); John Honeyman (1831–1914), to whom we owe elegantly spired Lansdowne Church, on Great Western Road, Trinity Congregational Church (now the Henry Wood Concert Hall), and Westbourne Church, Kelvinside. In 1888, Honeyman went into partnership with John Keppie (1862–1945). The following year they took on a new associate, one Charles Rennie Mackintosh.

The list of fine Glasgow architects included three generations of the Salmons, beginning with James Salmon (1805–88), whose son, James Salmon II (1873–1924) designed the remarkable 'Hatrack' building at 142–4 St Vincent Street in 1899. He was also responsible for laying out Dennistoun. William Leiper (1839–1916) practised a wide variety of styles, Dowanhill Church being one of his finest buildings. 'Greek' Thomson's son, John (1859–1933), was responsible for a number of schools and hospitals, among them Stobhill.

Victorian pietism led to the provision of so many churches that by the end of the more secular twentieth century, finding new uses for often large 'dead' churches, especially in the city, has become a major conservation problem. Rochead's St Andrew's Free Church, in Hanover Street, put up in 1843/4, is, for example, now a furniture warehouse, while his United Presbyterian Church in John Street at the moment of writing stands dangerously empty; proposals for its conversion to a restaurant have been stalled by the anti-drink attitude of its previous owners. (Odd that they should be allowed any say, one might think.) Alexander Skirving's (d. 1919) Langside Free Church, though 'A' listed (in Scotland, Grade 1, 2 and 3 Listed Buildings are categorized A, B and C), likewise faces an uncertain future.

Those still in use, and of outstanding merit, include the Kelvinbridge Stevenson Memorial Church in Belmont Street, the work of J.J. Stevenson (1831–1908); Kelvinside Hillhead Parish Church in Saltoun Street, modelled on the Sainte Chapelle, in the heart of Paris, by Campbell Douglas (1828–1910) and James Sellars (1844–88), which has fine stained glass, a richly carved pulpit and a noble organ; Camphill Queen's Park Church of 1875/6 by William Leiper (1839–1916); and Lansdowne Church near Kelvinbridge by Honeyman. Only the shell remains of the 1856 Caledonia Road Church of 'Greek' Thomson, following a fire in 1956, after which it was consolidated as an historic monument. Now it seems likely to be restored as a millennium project. His St Vincent Street Church of 1858/9, built, it is said, with Solomon's Temple in mind, is undoubtedly one of the city's most handsome buildings, with its Egyptian, Greco-Roman and Old Testament decorative suggestions. After the Church of Scotland vacated it, it was used for a time by a religious cult.

A word should be said about education in Glasgow. John Knox is commonly credited with having established Scotland's superior educational attainment by insisting on the creation, under Reformed Church auspices, of a school in every parish. Glasgow's Grammar School (later becoming the High School) dates from medieval times. The spread of schools in the city occurred early in the nineteenth century, though education tended to remain the prerogative of the better-off until the passing of the Education Act of 1872, the Glasgow School Board coming into being the following year. Established by popular vote, it immediately embarked on a school building programme, occasionally producing a masterpiece like Charles Rennie Mackintosh's Scotland Street School in 1906. Regrettably, however, the board insisted on Presbyterianism being taught in all schools, a policy that resulted in Roman Catholic separation, duly enshrined in the 1919 Act. Sectarian teaching should have no place in modern society.

Famous schools, whether independent, grant-aided or run by the Authority, include Hutchesons' Boys and Girls Grammar, the former founded in 1650, St Aloysius (1859), Notre Dame (1897), Allan Glen's (1853), Kelvinside Academy, the work of James Sellars (1878), and David Barclay's Glasgow Academy (1845) – his Kelvinbridge second home for it – now amalgamated with Westbourne Girls' School (1877). Two famous girls' schools, Laurel Bank (1903) and Park School (1880) have also amalgamated to become Laurel Park, itself now amalgamated with Hutchesons'.

Religious bigotry and disputation, stoked by the immigration of large numbers of Irish Catholics during the potato famine years, when Glasgow was able to absorb extra labour, though never as widespread or dangerous as in Northern Ireland, did at one time produce in Hugh MacDiarmid's words:

> Gangs of louts at every street corner
> Full of nothing but *ochiana* [mundane emptiness] . . .

Nevertheless, gang warfare reached such serious proportions in the twenties and thirties that it became the main preoccupation of Percy Sillitoe (later knighted) when he came from Sheffield to Glasgow as chief constable in 1931. Though the Catholic 'Conks' and the Protestant 'Billy Boys' and their like had been dispersed by 1939, such was the publicity they received that the novelist Alasdair Gray could write in 1984; 'Glasgow now means nothing to the rest of Britain but unemployment, drunkenness and out-of-date militancy.' That there is perhaps some truth in this was demonstrated by no less a person than H.R.H. the Duke of Edinburgh when at Brunei University in September 1988. Talking of foreign students coming to Britain, he remarked, 'I do not know how these students are going to integrate into places like Sheffield and Glasgow. I commiserate with them.' *Herald* readers were not amused.

VI

Both World Wars brought irreversible changes to the Glasgow way of life. Like the rest of Britain, Glasgow no doubt approached the 1914–18 War in a spirit of optimistic jingoism. While poetry in Scotland was at a low ebb in these pre-war years, there is no reason to suppose that the mood of the city differed from that expressed by Rupert Brooke in 'Now God be thanked who has matched us with this hour,' or Laurence Binyon's 'We step from days of sour division/ Into the grandeur of our fate.' He at least lived to see the reality of 'In Flanders fields the poppies grow/ Beneath the crosses, row on row.' Not much grandeur about that!

Some of those crosses stood over men from the twenty-six battalions of the Highland Light Infantry and the Cameronians (Scottish Rifles), as well as from the Cameron Highlanders, who had responded to an appeal to join up by Cameron of Lochiel in the *Glasgow Herald*. Though in fewer numbers, Glasgow men also played their part in the other fighting services.

The wives and children of those who volunteered for the ranks suffered initial hardship, no provision for welfare arrangements having been made. The Prince of Wales quickly organized a relief fund, to which Glasgow contributed £240,000 within six months. By September 1915, Lord Provost Dunlop was able to announce that more than 100,000 women and their families had 'received relief'.

In his history *The Highland Light Infantry* (some battalions of which were also known as the Glasgow Highlanders), L.B. Oatts relates:

> The Glasgow Highlanders lost four hundred and twenty-one all ranks at High Wood, but fought on until within six weeks their casualties had mounted to thirty-three officers and seven hundred and fifty men, which was just about all they had ... While struggling through snow and sleet, the 16th and 17th and the right Company of the 16th were decimated by machine-gun and rifle fire. But the survivors pressed on into the German Munich and Frankfurt trenches, which they held for eight days. At the end of it there were only fifteen left, who were then taken prisoner because they had become so weak from lack of food that they could no longer stand up ... After that, there were still two years of bloody battles to be footslogged through, the 15th and 16th H.L.I. being amongst those who faced Ludendorff's desperate assault in March 1918.

More than thirty Clyde yards and engineering works turned out ships, many of which fell victim to German U-boat attacks and had to be replaced. A considerable repair service was also carried out.

Women came into factories. Wearing long tartan skirts, they also took over from the men as conductresses on the extensive tramway service that linked the city's districts.

On the morning of 11 November 1918, a poster appeared in the office window of the *Glasgow Herald* emblazoned with a Union Jack and carrying the one word – VICTORY. A special edition of the paper was soon on sale; factory workers laid down their tools; a great crowd gathered in the streets and the Lord Provost proclaimed the civic joy from the back of a lorry in George Square.

In the between-the-war years, Glasgow became tainted with the 'Red Clydeside' smear. True, early in the nineteenth century, Glasgow had acquired a reputation for militancy as a result of the Chartist riots.

The Broomielaw c. 1850 – a bustle of trade and a forest of masts

The dilution of skilled workers with unskilled in the wartime munitions factories caused trouble, stimulated by the Clyde Workers' Committee. In spite of a visit from Prime Minister Lloyd George, trouble continued to smoulder. There was a resort to the law and some militants were imprisoned in Edinburgh, including the then Communist teacher, John Maclean, who subsequently became a kind of working-class saint, inspiring more bad verse by good poets than any other Scot.

On 'Black Friday', the last day of January 1919, a crowd of strikers outside the City Chambers was engaged by the police. Among those arrested was Emanuel Shinwell (later Lord Shinwell, a minister in the Labour government of Clement Attlee). Other members of the breakaway Independent Labour Party, which he helped to form, were James Maxton, Thomas Johnstone (author of a recently reprinted attack on the Scottish aristocracy, *Our Noble Families*, and a future distinguished Secretary of State for Scotland), John Wheatley (who became Minister of Health in 1924), and David Kirkwood, another future peer.

Partly as a result of dissatisfaction with the worsening employment situation, the Scottish National Party came into being in 1928, its founders including the traveller and writer R.B. Cunninghame Graham; R.B. Muirhead, whose family tanning business was at Bridge of Weir; the Duke of Montrose, whose seat Buchanan Castle, Drymen, is now a de-roofed ruin; novelist Compton Mackenzie and C.M. Grieve, the poet 'Hugh MacDiarmid'.

Dissatisfaction had come to a head in 1923, when coal-owners, faced with falling sales figures, proposed a cut in miners' wages and an extension of working hours. The Trades Union Congress (TUC) called for a sympathetic strike. King George V declared a national emergency. The TUC thereupon declared a national strike on 3 May, thereby coming into direct confrontation with the government.

As the strike clouds gathered, Lloyd George thundered: 'There is one thing I dislike about the situation more than anything else. There is a great similarity in it as to the methods that led to the Great War – desultory and dilatory diplomatic exchanges, leisurely negotiations, never touching the real issues, and then the parties hurling ultimatums at each other.'

The National Citizens' Union appealed for volunteers to help run essential services. They signed on in considerable numbers in St Andrew's Hall for the six days that the strike lasted, drove tramcars (my father among them), moved supplies and kept the services going. Glasgow's newspapers, the *Glasgow Herald*, the *Bulletin*, *Daily Record* and the three evening papers the *Evening Times*, the *Glasgow Evening News* and the *Citizen* combined to produce a slim sheet, *Emergency News*.

The TUC soon realized that it could not win and called off the strike, although it was some time before the miners returned to work. 'A victory for common sense,' declared Lloyd George. 'It has once more been demonstrated,' crowed the *Glasgow Herald*, resolving to employ in future only non-union labour, 'that the people of Britain will not accept the dictation of any section, and that the community has within itself resources, vitality and adaptability equal to the overcoming of any emergency.'

The following year, the government passed the Trades Dispute Act, prohibiting sympathetic strikes, an Act only repealed by the 1945 Labour Government.

The day after the General Strike ended, the *Glasgow Herald* carried an advertisement from the outfitter Messrs Paisleys for 'summer livery suits for chauffeurs in blue, brown, claret, green or grey' for £7 (with cap to match for 12s.6d. – 62 modern pence). A Rolls-Royce to go with the suit and cap would have cost a mere £1,900, while a humbler car you would drive yourself could be yours for as little as £200. A packet of cigarettes to smoke while you made your way to the Palais de Dance – there were nearly fifty of these establishments in Glasgow during the twenties, the most famous being the Plaza at Eglinton Toll, all offering new dances like the Black Bottom and the Foxtrot – cost only sixpence (2½ pence today).

Not only the coal industry was in trouble; the steel industry also had serious problems. In 1926, the closure of the Glengarnock works, producing the Bessemer that Stewart and Lloyd required for their tube-making business, led them to move to Corby to be closer to their English supplier. Tramp steamers were laid up in many a Scottish sea loch. Shipbuilding declined dramatically. By the end of 1931, unemployment in Scotland had reached almost three million. A year later, 30 per cent of the working population of Scotland, mostly around Glasgow, were without a job. Dole queues and straggling hunger marches became an all too familiar sight. Scotland divided into two social worlds. Right up until the outbreak of war in 1939, Rolls-Royces could still be seen parked outside quality shops like Russell, the fruiterer, in Great Western Road, a liveried chauffeur going in to carry out the order while his employer sat in the back seat. The abdication of Edward VIII in 1936, though of little enough social importance, added to the thirties' sense of foreboding and insecurity.

Some innovations, however, took hold, lightening the sense of gloom. After having set up studios in premises in Bath Street in the twenties, then retreating briefly to Edinburgh, the BBC established its headquarters at Broadcasting House, in the former Queen Margaret College, in Queen Margaret Drive. The first 'talkie' cinema, the Coliseum, opened its doors on 7 January 1929, offering the new medium in the form of Al Johnson in *The Singing Fool*.

A scandal had been caused in 1924 when a journalist, William Bolitho, published his pamphlet *Cancer of Empire*, which graphically described the appalling slum conditions in which many Glasgow families were still forced to live; but by 1939, 20 per cent of Glasgow's population occupied low-rent housing.

New public buildings, fewer in number than in the affluent Victorian and Edwardian days, were built and some were distinguished. The Union Bank of Scotland had James Miller design its headquarters (later to become the Glasgow head office of the Bank of Scotland) on the grandiose Victorian scale, though using more restrained Greek

Sauchiehall Street in 1949. The standard trams with covered top-deck were brought into service 1910–24

detailing. More original, though in a kind of new late-medieval style, Sir J.J. Burnet was responsible for 200 St Vincent Street (1925–7), with its soaring chimney-stacks and its figures on top of the entrance columns.

New churches continued to be built, notably the St John's Renfield Church in Beaconsfield Road, put up in 1927–32, with its Baltic-looking saddle-back tower, the work of Sir Robert Lorimer (1864–1929).

The Beresford Hotel by Weddell and Inglis, erected in Sauchiehall Street in 1938 to accommodate guests to the Empire Exhibition, originally had a front elevation of mustard and black faience but, sadly, overpainted, is now a student residence, Baird Hall. Distinguished, too, was the 1939 Cosmo Cinema by W.J. Anderson II, a dignified brick building with some glazed ceramic faience, though now much altered; and the 1939 circular Reading Room for Glasgow University by Harold Hughes (1887–1949) and D.S.R. Waugh.

Perhaps the most ambitious Glasgow building, and certainly one of the most admired, was Sir Owen Williams's Albion Street premises for the *Scottish Daily Express* (later occupied by the *Herald*, for a time) with its horizontal strips of opaque black and clear glass and its curtainwall glass and vitriol panels fronting the load-carrying frame.

I grew up in the Glasgow of the twenties and thirties, reaching the age of twenty-one a few weeks before the 1939 war broke out. Through these uneasy years one was aware of the certainty that one was growing up to war, probably a worse one than the previous so-called 'war to end wars', and therefore a war which one was unlikely to survive. I therefore joined a searchlight battery of the Territorial Army – the unit nearest to where I lived – after the Munich debacle of 1938 and was commissioned soon after in my father's old regiment, the Cameronians (Scottish Rifles). My war began with a sudden late-afternoon telephone summons from our holiday house at Innellan on the afternoon of 2 September, followed by a sail to Wemyss Bay on the *Duchess of Fife* and a journey to Glasgow on a darkened train from which the carriage light-bulbs had been hastily removed.

On the morning of 3 September, as the Second World War was declared, we had started piling sandbags against the battalion office's windows and Glasgow heard its first air-raid warning – a false alarm as things turned out. At sea it was a Glasgow ship, the Anchor-Donaldson liner *Athenia*, newly out of the Clyde on her way to Canada with child evacuees, that was to be the first casualty of the war at sea. Thus, the war that one hoped by some miracle might not yet happen but knew in one's heart could not be avoided, struck one of its first blows at Glasgow's young.

There was considerable bitterness among Clydeside industrialists just before and during the early months of the Second World War, because of a belief that an unfair proportion of government contracts since Chamberlain plucked the sting out of the Munich nettle had gone to the South. C.A. Oakley, who, during the war, was to become Scottish controller of the Ministry of Aircraft Production, and later Scottish controller of the Board of Trade, and who therefore has authority behind his opinions, has gone on record as saying:

An impression does remain that the English firms who doubled or trebled their capacity in the 1938-40 period – taking their opportunity of doing so at the taxpayers' expense – were willing to put their younger executives in charge of their new plant, and that the West of Scotland firms, who would not make any major extension to their factories, or open new ones, denied to their youngest executives comparable chances.

Unlike its predecessor the 'war to end wars', the war of 1939, so long expected, affected everyone from the start. This time there were no public heroics. The mood was one of sober resignation mingled with a curious amalgam of disgust, guilt and, inevitably, a fear of the unknown, perhaps best caught by the self-exiled W.H. Auden in New York:

> I sit in one of the dives
> On Fifty-Second Street.
> Uncertain and afraid
> As clever hopes expire
> Of a low dishonest decade ...

The decade was low and dishonest because most of us chose to shut our minds to the terrible things happening to the Jews in Germany and to the Ethiopians in Africa; dishonest, because most of us kidded ourselves into believing that without commitment on our part, something would somehow happen that would let us off the hook, the bad turn suddenly good and our islanded lives be no longer threatened or disturbed.

Long before it could be the time for voyaging back, when 'the lost traveller, with sun bleached hair/ Dazed on the gangway' could 'come again' from distant battlefields, six long years were to be lived through. This time, at least, no one thought it would 'all be over by Christmas', in spite of stories about friends holidaying in Germany in 1938 whose 'Baby Austins' had fashionable collisions with German tanks, which turned out to be made of papier-mâché.

Gas masks were a universal issue, and were supposed to be carried everywhere. Dave Willis, (1895–1973) then one of the most popular of the long line of 'Scotch Coamics', delighted Glasgow audiences with a song that went:

> In my wee gas mask
> I'm working out a plan,
> Though all the kids imagine
> That I'm just a bogey man.
> The girls all smile

And bring their friends to see
The nicest-looking warden
In the A.R.P.

Whenever there's a raid on,
Listen for my cry
An aeroplane, an aeroplane
Away, way up a-ky.
Then I'll run helter-skelter
But don't run after me.
You'll no get in my shelter
'Cause it's far too wee.

Children and old people were tearfully evacuated from Glasgow and Edinburgh to safer country places. Many of them drifted back again after about six months, when it began to look as if the urban dangers might not be as serious as had been supposed.

Other townies remained 'exiles' in the country almost for the duration. The novelist Robin Jenkins has dealt amusingly yet profoundly with the difficulties which the introduction of city children and their often difficult parents into rural families sometimes produced, in Guests of War (1956).

Air-raid shelters were built, those at the bottom of our gardens being dubbed Anderson shelters after Sir John Anderson, the home secretary in 1938. The entrances to tenement closes were faced with baffle-walls. Barrage balloons floated above the city.

Clothes rationing froze fashions. A scheme for food rationing had been prepared well in advance, but although delicacies, especially fruit, were often in limited supply, there was always enough to eat. Restaurants were limited to a maximum charge of five shillings per head, and it was astonishing how much continued to be offered for that sum throughout the war. Some food myths were created, like the supposed efficacy of carrots for increasing sharpness of vision at night in the severely blacked-out streets. (Woolton Pie, another war-time speciality also commended by the Minister of Food, Lord Woolton, contained carrots as a major ingredient.) Glasgow swallowed the carrot myth along with the lave (the rest).

There were shortages from time to time, particularly during the middle years of the war. Cigarettes were difficult to come by, and so was paper. The paper shortage sometimes made it difficult to meet the full demand for newspapers. It also forced some limitation on the number of books which could be published. Many of those that appeared used a poor-quality paper, which was often a dirty-grey when new and speedily yellowed in the post-war years. Books, though individually licensed for publication because of the paper shortages, were nevertheless in steady demand, as was entertainment of all sorts.

Driving at night, with masked headlights showing only little rectangles of light, was an unpleasant experience. Petrol was only available for essential purposes, though it was surprising how apparently unessential some essential purposes managed to seem. Even among the services in training, restrictions on transport were severe.

Public transport presented problems too. Glasgow's tramway service operated at a reduced level. Long-distance travellers found themselves faced with conscience-troubling posters asking: 'Is Your Journey Really Necessary?' To most people the need to struggle for a place in an overcrowded train arose only once a year at holiday time. Thousands of Glasgow men and women in the forces no doubt still have memories of long journeys to and from brief home leave, overcrowded in compartments or crushed in corridors.

Many of the Clyde steamers sailed out beyond the arms of the Firth to become mine-sweepers. An anti-submarine steel-net boom that stretched across the Clyde from the Cloch to Dunoon divided the estuary in two, Dunoon and the Holy Loch being served from Gourock, Rothesay and the Kyles of Bute piers from Wemyss Bay.

It is right and fitting to lay emphasis on the civilian population when considering Glasgow's 1939 war, since this was the first war affecting the United Kingdom in which those out of uniform were liable to be as dangerously involved as the soldiers at the front – a good prospect for the future of peace, I remember reflecting when air-raids started to take their toll of civilians on both sides. Scotland had to bear only a small share of the brunt of the air war launched against these islands by the Germans. Most of that share, however, was directed against Glasgow and the Clyde.

There was a minor daylight raid on 19 July 1940. The first night raid came on 18 September, when bombs dropped on George Square but missed the major buildings, Queen Street Station and the tunnel that leads into it. It did, however, remove the building at the east end of Royal Exchange Square, the site on which Glasgow Corporation Planning Department was later erected in an undistinguished early post-war style. Another bomb set fire to the cruiser

Essex at Yorkhill, causing the evacuation of the nearby Royal Hospital for Sick Children because of a danger that the ship's magazine might blow up.

The most serious attacks on Clydeside were made in 1941 when Clydebank and Greenock took the full weight. In the three days, or rather nights, between 13 and 15 March, 1,083 people were killed and over 1,600 injured, mostly in Clydebank, where only seven houses remained entirely undamaged. As a result, this town with a population of 55,000 had to evacuate its 50,000 or so survivors. Many of these folk were involved in vital production work and their spirit in quickly overcoming the need to travel substantial distances to and from work was wholly admirable.

Between 5 and 6 May, the raids against Greenock killed 341 people and injured 312. Whisky stores and sugar refineries were a major hazard in the fires that broke out. Worse still could have been the dangers that would have followed if the Admiralty oil storage tanks at Bowling, containing more than twelve million gallons, had been hit by any of the hundred or so bombs that the Germans tried to land on the site. 'Greek' Thomson's splendid Queen's Park St George Church was unfortunately totally destroyed by fire in the last raid on Glasgow, on the night of 23 March 1943.

Glasgow had thirteen raids in all and had dropped on it 183 high explosive bombs, thirty-seven parachute mines, three oil bombs and thousands of incendiaries. By comparison with what Bristol or Coventry endured, this was slight punishment. But the secretary of state for Scotland was later to describe the Clydeside raids as being 'as severe as any other areas of Britain'.

Towards the end of 1943, the course of the war turned. Because of this, and because German technology was consequently prevented from improving the range of its V-1 'flying bombs' and its V-2 rockets, Glasgow was spared the renewed ordeal that London and other English cities and towns had to face from rocketry long after the offensive power of the Luftwaffe against the civilian population had been broken by 'the few' in the Battle of Britain. Among the Spitfires that swept the Germans out of the skies was the City of Glasgow Fighter Squadron (602). Many other Glasgow men served in the Air Force, either in the Glasgow squadrons formed subsequently, or as individuals on Atlantic duties, protective and offensive, in the Far East and upon the Normandy beaches in the summer of retribution, 1944.

The loss of life among service personnel in the Second World War was mercifully much less severe than in the previous struggle, there being much less actual fighting. As the added names on war memorials show, about a third of the total of those killed between 1914 and 1918 fell between 1939 and 1946.

Conscription was introduced from the start of the 1939–45 War, and once again the territorial battalions of both the Highland Light Infantry and the Cameronians (Scottish Rifles) included many Glasgow men, enrolled or conscripted. It is probable that about 150,000 Glaswegians in all served in the armed forces. To many of these men and women, the war took them for the first time away from their native place, as it had done me when on a Sunday afternoon in 1942, walking in Lowestoft, I suddenly recognized the unmistakable lines of the Clyde steamer *Duchess of Rothesay*. There she was, lying in the harbour camouflaged in the grey paint of a minesweeper. I felt as if I had suddenly come upon an old familiar friend with whom I had shared happier days.

Glasgow's most important functions between 1939 and 1946 were probably as a sheltered port and as 'the arsenal of the Empire'. During the war years more than 300 merchant ships were built in Clyde yards. The total tonnage of 1,634,216 included HMS *Howe*, the aircraft carriers *Indefatigable* and *Implacable*, the battle ship *Vanguard* and a huge quantity of smaller ships, including submarines, corvettes, escort vessels and landing craft. More than 25,000 repair jobs were also rushed through, some of them major undertakings, like the putting-together of a ship blown into two sections by a mine.

The Clyde also became the chief port in the United Kingdom, handling about 80 per cent of our incoming merchant shipping. Some of the ships that arrived berthed at a specially built port in the Gareloch; others were unloaded at anchor in other lochs of the Clyde, a fleet of little ships and barges ferrying their cargoes to the nearest railhead. Fleets of fighting ships, British, Canadian and American, assembled in the Clyde. So did the Norway convoy of 1940 and others, including convoys to Malta and to North Africa.

Many of the D-Day landing rehearsals were carried out on the Clyde, and the famous Mulberry Harbours, without which the Normandy landing could not have been sustained, were organized in the Gareloch. More than a hundred Scottish firms were involved in making piers and other parts of this remarkable enterprise, all within a fixed delivery schedule.

The Clyde's great liners *Queen Mary* and *Queen Elizabeth* steamed 950,000 miles between them, carrying 1¼ million soldiers, the speed of their camouflaged hulls fortunately making them a difficult target for German U-boats.

Enormous quantities of ammunition and equipment were manufactured in and around Glasgow. Even the Kelvin Hall – peacetime home of exhibitions, carnivals and circuses – was turned into a factory where barrage balloons and inflatable rubber dinghies were produced.

Womenfolk spent their energies generously in running service canteens for visiting soldiers, sailors and airmen. It is said that about 90 per cent of American troops spending leave in the United Kingdom came to Glasgow. A tile showing a Free Dutch Army soldier, and presented to my mother and other Glasgow women who had organized wartime club facilities, stood by a fireplace in my parents' home long after a generation had grown up to whom the war was merely a piece of history.

There were local excitements, ranging from the surprising arrival of Hitler's deputy Rudolf Hess, who baled out of an ME 110 over Eaglesham on the night of 10 May 1941, to the dreadful explosion of a French destroyer, the *Maille Breze*, at Greenock on 30 April 1940, killing most of her crew and causing severe damage to the town.

Although an end to the war had so often seemed impossibly far away during these six long years, when it came at last, on 9 May 1945, Glasgow celebrated VE Day with energetic gaiety. According to the *Glasgow Herald* report:

> People of all ages, conditions and sizes who had been thronging the streets as if waiting for nightfall made George Square their resort when night settled down.
>
> Long before the lights had sprung up to shed beauty and carnival gaiety upon the Square, over which towered the mass of the Municipal buildings, the junketing had begun. Dancing had gone on intermittently among the young, the leadership of which seemed to fall upon high-spirited liberty men from the Navy.
>
> They danced jigs and eightsomes in front of the City Chambers, performed sweeping wonders with the palais glide, and wound in long serpentine columns, singing and laughing in happy eddies, round the staider islands of civilian sightseers.

VII

The 1945 election returned a Labour Government with a majority of 200, a result that to our European Allies seemed to smack of ingratitude to Churchill. After all, here was a man whose determination had at one stage seemed almost all that stood between Hitler and his territorial ambitions for the Third Reich. Just as the mood of realistic determination in which the 1939 War had begun differed from the feeling of exalted crusade which accompanied the outbreak of the 1914 War, so the mood of 1945 differed from that of 1918. With fighting less continuous and the expectation of survival among members of the armed forces much greater than the life expectancy of a week that faced the average second lieutenant on his way to the trenches in 1916, there was more time for thinking. Soldiers given compulsory instruction in current affairs were actively encouraged to plan the Brave New World that every generation feels so certain it can build out of the failures of the past.

Yet Glasgow played virtually no part in the political shift that brought the Attlee Government into power, only one seat – Kelvingrove, which Walter Elliott lost by a small majority to the Labour candidate J.L. Williams – changing party allegiance. Glasgow was represented in the 1945 House of Commons by five Conservatives, seven Labourites and two ILP members.

One result of the introduction of the newly created welfare state was that the progress towards improvements in the social services was plain for all to see. Perhaps because of this, in the immediate post-war years, strikes were few and comparatively small. It was not, of course, VE Day that finally marked the end of the conflict, but VJ Day, 15 August, 1945, when Japan capitulated after the dropping of two atomic bombs, that undoubtedly saved the lives of thousands of Allied soldiers, sailors and airmen. The severe cost to the civilian population of Japan, the nation that so aggressively entered the war at Pearl Harbor, has always seemed to me to have been, on balance, entirely justified.

The population of Glasgow reached its peak of 1,128,473 in 1939. Thereafter, it steadily declined, being 681,228 in 1991, but expected to be down to 635,000 early in the twenty-first century. From an acreage of 1,786 at the end of the eighteenth century, Glasgow covered about 50,111 acres at the end of the century.

In 1946, the Clyde Valley Plan envisaged an overspill policy whereby some of Glasgow's population would be transferred to other towns.

Not surprisingly, only the skilled for whom there were jobs, or those who brought jobs with them, were welcome. The new towns of East Kilbride, Cumbernauld, Glenrothes and Livingstone absorbed many more and were much more successful.

Glasgow's ways of earning a living also altered their pattern during the second half of the present century. As shipbuilding and heavy industry declined, service industries increased. No one in my youth seriously considered Glasgow to be a tourist attraction, but so it has increasingly become. Service industries and public administration account for an increasing number of jobs. Unlike many other places, however, relatively speaking, Glasgow has not substantially attracted the newer industries. As the city's *Economic Monitor* for Autumn 1998 put it:

> While the rise nationally in ... electronic high tech activities in terms
> of employment, output, exports and wealth generation has virtually by-
> passed Glasgow, and the city's overall contribution to Scotland's engi-
> neering product has fallen dramatically in recent years, local workers
> and businesses are nevertheless well placed to secure contracts from
> both the construction requirements (jobs/suppliers) of those particular
> projects and from the recruitment of production/office staff.

The Glasgow Development Agency, however, set up in 1991 to assist economic development in the city and attract new industries, in 1997 launched a £50 million strategic site programme, focusing on Cambuslang Investment Park; Robroyston Business Park; Pacific Quay; West of Scotland Science Park; Cardonald Park; Glasgow Business Park; and College Business Park. The benefits of this initiative are bound to be reflected in how Glasgow earns its living in the twenty-first century.

One benefit has been the steadily increasing interest of Glaswegians in their own environment. Perhaps to some extent this was stimulated by the wave of destruction in search of the new that the Corporation embarked upon in the post-1945 years, before the value of conservation had been properly appreciated and enforced by legislation. Today, we appreciate our Victorian and Edwardian heritage, even if, to enjoy it to the full, it is often necessary to look upwards from a traffic-safe standpoint.

Although post-1945 architecture, in Glasgow as in many other places, went through a bad period, partly under economic and other

Looking down Bath Street towards St George's Church, 1984

pressures, the city has increasingly added to its store of good things during the second half of the twentieth century. Sadly, cheapness has
often been the governing principle, as witness the all too numerous
Lego-like buildings (with no disrespect to that admirable Danish toy,
which can at least be taken down and put back in its box of an
evening). Nevertheless, quite a number of buildings have gone up that
might very possibly qualify for listing and preservation in some future
survey.

Increasingly, clients now deal with teams rather than with individual architects as in time past. Credit has therefore to be given to firms
rather than virtuoso 'names'.

If the forties and to some extent the fifties were mostly concerned
with 'catching up' after the depredations of the war years, the number
of outstanding individual buildings and housing schemes multiplied
during and after the sixties. Among the latter, for example, is the
Ladywell Housing Scheme of Honeyman, Jack and Robertson, put up

in 1964 on the site of the former Duke Street prison for women; Page and Park's sheltered housing in 1989 in the Cathedral precinct; Macrae, McBurn, Logan, Opfer's strikingly original 21st Century Tenement at Maryhill, a modern variant on a traditional theme, built in 1988; Derek Stephenson's flats in Langside Avenue and the 1986 Elder Park, Govan, by Simister and Monaghan.

Page and Park's Italian Centre courtyard of 1990 must be included. It is an attractive and popular venue in the Merchant City, the rehabilitation and restoration of many of the streets that once comprised tobacco-town Glasgow, itself an award-winning environmental improvement.

Among outstanding office buildings must certainly be counted that of the former BOAC at 85 Buchanan Street, by Gillespie, Kidd and Coia, built in 1966; the 1970 Heron House of Derek Stephenson, cleverly designed to blend with 'Greek' Thomson's St Vincent Street Church; Moir and Ellison's Scottish Amicable building of 1976, which catches the eye but does not discomfit Salmon's 'Hatrack' building next door; and Elder and Cannon's 1981 National Bank of Pakistan in Sauchiehall Street.

Among educational buildings, the Glasgow College of Building and Printing in North Hanover Street, the 1964 work of Peter Williams, has quiet distinction, as has the nearby 1986 Britannia Building of Glasgow's newest seat of higher learning, the Caledonian University. It is by the Keppie Group. Barry Gasson's Burrell Gallery is also distinctive. Another effective building of culture is the 1988–9 extension of the Tron Theatre, itself converted two decades ago from the old Tron building. In many ways, also outstanding is the London architect William Whitfield's Library and Art Gallery at Gilmorehill, its complex of close-related towers a notable feature.

Even in our multiracial secular age, some new churches have been added to the townscape. St Charles' Roman Catholic Church in Kelvinside Gardens is by Jack Coia (1898–1980), something of an old-style virtuoso even in the prevailing context of firm teamwork. His, too, is the 1966 Dennistoun Church, Our Lady of Good Counsel.

Other buildings too numerous to detail here have received awards or commendations from Europa Nostra, the Civic Trust in London or from the two Glasgow Award Schemes run by the Scottish Civic Trust.

From the new millennium's beginning, good things are also

Glasgow University, Gilmorehill, 1958

forthcoming, or promised. There is, for example, the proposed Bath House Hotel, Glass Murray Architects' arresting conversion of a former brewer's office in Bath Street, its unusual feature intended to be a full-height glazed façade. One of the most distinguished shopping malls in the United Kingdom must surely be the Buchanan Galleries, making it, with the St Enoch's Centre at the bottom end of Buchanan Street, Glasgow's main shopping street and the City itself the second shopping centre of these islands, after London.

Some years ago now, I was guest speaker at a Burns Night dinner in the south of England. Next to me was the local lady from 'the Big House'. She talked so much that, like Susanna in *The Marriage of Figaro*, I only had to watch that I said 'No' and 'Yes' in the right context. Suddenly, in particularly fruity tones, my dinner companion boomed: 'Tell me, how is that charming little district the Gorbals faring?' I nearly choked on my haggis. 'It isn't,' was all I could reply at the time. But things have changed here too.

The history of the Gorbals is synonymous with bad housing – a close-knit tenement slum community that in the 1960s became the subject of Spence and Matthew's social and architectural tower block experiment. When the infamous Hutchie E flats were finally demolished in 1987, a gaping hole was left where 100,000 people had once lived out their lives. How do you persuade people to live in an area that has been blighted so many times?

The Crown Street Regeneration project was set up in 1987 to address this issue and appointed Piers Gough to design a masterplan for the area. A decade on, few people who saw Gough's original presentation could have imagined the scale that the project would reach. Costing £85 million, the Crown Street Regeneration Project now stands as one of the largest urban regeneration projects in Britain, if not Europe. Part of the larger Gorbals Investment Plan, it has successfully shown that, given the right environment and standard of housing, people from all social backgrounds do still want to live in the Gorbals. The renewal of this area is an on-going scheme which will carry on well into this new century.

Glasgow does not have over-many vantage points from which a visitor can survey the grid layout of the city. To mark Glasgow's 1999 year as the United Kingdom's City of Architecture and Design, the firm of Page and Park renovated (at a cost of £12.25 million) the tower in Mitchell Street and Mitchell Lane, known as The Lighthouse, originally a watertower for a large office (and in which Charles Rennie Mackintosh had at one time a designer's hand), adding an airy extension. The Lighthouse now includes exhibition space, cafés, shops and appropriate technical facilities. Said the director of Glasgow 'Year', Dejan Sudjic: 'The new work is a camera for looking at the city.' Onetime home of the *Glasgow Herald* the Lighthouse was described in a report in that paper as being 'a signal tower for world news, publishing the latest news bulletins from far and wide,' but now having undergone 'a remarkable transformation to become not only a showpiece for Glasgow's Year of Architecture and Design, but a beacon of light which is showing the way for design all round the globe into the twenty-first century.'

In the meantime, the rise in tourism has led to an increase in the number of new hotels and restaurants in the city. It would not be too much to claim that with the establishment of new, covered shopping

'The Lighthouse' building in which Mackintosh had a hand. It was converted in 1998 to a conservation centre, exhibition space and restaurant by the architects Page and Park

centres – The Forge, Braehead Park, St Enoch's Centre, Prince's Square and the Buchanan Galleries with its adjacent blocks – Glasgow is now, in all probability, the finest shopping centre in the United Kingdom after London with a '£2.5 billion baseline spend,' to quote the *Economic Monitor*'s unlovely jargon for possible customer spending power.

Statistics are dry things, however essential to planners and economic strategists. Even so, every now and then they take the general reader by surprise. I was certainly so taken when I read that 'the University of Glasgow, with some 5,300 employees, is one of the largest employers in the city' – particularly when I further learnt that Glasgow's other two universities, Strathclyde and Glasgow Caledonian, together employ an additional 5,190.

Other interesting statistics reveal that at the century's end, public administration with 97,083 employees tops the comparative jobs list; followed by banking, finance and insurance with 64,223, closely rivalled by distribution, hotels and restaurants; as compared to 3,288 in manufacturing.

Various factors play a part in persuading companies to locate in Glasgow, apart from such purely practical considerations as availability of labour, good communications and central position for marketing operations. The urban environment, the arts, sporting facilities are all good draws, and outstandingly beautiful countryside – Loch Lomondside (itself the gateway to the Highlands), the Firth of Clyde, the Ayrshire coast – can be found on Glasgow's doorstep.

How Glaswegians and visitors to their city enjoy themselves is the subject of a later section of this book. First, though, who were, and are, the Glaswegians, the famous and the infamous, and the ordinary daily folk?

2   The People

I

IT IS IMPOSSIBLE to pick out traits or idiosyncracies which can be said to depict the character of a particular place. Society has its layers and influences, created by the differing levels of wealth and, consequently, lifestyles that shape themselves within it, represented to some extent by consciousness of what is often defined as 'class'. Thus, Edinburgh, as the headquarters of Scottish government, the law and the Church, has a large and influential middle class, together with its colder North Sea climate, leading to the overworked sobriquet: 'East-windy, West-endy.' Hence that city's friendly rivalry with Glasgow – a rivalry acknowledged and written about by Glasgwegians more often than by the 'good burghers of Edinburgh', as Bernard Levin once called that city's inhabitants. Rivalry, real or imagined, certainly fuelled the journalism of Jack House (1906–91) for many a year. There used to be a joke told about a visitor arriving in both cities about tea-time. 'You'll have had your tea?' asked the Edinburgh lady. 'Will you have some tea?' asked the Glasgow hostess. But it is not really a joking matter. As George Blake remarked: 'Many a good Scots cause has been lost through the absurdities of this intercity rivalry.'

While the social reserve, no doubt encouraged by the handsome, rather aloof dignity of Edinburgh's late eighteenth- and early nineteenth-century New Town, is noticeable, in all probability much the same sort of class withdrawal was probably equally noticeable in the handsome Victorian edifices of the Park Circus area or Kelvinside in their pristine heyday. Glasgow, a major centre of commercial enterprise, harboured, however, a greater proportion of what Victorian commentators would have called 'the working class'.

Though Edinburgh's 'lands', with their narrow-based, high-laired dwellings, housed a reasonably diverse social mix, after 1768 when James Craig's New Town of Edinburgh was begun, the better-off 'emigrated' to the northern side of what is now Princes Street, and the social divisions widened, in recognition, as it were, of the physical divide.

In Glasgow, on the other hand, the form of housing from its period of expansion was of a more communal nature. Earlier Glasgow housing consisted mostly of one- or two-storey houses, often in narrow wynds and vennels, carrying open drains that became breeding-grounds for typhus and other diseases: but from about 1840 onwards, the characteristic Glasgow form of dwelling, originally intended mainly for the working classes, though later in more commodious proportions also occupied by the professional class, was the tenement. Typically of four storeys (although it could occasionally be of three or five) the tenement was built first of grey sandstone from local quarries such as Westfield, near Rutherglen, though from about 1910 of red sandstone quarried either in Annan or elsewhere in Dumfriesshire. The tenements consisted of a tiled common close with two flat entrances off it on the ground floor, and at the back a staircase leading to landings off which two opposite doors led to other flats. Sometimes the ground-floor flat had a main door entering off the street through a small garden. Tenements were built in three- (sometimes four-) sided blocks with a drying green in the middle. In the early tenements, sanitation (if provided) was by means of a common landing lavatory, or 'cludgie'. Each flat contained a box bed, usually in the kitchen. Originally with one room and kitchen – 'single ends', as they came to be known – tenements were soon developed to provide two- or three-room flats.

During Glasgow's vast population expansion, overcrowding became endemic, in spite of ticket men descending in the 'wee sma oors' to ensure that the permitted number of dwellers was not being exceeded. 'Backlands', usually jerry-built, were also sometimes erected in the back courts, thereby further increasing Glasgow's appalling density problem, for long the worst in Europe, and helping to create slum conditions.

On the other hand, even in such circumstances, there developed a neighbourliness and group loyalty that, bonded perhaps by the frequent working-class sense of insecurity, tended to produce that warmth and greater friendliness that for many generations visitors have found to be an unchanging quality among Glaswegians.

The folk-poet Adam McNaughton (b. 1930) indulged in some not uncommon sentimentality when he wrote:

> Where is the Glasgow where I used to stay?
> The white wallie close done up wi' piped clay
> Where ye knew every neighbour frae first floor to third
> An' to keep your door locked was considered absurd.

Times, alas, have changed and to keep your door unlocked now might sooner or later get you into trouble with your insurance company.

In very bad 'prentice schoolboy verse, I recorded my feelings for Glasgow in a line that contained a metaphor of appalling ineptitude, but that nevertheless summed up one aspect of the city's character:

> Warm heart of Glasgow with the generous hand.

Apart from the fact that as poetry, it might qualify as one of the worst lines ever written, factually generosity is an often commented-upon Glasgow feature.

Various attempts have been made to depict the Glasgow man. On the principle of Ladies First, we should perhaps begin with the French lawyer and geologist, Faujas de Saint-Fond, who, when on an extensive tour of Scotland in 1784, was struck by the comeliness of Glasgow women. He wrote:

> I was greatly astonished, in a climate so cold and moist as that of Glasgow, to see the greater part of the lower class of women, and even many of those in easy circumstances, going about with bare feet and bare heads, their bodies covered only with a bodice, petticoat and a cloak of red stuff, which descends to the middle of their legs; their fine long hair hanging without any other ornament than a simple curved comb to keep back what would otherwise fall over their faces. This garb of the females, quite simple as it is, is not without grace, and since nothing impedes their movements, they have an elegance and agility in their gait so much the more striking, as they are in general tall, well made, and of a charming figure. They have a bright complexion and very white teeth. It is not to be inferred, because they walk bare-legged, that they are neglectful of cleanliness; for it appears that they wash frequently, and with equal facility, both their feet and their hands.

J.H. Muir, the pseudonym of James Bone (later, a Fleet Street editor), wrote in *Glasgow in 1901*:

> The man in the square hat has been described as the typical Glasgow man, because it is he that is seen most often in the business parts of the city. But we do not forget that he is not the cause, but the product, of her greatness. To a superficial eye he would seem to be a parasite buying and selling what other men produce, and yet he renders services to his fellows which justify his existence. Still, it is not he who makes Glasgow a centre of industry and a home of manufacture. That is a man of quite another kind, who is rarely seen on the streets and, save to his own circle, is hardly known even by head-mark. He is to be found in the engine shops of Springburn or Govan, in the shipyards by the river, in the factories of the South Side and East End. We would gladly describe him, but we know him only by name.

So it was then, and probably was for another thirteen years or so.

An American professor of administration, Frederic Clemson Howe, looked in on Glasgow in 1905 while on a tour of European cities. He visited Dalmuir Sewage works, where an old employee told him how the sewage was collected; how it was separated by chemical treatment; how the

> water was purified before being poured into the River Clyde. It was so pure, he said, that it was fit to drink. He offered me a glassful, but I told him, I wasn't feeling thirsty at that moment. So he drank it himself. He told me how much the city received from the sale of the sludge as fertiliser. He explained the process as a gardener might describe the cultivation of some rare flower he had given his life to producing. The man had been in the city employ a long time. There was little dignity and less pay about his position. But he was a citizen of no mean city, and he was proud of his job. It was all so important to him, he felt it must be equally important to the rest of the world. Enthusiasm and interest, devotion and pride – these are the characteristics of Glasgow citizenship.

The author George Blake, though the prototype of the Garvel of his novels was Greenock, knew Glasgow well as a one-time editor of its *Evening Citizen* newspaper. He maintained, in *Heart of Scotland* (1934), that while Glasgow 'has the faults inherent in a fairly recent

Glasgow folk in St Vincent Place, 1914

industrial growth, it has the interest of diversity. He would be a poor observer who did not see in Glasgow one of the most diverting communities in Christendom,' adding that 'it may confidently be maintained that here is the liveliest community in Scotland. This fantastic mixture of racial strains, this collection of survivors from one of the most exacting of social processes, is a dynamo of confident, ruthless, literal energy. The Glasgow man is downright, unpolished, direct and immediate.'

The men whose driving initiatives raised Glasgow to its industrial zenith were ruthless entrepreneurs – men like shipbuilder and engineer David Napier; shipbuilders Alexander Stephen and Charles Connal; industrialist Sir Charles Tennant; coal-owners and iron-masters, the Bairds of Gartsherrie and their contemporaries. All were rugged individualists, usually members of the Conservative and Western Clubs and shared yachting as their hobby. Indeed, the most ambitious yachtsman of them all, Sir Thomas Lipton (1850–1931), who three times unsuccessfully challenged the United States for the America's

Cup with his great yachts *Shamrock One, Two* and *Three*, was the owner of a highly successful chain of grocery stores and a provision merchant specializing in tea.

Recently, an academic publicly deplored what he deemed to be the present-day lack of entrepreneurial skills among the young in Scotland. It does sometimes seem that way, though the lack of native inventiveness and investment in Scottish enterprise is surely the fault of an older generation. In any case, as Sydney Checkland remarked in his excellent economic study *The Upas Tree* (1976):

> It is no good yearning for a return to the age of the tycoons of Victorian times, for management is now a very different function, to be carried on in very different conditions. Similarly, though regional loyalty must still play an important part, it is no longer possible to think of management as a locally varied product, bound to its place of origin. As with a football team, talent must be sought where it is to be found, it must be attracted by free choice, and it must be paid for on the appropriate scale ... On the labour side there can be little doubt that Glasgow and the West of Scotland have acquired a bad reputation in industrial relations, which compounds the difficulties of the region. Though conflicts between management and men have perhaps been amplified beyond their true dimensions by the emotive label of Red Clyde and by the media, they are nevertheless a reality, of which the rest of Britain is very conscious. Such a situation and such a reputation are, indeed, what might be expected from an area with such an economic base (containing as it did a higher proportion than the national average of strife-prone industries).

In this connection, it sometimes seems that whatever the cultural achievement of sustaining the national identity may have been, it has become obvious that the industrial and commercial base is seriously flawed. Over and over again, when a Scottish company becomes successful enough to attract hostile take-over bids from English companies competing in the same field, Scottish shareholders quickly forget their sense of nationalism in the rush to make a profit selling their shares. I sometimes think that under these circumstances no Scottish concern is ever going to survive for long on the crest of viable success, because English or foreign money speaks louder than pride in Scottish industrial or commercial achievement. We are thus bound to be, in that sense at least, forever a nation of losers.

Much of the pride Glasgow evokes is of a distinctly romantic nature, as when Sir Compton Mackenzie, in his rectorial address of 1931 to the students of Glasgow University said:

A few weeks ago from the Campsie Fells I gazed down at Glasgow. From a mass of dark cloud the sun, himself obscured from where I stood, sloped his golden ladders into the rain-washed city, which lay with her spires and chimneys, with all her towers and tenements and sparkling roofs, like a vision of heavenly habitation. I have looked down over Athens. I have looked down over Rome. With beauty unparagoned the glory and the grandeur of the past have been spread before my eyes; but in that sight of Glasgow something was added which neither Rome nor Athens could give – the glory and the grandeur of the future, and the beating heart of a nation.

A far remove that, from Aberdeen-born poet G.S. Fraser's 'Glasgow, that damned sprawling evil town!'

In *The Heart of Scotland* (1934), George Blake made this assessment:

The Glasgow man is downright, unpolished, direct and immediate. He may seem to compare in this respect with the Aberdonian, but in him there is none of that queer Teutonic reserve, which is so apt to affect human intercourse with the native of Buchan. That he is a mighty man with his hands, the world knows and acknowledges; that he is nearer the poet than his brothers in the other cities is less obvious but equally true. He has the 'furious' quality of the Scot in its most extreme form. He can be terribly dangerous in revolt and as terribly strong in defence of his own conception of order. He hates pretence, ceremonial, form – and is at the same time capable of the most abysmal sentimentality. He is grave – and one of the world's most devastating sardonic humorists.

Charles Oakley, whose book *The Second City* (1946) had many perceptive things to say about Glasgow and Glaswegians, has analysed the character of the Glaswegian perhaps more extensively than anyone else.

A great many people have been grateful for having, at a hazardous moment, a Glasgow man on their side. In matters concerning his own self-interest – or, at least, what appears to him his own self-interest – he is a realist and an opportunist, ever, like Kennedy Jones, with his eye on the main chance. With his roots in the soil, he has a good understanding of his fellow-men, and he can usually be depended upon, as Sir John Moore was when carrying out the re-training of the British infantry soldier, to concentrate on what really matters while handling those under him humanely. He drives the men in his charge, but mixes with them, and is never 'standoffish'.

To what extent is the common impression that he is a solitary man really accurate? He likes to be alone, is reticent, and does not mix so readily with his fellow-men as the Englishman does – the Glasgow 'pub' is a dismal place, quite lacking the warm geniality of the London pub – but he is, nevertheless, the better host. Scottish hospitality has a world-wide reputation, and the American and Dominion troops, who spent their leave in this country made no secret of their view that they were better looked-after in the North than in the South. Yet the Glasgow man lacks the social graces – he is reluctant to say please, thank you, I'm sorry, or excuse me – and he is apt to push people out of his way rather crudely and often unnecessarily. He glories in being outspoken, sometimes without realising that an inaccurate or ill-advised remark is not rendered any the less accurate or ill-advised by being candid.

The outstanding weakness of some Glasgow people is perversity. Contra-suggestibility is found in every community throughout the world; but, alas! the percentage of Clydeside people, who seem disposed to do the opposite of what is suggested to them, is on the high side. As a recent Medical Officer of Health for Glasgow remarked, 'the people of Glasgow are inclined to be thrawn.' They always want the one brand of toothpaste not in stock, to ride on the crowded tramcar rather than on the empty one behind, to go among the Celtic supporters at a football match and cheer for the Rangers. Their predilection for jay-walking on busy streets is probably the most unfortunate feature of their social behaviour. Believing that he has a prior right on the roadway to automobiles, the perverse man expects them, even if the traffic lights are in their favour, to make way for him, and he will walk scowling in front of motor-cars, daring their drivers to knock him down. Thus he makes visiting motorists – including those who might consider building new factories in Glasgow – ill-disposed towards his city on their first contact with it – and first impressions have a habit of lasting.

Perhaps this unreasonableness has its origin in the Glasgow man's endeavour, a worthwhile endeavour, to preserve his individuality. In integrity, for instance. The reputation of the Scottish Insurance companies in the United States is still high because, unlike some American companies, they did not haggle over claims at the time of the San Francisco earthquake. And it is worth noting how often the Glasgow man, who has had a business failure, succeeds later in meeting his creditors in full. Sometimes his children do it for him, after his death. The goods he makes are of first-rate quality. The last battle in the struggle between craftsmanship and mechanised production is likely to be fought in Glasgow. Pride in personal appearance can be seen in any street. The Glasgow business man and his clerks and his typists are usually better dressed than their opposites in London – although the latter are sublimely unconscious of their relative, and, indeed, actual dowdiness. Contrast, too, the bearing of the Glasgow bus drivers and conductors in their tidy, well-pressed green suits and that of the mussy London bus drivers and conductors.

The Glasgow man's concern about his appearance arises from his self-consciousness. In comparison with the extroverted Southern Englishman or Lancastrian, the Glasgow man is highly introverted. He is, for instance, shy about singing in public and, as J.H. Muir remarked, he would not for his life lower himself to be seen in a tramcar blowing his child's nose. But he is much the more likely among parents to take that child on an annual visit to the pantomime and, when he grows older, to give him a better start in life.

The Glasgow man has the reputation of being stubborn, and wits sometimes tell stories about the awful spectacle to be seen when two Glasgow men push their chins in each other's faces, both actuated by the necessity for maintaining profound and inviolate principles. Much of this misrepresentation is nonsense, although the Glasgow man does not have the Londoner's sense of compromise, and the lack of it is apt to be a handicap in the conduct of his affairs. Yet he often derives great moral force from his principles – witness, for instance, the courage of the Covenanters and the sacrifices made by many who took part in the Disruption of the Established Church. He came out of his stand against professionalism in sport with a great deal more dignity than his opposites in England. And, although he is quite capable of being astute when arranging a deal, he is not a 'smart alick' or a 'double-crosser'. The word of the Glasgow business man stands perhaps a little higher than the word of the business men of certain other towns.

Edinburgh-born Naomi Mitchison (1898–1999), in the notes for her greatest novel *The Bull Calves* (1947), had this to say about Glasgow:

I know Edinburgh well enough. I feel easy there in my birthplace, the beautiful northern city, the half alive, emptied capital, the lilac-smelling squares of the New Town, the great amethyst shadow of the Castle rock. Yet now, surely, I know Glasgow better. And I am always in two minds about this Glasgow. Edinburgh has two faces, one of beauty and order and the possibility of civilization: the other of conservatism and the dead hand – a little enthusiasm over the preservation of past beauty but none over the creation of new beauty along new lines. And Glasgow also has two faces. Neither is of beauty or order. It is a disgustingly ugly town, a huddle of dirty buildings trying to outdo one another and not succeeding, an overgrown village with no decent architecture except Blythswood Square and a few half-forgotten terraces, its ancient buildings hardly to be seen through the mess and squalor that surrounds them. Glasgow, 'the most uniform and prettiest town' that Burt saw on his eighteenth century tour! The population is as ugly as the buildings. Walk down the Gallowgate; notice how many children you see with obvious rickets, impetigo or heads close clipped for lice; see the wild, slippered sluts, not caring anymore to look decent! There is something queerly inappropriate about their bobbed heads, since shortened hair should either be elegantly dressed or else glow and wave with brushing; they have no money for hair-dressing, no energy for brushing; they went down with their men into the hell of unemployment and vile housing. They do not speak any real variety of Scots, but a blurred, debased English, or – since 1942 – American. They lost everything, even the courage and solidarity that stopped London from panicking desperately during the blitzes, as Glasgow panicked in 1942. The other thing that will give you a good scunner in Glasgow is any place where the prosperous Glasgow businessmen congregate to eat – or drink. They have full as little use for beauty as those out of whose bodies the profits were made.

But yet through all one's anger against Glasgow, there is the other side. It is alive, it is full of hope and people wanting to be educated, wanting to try out something new, even if they don't rightly know what it is. And it is friendly – dirty and friendly and hospitable as a great slum tenement building or a Highland clan stronghold two hundred years ago. And it might be great and beautiful.

A great novelist and a distinguished member of the famous Haldane family, her views could be oddly idiosyncratic. She once accosted me in the Glasgow Saltire Club, long since vanished, where we were both having an early supper. She wanted to know what was on that night in Glasgow's theatres. Being at that time music critic to one paper and temporary drama critic to another, I responded to her request. 'Donizetti's *Don Pasquale?*' she questioned. 'What's the plot?' I outlined it in some detail. 'And who is singing?' This information I also provided. 'There's only one thing,' she said. 'What's that?' I asked. 'I don't like Donizetti's music.'

In the days of its growing prosperity, Glasgow learned to think big. Now, in its days of contraction it has had to think smaller, though not small. It seems improbable that it will ever again be the major industrial centre that once made it, as well as 'The Second City of Empire', 'the workshop of the world'. Checkland again: 'There is the further circumstance that advanced economies show signs of continuously shrinking the manufacturing sectors and expanding the service element. It may be that the future of a city like Glasgow will lie more in providing commercial premises and service jobs of one kind or another rather than industrial ones.'

Yet it shows every sign of attracting businesses from more vigorous economies wishing to establish a base with easy access to mainland Europe. Often they locate in Scotland enticed by generous government grants. The drawback to this arrangement is that in leaner times such firms tend to pull in their tentacles, so to say, and close their overseas factories. If they have received hefty grants from this or that government, taxpayers' money is thereby lost, to very little ultimate purpose.

Obviously, Glasgow's future depends on the future of Scotland. I happen to believe that the days of the competing nation state are over; that integration is essential, both for economic stability and to ensure the preservation of peace. It surely makes little sense for Scotland totally to sever its union with England? A Scottish army, a Scottish navy, a Scottish air force? On the other hand, if the eminently sensible solution of a devolved Scottish parliament is to work, Scots will need to recover and sustain the self-confidence of much earlier years; not just among the future leaders of Scottish enterprise, but among ordinary Scots, Glaswegians included.

For far too long they have been affected by debilitating unbelief in their own potential abilities; for too long half convinced that because of past production successes, the world still owes them a living; and for too long victims of the notorious old-fashioned Scots cringe factor, initially brought about by urban tycoon management and absentee land-

lord ownership. Somehow or other, Scots – and, in this context, especially Glaswegians – have to learn to master the enterprise, vision and
energy of the entrepreneurs of earlier days, but within the more restric-
tive circumstances of a modern civilization.

II

Irish immigration during Glasgow's expanding days, fuelled by the
Potato Famine (1846), which the British Government did little
enough to relieve, helped to turn the Gorbals – for long Glasgow's
most notorious slum, though probably not its worst – into a synonym
for appalling living conditions. The area inspired, more than a century later, Robert McLeish's play *The Gorbals Story* (1954) and Sir Arthur
Bliss's ballet *Miracle in the Gorbals*, choreographed by Robert Helpman.

Leslie Mitchell (1901–1935), who wrote under the pseudonym of
Lewis Grassic Gibbon, and who collaborated in 1934 with C.M.
Grieve (1892–1978), the poet Hugh MacDiarmid, to produce a fierce
survey of the national fabric, *Scottish Scene* (1934), wrote of the
Gorbals at a time when Eastern European refugees were further
increasing the social pressures.

> It is coming on dark, as they say in the Scotland that is not Glasgow.
> And out of the Gorbals arises again that foul breath as of a dying beast.
> You turn from Glasgow Green with a determination to inspect this
> Gorbals on your own. It is lovably and abominably and delightfully and
> hideously un-Scottish. It is not even a Scottish slum. Stout men in
> beards and ringlets and unseemly attire lounge and strut with pointed
> shoes ... In the air the stench is of a different quality to Govan's or
> Camlachie's – a better quality. It is haunted by an ancient ghost of good-
> ness and grossness, sun-warmed and ripened under alien suns. It is the
> most saving slum in Glasgow, and the most abandoned. Emerging from
> it, the investigator suddenly realises why he sought it in such haste from
> Glasgow Green; it was in order that he might assure himself there are
> really and actually other races on the earth apart from the Scots!

More than half a century after that was written, our multi-racial society – however socially broadening, the inevitable price of collapsed
colonialism – happily ensures that no such reminder of the fatuity of
racial pride survives.

In 1912, when playwright James
Bridie was still briefly a practising
doctor under his own name, O.H.
Mavor (1888–1951), he attended a
maternity call-out to a slum
dwelling, not in the Gorbals, accompanied by a friend. He recounted the
incident in his autobiography, *One
Way of Living* (1939):

James Bridie (1888–1951), drawn by
Sir William Oliphant-Hutchison

Among the silt into which Matthew
White and I dived and delved was a
house near the Municipal Buildings
and back to back with a fire station.
It had been a noble house in its time
but was now farmed out. There was
no light in the rotten staircase, and
we had to pick our way over and
among drunken men lying among
their gastric contents ... Among the rags and filth of the little Irish home
the patient and her mother were having a first class row. The Virgin and
the Saints were being invoked to the accompaniment of words from a
rather less exalted vocabulary. The baby was just about to be born. I had
to conduct the confinement myself. I was protected by a cold in the head
from the atmosphere in the room, but Matthew White had to retire to the
street to be ill. Before the *accouchement* I am sorry to say we had to lift our
hands to a woman, not in the way of kindness. We threw the grandmoth-
er downstairs and didn't see her again. It was a fine, healthy boy ...

In the morning I looked out of the disreputable window and saw the
firemen's wives cleaning up before breakfast on the verandas of their
tidy little flats. The sun was shining – not, indeed, into the room where
I stood ...

Cleanliness and honour and filth and dishonour were pretty evenly
mixed in the 'district'. Among other things, I found that the caste system, which provides such engaging little comedies among the well-to-
do, was held here with a desperate passion. The respectable poor saw
their children walking on rotten planks. At any moment they might fall
into the cesspool and be drowned. The badge of rank was cleanliness,
and cleanliness was preserved in bug-infested houses with one tap in a
kitchen sink as the only instrument.

One of the mildly annoying aspects of my friendship with Hugh MacDiarmid, who lived for some two years in the basement flat in the home of artists Walter and Sadie Pritchard, almost back-to-back with my father's house in Athole Gardens, was his wife's frequent disparagement of what she called my 'middle-class upbringing'. Nobody is responsible for the circumstances into which they are born and such chip-on-shoulder accusations are, indeed, a variant of racism. As I once said to a famous Scots novelist, bleating on about his humble origins: 'Nobody gives a damn about what you were. They are only interested in what you are.' If you are a writer, indeed, you must become classless, your only responsibility being to humankind as a whole.

I do, however, remember the Glasgow occasion when I broke free from both the class system and from the art-for-art's-sake fallacy that, for a while, I embraced in my early youth: I commemorated the occasion in 'Unpaid Engagement'.

The first time that I felt uncomfortable
about the fitness of things was when a charity,
to which my school gave yearly donations,
conveyed me, as a schoolboy, to a poorhouse
to play the violin with others for
the docile inmates. We were heard politely
through scratchings and the scliffing grunts of bows
by women with no teeth to brace their smiles;
old men who gristled stubbly beards; officials
procuring routine patronised applause,
glazed with the boring thanks of disapproval –
leadership gratituding, come what may!

From the hired outlook of the homeward car,
through slums we never knew crowded existence
we saw small ragged children; barefoot streets;
unwinding wobbled iron hoops, which clattered
flat on the cobbled stones; and through the open
rear window, smelt the name of poverty;
past spilled pub-corners propped by argued loungers,
the crumpled white cravats of unemployment
scragging at fag-ends and exhaling laughter
(whatever could they find to joke about?)
The car went gliding through the business quarter

where ordered office was the time of day
and tramcars squealed at corners tight with shoppers
whom life had put upon a settled way;
back to the West End, with its prospered houses;
back to the edge of my secure good fortune,
leaving behind some part of certainty.

What was there that a violin could say?

That 'secure good fortune' was centred in our home, first at 11 Ashton
Terrace, then a private road linking Byres Road and University
Avenue. The houses on the north side went up in the 1850s, those on
the south side later, about the turn of the century, and were residences
for the university professors. One of them had a peculiar fascination for
me as a teenager, because it then housed a professor's wife who, reputedly, had tried (and failed) to pass her driving test no fewer than thirty-six times, causing a nervous breakdown among several examiners,
before the powers-that-be ruled that she could no longer apply for a
test.

Today, only half of the south side survives, including our umquhile
(one-time) house, the rest having been demolished to make way for a
new road system.

III

When a city wishes to establish its credentials as a hotbed of genius it
usually lists the painters, poets, novelists or composers who have
spread its name abroad. Of composers, Glasgow has had few enough:
Cedric Thorpe Davie (1913–83) is the only name that springs readily
to mind, though Borderer Francis George Scott (1880–1958) spent
many years as lecturer in music at Jordanhill Training College for
Teachers, and after his retirement continued to live and compose at his
house, 44 Munro Road. He must therefore have written many of his
finest songs in Glasgow, and with his leonine features and shock of
white hair, was a familiar figure striding around the West End on his
daily walks.

Another Glasgow musician, Erik Chisholm (1904–65), studied com-
position under Sir Donald Francis Tovey (1875–1940) in Edinburgh.
After touring Canada, he returned to Glasgow where he functioned as

an organist and the conductor of the Glasgow Grand Opera Company, with whom he gave the first British performance of Mozart's *Idomeneo* and several Berlioz operas, including *The Trojans*. In 1930 he founded the Active Society, to promote contemporary music. Under its auspices he brought to Glasgow, among others, Bartok, Hindemith and Sorabji. In 1945 he went to Singapore as conductor of the Symphony Orchestra there and in 1947, he became principal of the Cape Town School of Music. It was no small disgrace to Scotland that such an energizing force should have to go abroad to find an academic appointment.

His own compositions include two symphonies, the ballets *The Forsaken Mermaid* and *The Pied Piper of Hamelin*, as well as an overture, *The Friars of Berwick*, the *Straloch Suite* for piano and strings and other chamber music pieces.

He was a man of immense energy and infectious enthusiasm – qualities that, however, he did not succeed in transferring to his own music; though some of his best piano music has been recorded on compact disc by Ronald Stevenson, himself a composer.

Glasgow novelists and poets are dealt with in my discussion of literature as a pastime. Despite the international fame of the painters forming the group known as 'The Glasgow Boys' (many of whose members were not actually from Glasgow) and of the Glasgow School of Art as a centre of design and teaching excellence, it should really be the early Glasgow industrialists who head the Glasgow celebrity role.

Novelist and story-teller Neil Munro (1864–1930) makes Erchie, the 'Droll Freen' of several of his tales, report King Edward VII as (improbably) having said on arriving at Queen Street Station from Edinburgh and surveying George Square: 'Whit'na graveyaird's this?' Most of the statues do not, in fact, commemorate Glaswegians, but rather people who visited the city, including Queen Victoria and Prince Albert, the work of Baron Marochetti of Vaux. The statue of Sir Walter Scott by Greenshields and Ritchie, standing on David Rhind's Doric column, erected in the centre of the square in 1837, was the first of its kind to be put up in Scotland.

C.E. Ewing's statue of Robert Burns, put up in 1877 and costing £2,000, was reputedly paid for by public subscription; William Ewart Gladstone (1809–98), a robed bronze figure on a granite base was by William Hamno Thorneycroft, celebrating Gladstone's election as lord rector of Glasgow University in 1877 (his rectorial address was delivered in the Kibble Palace in the Botanic Gardens). Another such is Sir

Robert Peel (1788–1850), who had been elected lord rector in 1836, and who was given a magnificent reception in a building specially constructed for the occasion in a Buchanan Street garden (when the huge rock, later blasted away, was made a central feature) and at which Gladstone was a speaker. Then there is the soldier, Colin McIver, who took his mother's name of Campbell, fought at Corunna with Sir John Moore, became, first Sir Colin Campbell and, after service during the Indian Military Campaign (including the relief of Lucknow) was created Lord Clyde and sculpted by J.H. Foley. Glasgow-born Sir John Moore (1761–1803) himself, indeed, is represented by a Flaxman statue, said to be made from a smelted-down cannon. Mossman's statue of the poet Thomas Campbell was also paid for by public subscription in 1871. Campbell, three times rector of the university, was the son of a tobacco lord. James Watt's statue by Sir Francis Chantry went up where it still stands, in 1832 – several of the rest have been brought in from other parts of the city, where they originally stood. Then there is the gentleman holding out his hat, in less sophisticated days frequently a receptacle for balls or stones thrown up by small boys. He is James Oswald, again the work of Marochetti. Oswald was a Whig, and one of the first Glasgow MPs to be elected to the reformed parliament of 1832.

Few businessmen are there. Of those so commemorated elsewhere in the city, there is the monument to the founder of a once-famous drapery business, James Arthur (1819–61). It is said that the sculptor, G.A. Lawson, never saw his subject in the flesh. Astonishingly, it was paid for by former employees in the business.

Two other notable statues should be mentioned, though neither is of businessmen. That of William Thomson, Lord Kelvin (1828–1907), by A. Macfarlane Shannon, sits deep in thought on Kelvinbridge in Kelvin Way. Perhaps he is pondering the answer he gave to the students, who, when they wanted to erect a solid square steeple on their university tower, were warned by Kelvin that the structure could not carry such a weight; hence the fretwork spire put up in place of it, and the anonymous statue of that great benefactor to humanity, Joseph, Lord Lister (1827–1912), who discovered the beneficial use of antiseptics in operations.

Though Glasgow, on the whole, has been somewhat tardy in erecting statues to its captains of industry, no doubt many of them achieved what they did in order to amass private fortunes. Some as employers were probably little better than omnipotent tyrants in their own small world. Others, however, do seem to have been inspired by a genuine urge to be of service to their fellow citizens. Their achievements are too numerous to describe in detail, but a few of those who made particularly significant contributions should be chronicled.

One obvious candidate for mention is Dumbarton-born Patrick Colquhoun (1745–1820), who served his apprenticeship in the tobacco plantations from the age of sixteen, but who, by his twentieth birthday, was already established in Glasgow as a youthful tobacco lord. When in 1782 the provost, Hugh Wylie, died facing financial ruin, Colquhoun succeeded him in office, restoring the city's self-respect. He headed the committee that completed the Tontine Hotel. In 1783, he founded the Glasgow Chamber of Commerce, the first to be established in the United Kingdom. At the height of his fame he went to London, where for thirty-one years he ran an establishment that auctioned Glasgow cotton and linen fabrics. He became a London magistrate, publishing several pamphlets on economic matters and creating a police force and a police patrol for the River Thames. He was also active in organizing soup kitchens for the destitute. Given an honorary Doctor of Law degree by Glasgow University and made a freeman of Edinburgh, he was buried in St Margaret's Chapel, Westminster, where he is commemorated by a plaque. Parliament is 'kirked', to use the Scots term for such events, in St Margaret's to this day.

One of the early outstandingly successful businessmen was Kirkman Finlay (1772–1842). He first came to prominence as second-in-command of 'a corps of Gentlemen Sharpshooters,' part of the volunteer force, which included eight infantry battalions, mustered to resist a threatened Napoleonic invasion. An immense review, which also included men from Dumbarton and Hamilton, was held on Glasgow Green in the autumn of 1804, the Dumbarton contingent eventually becoming the Glasgow Light Infantry. The destruction of the French and Spanish fleets off Cape Trafalgar by Nelson on 21 October 1805 was commemorated by the Nelson monument, an obelisk and plinth on Glasgow Green by David Hamilton, created in 1806 at a cost of £2,000 raised by public subscription, one of the first to the victorious admiral commander to be erected. It was built by a local builder and mason, Andrew Brocket.

Finlay's father died in 1790 leaving his business to his eighteen-year-old son. Kirkman Finlay soon began expanding it, until the firm of James Finlay was the most important cotton yarn business in Scotland.

He then founded a London house to handle the contraband business in the face of Napoleon's blockade, the London house eventually merging with Baring Brothers. Finlay was also largely responsible for breaking the London port monopoly for hauling all goods going to and from the East Indies, later achieving a similar liberalism as regards the conduct of the China trade.

Finlay, whose spinning mills were among the earliest to be operated by steam, was said to be an 'aggressive, astute, contentious, indomitable manufacturer and business man,' chosen on no fewer than four occasions to be chairman of the Chamber of Commerce. He was an MP for the local burghs from 1812 to 1818 and lord provost for the year 1812, when, on his election, his fellow citizens had him drawn 'in an open carriage from the Town Hall to his Argyle Street house'. Silver medals were struck to mark the occasion.

In Scotland, great success often produces a critical reaction. So it was with Kirkman Finlay. On one occasion he was hung in effigy from one of the pillars of the Tontine. On another, two troops of cavalry had to do a fast ride from Hamilton barracks to disperse a crowd threatening to destroy his house. He had David Hamilton build for him the splendid Castle Toward on the Clyde coast looking across towards Bute.

The university students elected him their lord rector in 1819, but turned him out the following year. Nor was he re-elected to his parliamentary seat, eventually returning to the House only with the aid of a rotten borough in Wiltshire – rotten boroughs at one time were imaginary constituencies which nevertheless returned members of parliament. His unpopularity with ordinary people was largely due to his support of the much disliked Corn Laws of 1815, devised to protect farmers, but resulting in dear bread. He was also disliked for opposing Peel's bill to regulate the hours of labour of employees, believing that such an intervention would 'tend to paralyse industry and injure the manufacturing and commercial prosperity of the country'.

Worse was to come. A meeting of workers took place on 29 October 1816 at a field at Thrushgrove, in the east end of the city. It was attended by more than 40,000 people. Its first concern was to pass a resolution urging the repeal of the Corn Laws; but it also passed resolutions on working conditions in factories, Catholic emancipation and the by now widely supported need for Parliamentary Reform.

The government became alarmed, especially after a cotton weaver, Andrew McKinley, was arrested in February 1817 for having signed an oath urging the overthrow of the Government. The case against him fell through, because a witness for the Crown admitted to having been paid to testify. In the *Reformer's Gazette*, the editor, Peter Mackenzie, thereafter alleged that McKinley had been trapped into signing the oath by a Government *agent provocateur*, employed for that purpose by none other than Kirkman Finlay, but paid for out of the purses of other affluent names.

Proverbially, it is often best to let sleeping dogs lie; but nine years later, Finlay chose to write a letter to a Glasgow paper denying the accusation, which hearsay led him to believe was about to be reiterated by Mackenzie. Mackenzie thereupon published a pamphlet outlining the nature of his evidence. In the House of Lords, Earl Grey declared that there could no longer be any doubt that the alleged treasonable oaths in Glasgow were administered by 'hired spies and informers'.

In April 1820, a General Strike was called for and large numbers of workers came out, mooching about the city streets. As a precaution, the government called out 5,000 regular troops, the so-called Old Guard of Glasgow, under the command of Samuel Hunter, editor of the *Glasgow Herald*. Further troops were sent from Edinburgh and there were also reinforcements of Dragoons and Hussars.

Ill-advisedly, about one hundred weavers and mechanics armed themselves with pikes, guns and pistols and gathered around the hill on which the Necropolis now stands, prior to setting out to join a supposed, but non-existent army, rumoured to be mustering at Falkirk. There was no such army. Learning of their mistake, the weavers turned tail, but before reaching the city were intercepted by a troop of Hussars. A battle of sorts ensued in which many were wounded. The weavers' ringleaders were apprehended and thrown into Stirling Castle.

Two of them, including Andrew Hardie, grandfather of Keir Hardie, one of the founders of the Labour Party, were subsequently hanged and beheaded at Stirling. The other sixteen sentenced to death were reprieved and transported to Australia. James Wilson of Strathaven was subsequently executed in a similar manner before a huge crowd outside Glasgow's Justiciary Hall. Kirkman Finlay was one of those who publicly congratulated the government for so effectively having suppressed the revolt.

Another taking a similar stance was James Ewing. Thereupon, with James Oswald, Ewing went to parliament as the other Reform

Parliament MP. He was long remembered with distaste by many ordinary Glaswegians, however, for having sentenced the weaver James Wilson to death. James Ewing (1775–1853), commonly known as 'Crow' Ewing, had his mansion at the top of Queen Street, where the railway station now stands. He was an accountant and something of a scholar. He was left a plantation in Jamaica by an uncle, and so inherited considerable wealth. With several business interests in the Caribbean, he was for many years chairman of the East India Association. He was also the first chairman of the Royal Exchange, built around William Cunninghame's mansion in what is now Royal Exchange Place. He also set up the Necropolis cemetery and promoted the building of Duke Street prison. He was one of the original members of the Glasgow Bank and of the Glasgow Savings Bank.

He laid the foundation of the Jamaica Street Bridge in 1833, having become dean of guild in 1815. He was lord provost in 1832. He soon stood down, however, to allow the first Reform Town Council to elect its own man.

Then there were the chemists. Charles Tennant took out a patent for his bleaching powder in 1789 and founded the St Rollox works, famous for its great chimney. It was to become the largest chemical works in the world, though it created disfiguring heaps of soda waste that were only removed in our own day. Tennant's produced sulphuric acid, chloride of lime, soda and soap. The other great Glasgow chemist, Charles Mackintosh, became a partner with Tennant in the Hurlet and Company's Alum Works, which produced ammonia. Mackintosh hit upon the process for producing waterproof cloth, thus giving his name to that protective and very necessary Glasgow-originated garment, the mackintosh, or 'mac'. He is credited with remarking: 'I fear that the development of the railways will destroy the need for waterproof coats,' a fear that has proved unfounded.

The grandson of that first Tennant, Sir Charles Tennant (1823–1906) was a partner in the firm when he was just twenty. He became a director of the Tharsis Sulphur and Copper Company, which imported Spanish pyrites. Having refused the chairmanship of the rival company, Rio Tinto, he became in 1872 the first chairman of the Steel Company of Scotland, which promoted with rewarding success the Siemens and Martin acid process for making steel.

His other activities included setting up a company to mine gold in India, a move that advanced his already considerable fortune. He became a member of the building committee for the Forth Railway

Bridge as well as chairman of the Nobel Dynamite Trust founded, ironically, by the same family who established the Nobel Peace Prize. When the Swiss inventor Ludwig Mond discovered a new process for making alkali-soda, Switzerland's Bruner-Mond Company for a while competed with St Rollox. Amalgamation in 1891, however, led to the formation of the United Alkali Company, with forty-eight factories and Sir Charles Tennant being made president. Further amalgamation eventually resulted in the formation of ICI, though by then Sir Charles had retired.

Sir Charles, Liberal MP for Partick and later the East Borders, is, however, now best known as the father of that sharp-tongued wit Margot, who became the politician Herbert Asquith's second wife.

No survey, however brief, of Glasgow's industrial activities would be complete without the inclusion of David MacBrayne, the Glasgow-born grandson of the founder of the Burns Steamship Company.

In 1842, a group of Glasgow merchants, including Campbell of Tullichewan, Hunter of Hafton and Finlay of Castle Toward, built the steamship *Duntroon Castle*. Their subsequent steamers were all named after castles. The company, however, failed three years later and its ships were sold to G. and J. Burns. The new owners thereupon made a vigorous effort to dominate all Clyde steamer traffic, running their vessels to any point at which there was a pier for them to call, at a level tenpence per passenger. This venture failed in 1848 and ownership of the vessels then passed by purchase to the David Hutcheson Company. This was a family arrangement, David and Alexander Hutcheson and the Burns brothers being related to each other, and to the man who became their junior partner, their nephew David MacBrayne.

The opening of the Crinan Canal had resulted in increased traffic to the West Highlands by track-boat and from Crinan to Oban by the steamer *Brenda*. In August 1847, the Queen herself had travelled to the West Highlands by this route, thus giving it the title 'Royal Route'

David MacBrayne (1818–1907), ship-owner. His ships provided a vital link between Glasgow and the west coast

– a name used publicly until 1956, when the steamer *St Columba* with her distinctive three black-topped red funnels was taken out of service and the Glasgow to Ardrishaig sea route was abolished.

Messrs Hutcheson developed this traffic, at first with the *Shandon*, a paddle-steamer bought from its previous owners, Thomson and McConnell. Then, in 1855, they put on the route their own newly built 'crack' steamer, the first *Iona*. Seven years later, like so many Clyde steamers of her day, she was sold to run the American blockade, but before getting anywhere near America was sunk off Fort Matilda in a collision with the *Chancellor*.

Iona No. 2, built the following year, was also sold to run the blockade, but sank in bad weather off Lundy Island, on her way to America. In 1864, the third *Iona* was built. She remained in service until her seventy-first year, the 'crack' steamer the expanding public demanded.

David Hutcheson retired from the business in 1876. When his brother Alexander also retired two years later, David MacBrayne was left as sole owner. He inaugurated his control with the building of the *Columba* in 1878, arguably the finest of all the Clyde steamers. Thereby MacBrayne regained the supremacy of the Clyde, which had been briefly threatened by the luxurious rival *Lord of the Isles*. In 1909, a journalist could record: 'Today the MacBrayne fleet consists of thirty-three steamers manned by more than a thousand officers and men, to say nothing of the five hundred employees on the shore. Outwith the Clyde, the vessels sail to every port and island, from Islay to Thurso, and perform a service only differed in degrees from that of the Cunard fleet of Mr MacBrayne's cousin, Lord Inverclyde.'

Robert Napier (1791–1876), the 'father of Clyde shipbuilding', was the son of a Vale of Leven blacksmith and millwright and cousin of David Napier (1790–1876), son of the

David Napier (1790–1876), shipbuilder and the 'father' of marine engineering on the Clyde

man who had built the *Comet's* boiler in 1812. Young Robert was educated at Dumbarton Grammar School and for a time apprenticed to
Robert Stevenson, builder of the Bell Rock lighthouse.

In 1815, Napier set up business on his own in Greyfriars Wynd,
Glasgow, before succeeding his cousin, David, in the occupancy of
Camlachie Foundry, established in 1814. Among his first orders was
one to supply the Glasgow Water Works Company with large iron
pipes. In 1823, he produced an engine for the paddle-steamer *Leven*, so
good that it outlasted several hulls. It was for long preserved at the foot
of Dumbarton Castle by Napier's two sons as a memorial to their
father. By 1828, he found his engines in such demand that he moved
to larger premises.

James Cook (1761–1835), a young millwright from Kirkcaldy, set up
a small workshop in 1788, near St Enoch's Square, specializing in plantation machinery, although he also built the first marine engine on the
Clyde. (The *Comet* had been powered by a land engine.) Cook later
moved to Tradeston. Though he eventually succumbed to the Napiers'
competition, he is generally regarded as 'the father of engineering in
Scotland', particularly since so many later successful engineers passed
through his works as apprentices.

Another outstanding industrialist was Sir John Ure, undoubtedly
inspired by the ideals of public service. Miller and flour merchant and
twenty-seven years a councillor, Sir John Ure became dean of guild,
was for fifteen years chairman of the Clyde Navigation Trust and from
1881 to 1883 lord provost, during which time he refused a knighthood
from the prime minister on the grounds that 'he was contented with
the generous recognition of his services given him by his fellow-citi-
zens'.

A notable benefactor to the city was Sir James Bell (1850–1929) of
Bell Brothers and McLellan, steamship owners, an 'incessant driving
force' popularly said to be 'one of the last of Glasgow's "old style" businessmen, whose sole word was law.' He gave Bellahouston Park to
Glasgow. He was twice lord provost – in 1892 and again in 1895. He
was one of the first to encourage the introduction of electricity to
Glasgow, in 1893 switching on the first street current. In the same year
he laid the foundation stone of the Eastern Sewage Works, which
marked the first step towards the purification of the polluted Clyde.
During his terms of office, too, the Corporation took over the expanding tramway service, hitherto in private hands. He became vice-
commodore of the Royal Yacht Club, chairman of the Clydedale

Sir James Bell (1850–1929), a member of a famous Glasgow family who became Lord Provost of the city

Bank, chairman in 1887 of the syndicate that built the steam yacht *Thistle* – later to become the German Emperor's *Meteor* – and he was chairman of the Royal Glasgow Institute of Fine Arts from 1887 to 1898. The owner of a fine collection of paintings at his home in Kilwinning, he played a leading role in having the Kelvingrove Art Galleries built out of the profits of the 1888 Exhibition, in time for its inauguration during the 1901 Exhibition, of which he was also vice-chairman.

Sir James Bell had been preceded as lord provost by his fellow Exhibition vice-chairman, Sir James King (1830–1929), who had also preceded Bell as chairman of the Clydesdale Bank. King, apparently, was genial and much liked, whereas Bell was dour and severe. The family company of which King became a partner when twenty-one was the Hurlet and Company Alum Company, although he was chairman also of many others. Lord provost by invitation, 'because it was found impossible to secure a suitable candidate within the Council,' he held office during Queen Victoria's Jubilee (1887), the International Exhibition of 1887 in Kelvingrove Park and the official opening of the municipal buildings, which took place in the same year.

John Matheson, a leader in the textile trade, helped found the Choral Union, promoted the building of St Andrew's Halls and occupied the chair when the new building was officially opened on 13 November 1877.

The main figure in the textile trade, however, was surely David Dale, who founded New Lanark, on the upper Clyde. This model village was furnished with the latest equipment by Sir Richard Arkwright, whom Dale had invited to Scotland. Dale's daughter married Robert Owen (1820–1902), who eventually took over from his father-in-law. Owen, a man of social conscience who pioneered improved working and housing conditions for his workers and was instrumental in founding a village store that was to become one of the earliest cornerstones of the Co-operative movement, eventually left New Lanark for the United States, setting up a similarly enlightened establishment at New Harmony in Ohio. It has been preserved as a conservation area, as has the village of New Lanark, now one of the most popular tourist attractions in Scotland. It is a matter of some pride to me that during my period as the Scottish Civic Trust's first director, at the behest of the last provost of Lanark, Harry Smith – later the first highly successful chairman of the New Lanark Conservation Committee – the trust played an early part in setting in motion now well-established conservation procedures that helped save it.

Without a doubt one of the best-known of all Scots internationally is the architect Charles Rennie Mackintosh (1868–1928). He was born in Glasgow, the son of a police superintendent. The future architect attended Allan Glen's School and the Glasgow School of Art (then in the MacLellan Galleries), gaining the Greek Thomson Travelling Scholarship, which enabled him to study in Italy and France. On his return to Glasgow in 1884, he joined the firm of Honeyman and Keppie. Wisely, they allowed him to exploit his own ideas. He soon evolved a highly personal style, combining a 'new look' interpretation of the Scottish vernacular with the ideas of the Arts and Crafts movement and the still newer mannerisms of Art Nouveau. Indeed, he became an honorary member of its most famous Continental manifestation, the Viennese Secession in 1902. Soon made a partner in the firm, he received two important commissions. One was Windyhill, home at Kilmacolm for Glasgow businessman William Davidson; this work led to the commission to put up Hill House for Walter Blackie in upper Helensburgh. Built between 1902 and 1904, it is now safe in the ownership of the National Trust for Scotland.

Mackintosh's public buildings included the Martyr's School (1895–98), the Scotland Street School (1904) and his only church, Queen's Cross Church (1897–99), since 1977 the headquarters of the Charles Rennie Mackintosh Society. In 1999 the society was able to acquire the former Glasgow Herald building in Mitchell Street, another Mackintosh work, now restored as the Lighthouse Exhibition Centre.

Most important of all, of course, is his Glasgow School of Art on Garnethill, built in two phases because of financial shortages – 1897 to 1899 and 1907 to 1909.

The school's head, Francis Newberry (1855–1946), popularly known as Fra Newberry, had long been anxious to move from its cramped Sauchiehall Street premises. Newberry persuaded the gover-

Charles Rennie Mackintosh (1868–1928), Glasgow's most famous architect. His masterpiece is generally regarded to be the Glasgow School of Art

nors to acquire the Garnethill site and inaugurate a competition for a new building, not to exceed a cost of £21,000.

Many Glasgow architects submitted entries, working to the director's very exacting specifications. Thanks to Fra Newberry's prescience and persistence, however, the commission went to the youthful Mackintosh. The young architect rewarded Newberry by producing what is generally regarded as Mackintosh's masterpiece.

The astonishing thing is that thereafter, during his lifetime, Mackintosh received more honour in Vienna, Berlin and Dresden than he did in his native city. Apart from a characteristic doorway to the premises in Blythswood Square, then occupied by the Lady Artists' Club, designed in 1908, and the buildings already mentioned, very little survives. Even his House for an Art Lover, the design for the exterior of which failed to win a German competition in 1901 (on a technicality) was only realized during the closing years of the previous century, given interiors by Professor Andy MacMillan. Built on the site of the long-demolished Thornhill House, it now functions as a postgraduate school for the Glasgow School of Art, but is open to the public.

Mackintosh's associates in what became known as the Glasgow Style were art designer George Walton (1867–1933); book designer and binder Talwin Morris, a teacher and designer who married Margaret Macdonald, also a designer, like her sister Frances, who married Mackintosh; Jessie Newberry (Fra Newberry's wife); interior designer John Ednie and George Logan, a furniture designer. Because of their fondness for stylish elongated figures as decorative motifs, they became known as the 'Spook School', but exercised enormous influence and to this day still influence a wide range of work, some of it described by the irreverent as 'Mockintoshery'.

In 1896 Mackintosh was introduced to Kate Cranston (1849–1934), daughter of a George Square hotel owner. Her brother, Stewart, was a tea importer who first served tea from his business

Kate Cranston (1850–1934) whose tearoom became a feature of Glasgow social life

The Willow Tearoom, Sauchiehall Street, opened in 1902 and was thought by some to be the finest of them all. Mackintosh had been given a free hand in its design

premises. Together they opened a new tearoom in Queen Street in 1901, followed by 'The Willow' in Sauchiehall Street in 1904 (which still survives in modified restored form and where some of Margaret Macdonald's faience panels may still be seen), followed by others, now long since gone.

Mackintosh designed furniture, interiors and accessories for Miss Cranston. An anonymous wit of the time observed that he 'elevated the Glasgow buddies' high tea to the height of a Japanese tea ceremony'. Everything was impeccable – even the flowers, carried daily in a donkey-cart driven by a boy in green uniform.

Dressed in a blend of bygone fashions and current styles, striking and elegant but never *outré*, Kate was said to be 'the first to discover in Glasgow that her sex was positively yearning for some kind of afternoon distraction that had not yet been invented'. She certainly invented it, presiding regally at the cash desks of her various establishments until the death of her husband, a Major Norris, in 1917, when she sold her tearooms. They nevertheless survived for some years, more or less intact; but when the Ingram Street premises were eventually sold for other purposes after the 1939–45 War, Glasgow Corporation, besotted with worship of the 'New' and under public pressure, agreed to store the Ingram Street interiors against possible future exhibition use. They did so in such a fashion that some of Mackintosh's work was irretrievably damaged.

Mackintosh himself relinquished his partnership and his practice in 1913 and retired to Suffolk to paint pictures, though not before designing one further distinguished home in Northampton, for the model railway-maker Bassett-Lowke.

It would be wrong to give the impression that all the men who helped to shape Glasgow belonged to the nineteenth century. There was, for example, Sir A. Steven Bilsland (d. 1970), the eldest son of a former lord provost, Sir William Bilsland, and, like his father, in the

The 'Dutch Kitchen' in Miss Cranston's Argyle Street tearoom which opened in 1897, after being converted by Mackintosh from existing premises

food manufacturing business. Steven Bilsland had served in the 1914–18 War with distinction and was actually the youngest man to become president of the Glasgow Chamber of Commerce with the exception of its founder, Patrick Colquhoun.

Bilsland had been one of those involved in the setting-up of the Glasgow Development Board in 1930, the aim of which was to attract new industry to Glasgow, where there were empty factories a-plenty. The policy did not succeed, and the board was disbanded in 1950, to be succeeded by the Scottish Council for Development and Industry.

Sir Steven, an advocate of attracting businesses to new sites, was the prime mover in establishing 'industrial' estates on the English model, arguing that they offered attractive possibilities to new industries. Though the idea was supported by the Chamber of Commerce, the business community was unenthusiastic. Nevertheless, Hillington was set up as the first industrial estate. It was officially opened by Queen Elizabeth in 1938 and has prospered ever since, as have others created subsequently elsewhere in the city.

Bilsland then became chairman of the newly formed Scottish Committee of the Council for Art and Industry. But his energy was unbounded. He was a member of the Management Council of the 1938 Empire Exhibition (of which Sir Cecil Weir, another distinguished industrialist, was chairman); chairman of the Hillington Industrial Estate (enormously strengthened by the arrival of Rolls Royce); and for most of the 1939–45 War, commissioner for Civil Defence in the West of Scotland. His post-war roles included those of chairman of the Scottish Council (Development and Industry) and chairman of the Scottish Industrial Estates Corporation, as well as chairman of the first Scottish Industries Exhibition, held in the Kelvin Hall in 1949. Among his business interests were his governership of the Bank of Scotland, his presidency of the Scottish Amicable Life Assurance Society and several directorships, including Colville's, John Brown and the Burmah Oil Corporation. He became Baron Bilsland of Kinrary, a Knight of the Thistle and in 1949 one of the most worthy recipients of the St Mungo Prize – instituted by Alexander Sommerville, Glasgow businessman and reputed inventor of the square-toed shoe – which is awarded every three years to someone who has given outstanding service to the city of Glasgow. Others who have received this prize have included the first recipient, Dr Tom Honeyman, who made Glasgow art-conscious again (1943); Sir Alexander Gibson, the 'true begetter' of Scottish Opera (1970); and Glasgow journalist and historian Jack House (1988).

Associated with Bilsland, in what was virtually a renaissance of Scottish industry after the slump of the twenties and early thirties were, of course, Sir Cecil Weir (1890–1960) and Sir James Lithgow (1883–1952). Commenting in the *Glasgow Herald* on the death of Lord Bilsland, however, C.A. Oakley observed that 'unfortunately he did not have an evident successor'.

Sir William Lorimer (1850–1931) formed the North British Locomotive Company, the largest in the world, taking over the pioneering Hyde Park works of Newton, Reid and Company and the Queen's Park works of Henry Duibs, as well as Sharp, Stewart and Company of Manchester, who had also set up near the Hyde Park works in 1884. All came under Lorimer's control in 1903, Sir William Arroll being one of the directors.

Andrew Stewart (1832–1901) took up the making of iron pipes in 1860, setting up his business in St Enoch's Wynd, in due course partnered by his brother James. When St Enoch's Station was mooted, the Stewarts moved to Coatbridge, which was by this time becoming a centre of heavy industry. He took over rival companies, so that by the end of the century, A. and J. Stewart could supply virtually every kind of tube for which there was a demand, especially after 1903, when the firm Lloyd and Lloyd of Birmingham amalgamated to become Stewart and Lloyd, under the chairmanship of Andrew's son, J.G. Stewart. Andrew Stewart, however, is perhaps more directly remembered today as the founder of the Adam Smith Chair of Political Economy at Glasgow University.

Other outstanding industrialists who should be noted include Sir William Arroll (1839–1913) of Houston, Renfrewshire, the son of a manager in Coates thread works, which young Arroll entered as a spinner at the age of nine. He next served an apprenticeship in the boiler- and bridge-building works of Laidlaw and Son at Barrowfield, setting up his own boilermaking business in 1868. He then moved to Dalmarnock, where his iron works produced bridges and by the end of the century ran the biggest structural engineering firm in the United Kingdom. The replacement Tay Rail Bridge was his, and, as is not always realized, London's Tower Bridge (1894), as well as the Forth Rail Bridge (1898).

The shift from manufacturing industries to service industries has continued apace. Very few ships now come from Clyde yards, though there has been some construction work on oil rigs; and the world's locomotives are no longer made in Glasgow. There are, of course, some new high-tech initiatives, and the tourist business has developed into a potent force. But the Ring Road, Abbotsinch Airport and the two great bridges over the Clyde – the Kingston Bridge in the city and the Erskine Bridge by the site of an old chain ferry – at least give a modern sweep to Glasgow. Now that the Empire, of which it was once the 'second city', has long since gone, Glasgow's population is creeping down towards 600,000; far short of its brief million-plus days immediately before the 1939–45 War.

3   Pastimes

I

IT MAY APPEAR to some unseemly that religion should be classed as a pastime, even by an octogenarian agnostic who since he was four-teen has shared Hume's belief that since we know nothing of this world until we come into it, reason suggests that we shall know nothing when we leave it. For some Glaswegians, however, it does seem to have been something of an obsession – compensation for the frustration, brittleness and brevity of life, perhaps. After all, its Cathedral Church lies at its very heart.

From Glasgow's Catholic bishop Michael in AD 1115 to the last Catholic archbishop, James Beaton, who served from 1551 to 1576, through the fourteen Reformation archbishops and the subsequent twenty-two Presbyterian ministers, the cathedral has featured strongly in Glasgow's story, even if only indirectly.

There were the events that played a major influence during the incumbency of the great clerics: Bishop Achaius, who rebuilt the burned-out wooden cathedral in stone; Ingelram, who fended off the claims of superiority of the See of York; Jocelin, who obtained Glasgow's burgh and market rights from William the Lion and estab-lished that the See of Glasgow was subordinate only to the Pope in Rome; William de Bondington, who built the lower church and choir; Robert Wischard, who supported Wallace and Bruce against Edward I and suffered English imprisonment for twelve years for his pains; William Rae, who built the first stone bridge over the Clyde; William Lawedre, who put up the central tower and part of the chapter-house; William Turnbull, who founded the university; and Archbishop Blacader, the last to help build the cathedral. Gavin Dunbar burnt two heretics at the east end of the cathedral in an attempt to defend the old faith; and James Beaton, the last Roman Catholic archbishop, saved the choir's records and relics by decamping with them to France (though they were eventually returned). Then there were the Reformation archbishops, like the other James Beaton, under whom the Church's lands became a temporality, Church lands granted to (or seized by) lay persons, in 1567 in favour of the Duke of Lennox (although the Cathedral lands went to Walter Stewart of Minto); enthusiastic Episcopalian James Spottiswoode; Andrew Fairfoul, who persecuted Covenanters; Arthur Ross, who hanged them and John Paterson, who finally realized the old faith's game was up.

The General Assembly of 1638, which abjured Episcopacy, established Presbyterianism and contributed to the outbreak of Civil War against Charles I, was one religious high-point, taking place in Glasgow and adjourning on 20 December on what was said to be 'a blithe day for all'. The troubles had well and truly begun.

Charles II's attempts to restore Episcopacy failed, after which the Glasgow bishops appointed during his reign gave place to ministers, when William of Orange brought back Presbyterian worship in 1688, an event Burns and others habitually referred to as 'the glorious revolution'. The first minister, David Wemyss, was appointed in 1565 and served for fifty years. The succession continues.

From then until the end of the eighteenth century, during which time small groups of Roman Catholics had to meet in each other's houses, Catholicism in Glasgow was all but annihilated.

The first resident priest returned (from Banffshire) in 1792 and gradually the persecution of Catholics slackened. The arrival of Highland and Irish workers, mostly Roman Catholic, during the last two decades of the eighteenth century led Kirkman Finlay to establish a Roman Catholic school in 1817. But they soon outgrew the small chapel in the Calton that they used as a place of worship, so between 1814 and 1817 the grandiose St Andrew's Cathedral went up at the foot of Clyde Street, fronting the river. The increasing number of Irish immigrant labourers arriving in the nineteenth century led to the growth of resentment and anti-Popery in the city, especially where jobs seemed threatened. This pressure was somewhat relieved with the setting-up of the Irish Free State in 1921, though lamentably, as the composer James MacMillan has recently complained, traces of sectarian bigotry still survive.

Baptists can be traced in Glasgow from about 1770. They now have some twenty churches throughout the city. Episcopalians were, of course, in some measure 'discouraged' until the repeal of the last of the Penal Acts in 1792. Since 1750, however, they had had their publicly subscribed-for church St Andrew-by-the-Green (Glasgow Green) built for them by Andrew Hunter, a talented mason who was, however, excommunicated from his Secessionist Church for so doing.

Though John Wesley (1703–91) twice visited Glasgow between 1751 and 1790, the first Methodist Chapel, in John Street, was opened only in 1787. George Fox, founder of the Quakers, came to Glasgow as early as 1657 and a small group was established in 1687, but the sect for long encountered considerable opposition in the city.

The Italians who settled in Glasgow came mostly around the end of the nineteenth and the beginning of the twentieth centuries, often setting up ice cream parlours or fish-and-chip restaurants. It has been estimated that there are now more than 20,000 Glaswegians of Italian descent, mostly Roman Catholic. There has never been any anti-Italian feeling in the city.

The early Glasgow Jews were mainly merchants. Their first synagogue was put up in the High Street in 1823. The Jewish community steadily increased in numbers during the nineteenth century, tending to congregate on the south side of the city. Their first major centre was the Great Synagogue in South Portland Street, built in 1900 and closed in 1974. The Jewish community is now mainly resident in and around the suburb of Newton Mearns, the Garnethill Synagogue of 1879 their principal place of worship. Despite the remnants of anti-Jewish prejudice – at its height in the twenties and thirties and fired, I always thought, by jealousy of Jewish business astuteness and success – Jews have thoroughly integrated themselves into Glasgow society, providing the city with several lord provosts and the Westminster parliament with numerous distinguished MPs and ministers.

Lascar sailors were among the first ethnic groups regularly seen in Glasgow. Indians began arriving in the 1920s, in search of employment.

The Sikh community in 1941 opened their temple in South Portland Street, and now also have a cultural centre in the West End. By the end of the 1939–45 War there were enough Muslims in Glasgow to enable them to establish a temporary mosque in Gorbals Street. At first they were mainly pedlars or shopkeepers, but gradually they took over transport jobs, becoming drivers or conductors. In recent years there has been a steady increase in the number of Asian doctors and nurses in the National Health Service and other professional occupations. In 1984, Muslims opened their Central Mosque, one of the largest in Europe, on the south bank of the Clyde. Indeed, native-born Muslims now form an integral part of the Glasgow scene, most of which is now in any case secular in orientation rather than religious. Tolerance is thus the essential factor in social harmony.

> Colour of skin, belief or unbelief,
> the shade of politics with which you side,
> for what strange thoughts you hold a watching brief,
> which nation chanced your birth or fires your pride,
> only one creed befits a man or woman –
> the simple decency of being human.

II

Keeping abreast of news and current affairs is a daily pastime that can become a compulsive addiction. It is, I suppose, in part entertainment, in part extending our knowledge of the state of the human condition. In days gone by, news was often slow and hard to come by. The first regular Glasgow newspaper was probably the *Glasgow Courant*, which came out three times a week, the first number appearing in November 1715. It soon changed its title to the *West Country Intelligence*, perhaps in an attempt to widen its readership; but it ceased publication with the sixty-seventh number in 1716.

The next venture, the *Glasgow Journal*, was a weekly, first published in 1741. In 1845 it was absorbed by the *Glasgow Chronicle*, which had been launched in 1811 as a Whig organ and which continued until 1857.

In 1783 the *Glasgow Advertiser* first appeared, soon changing its name to the *Glasgow Herald*. It is still Glasgow's essential daily, though after 1992 it dropped the city's name from its title.

The *Glasgow Mercury* lasted from 1778 to 1796. The *Glasgow Courier*, founded in 1791, survived until 1833, its first editor being the poet William Motherwell (1797–1835).

Other papers that engaged Glasgow readers for varying periods included the *Glasgow Free Press* (1823–35), the *Scots Times* (1825–41), the *Scottish Guardian* (1832–61) and the *Reformer's Gazette* (1832–64), metamorphosing itself during its existence as the *Reformer's Gazette* and the *Glasgow Reformer*. Smaller ventures included the radical *Liberator* (1833–38) and the *Glasgow Constitutional* (1835–55).

James Hedderwick (1814–97) newspaper proprietor, who attended Chopin's Glasgow concert

In 1842 Dr James Hedderwick (1814–97) set up the weekly *Glasgow Citizen*, fathering nominally, so to speak, the *Evening Citizen* in 1864, one of the city's first evening papers. It lasted until 1974, when the coming of television wrought havoc among both evening papers and illustrated news magazines.

The *North British Daily Mail* first appeared in 1847. Sold to Lord Northcliffe in 1901, it became the *Daily Mail*, before adopting its present name, the *Daily Record*.

The *Glasgow Sentinel*, with various minor name-variants, lasted from 1850 to 1877. The *Glasgow News*, which began life in 1873, became the *Scottish News* in 1886 and ceased publication in 1888.

The *Evening Times*, now the sister paper of the *Herald*, first came out in 1876 as a daily evening paper and is the only one of Glasgow's three evening papers to have survived today.

The *Glasgow Observer* (1885) added the *Catholic Herald* to its title in 1895 and in 1939 became the *Scottish Catholic Herald*. The lively-minded left-wing paper *Forward*, founded in 1906, lost much of its rugged literary and political Scottish character on being absorbed by the *Socialist Commentary* in 1956.

Others from our own day that have died the death include the *Glasgow Evening News* (1915–57) and the popular pictorial *The Bulletin and Scots Pictorial* (1915–60), of which I happened to be the last music critic and an occasional leader-writer.

Still published today are the *Daily Record*, Scotland's best-selling newspaper, with about 760,000 readers (not all, of course, in Glasgow); the *Herald*, with about 124,000 readers (a 'must' for informed Glaswegians); and the *Evening Times* (faithfully read by about 164,000 in spite of increased competition of television and radio early evening news bulletins).

Periodicals have mostly been short-lived. Those originating in

Glasgow during the first half of the nineteenth century, apart from radical publications during the 1820s and 1930s, included the *Glasgow Looking Glass* (1925/6) and the *Looking Glass* (later the *Northern Looking Glass*, running to nineteen issues). In the latter half of the century there were the *Bee*, *Sphinx*, *Chiel*, *Traveller*, *Detective*, *Prompter* and *St Mungo*, all short-lived; and, best of all, the *Baillie*, which appeared from 1872 to 1926. More recently, the *Glasgow Review* (1944) lasted ten years, the *Glasgow Magazine* (1982) three, while *The Scottish Review*, which ran through thirty-two issues, appeared between 1970 and 1982.

III

Reading a daily newspaper is a pastime indulged in whether at home or on holiday. Enjoying a holiday, however, is the most significant and best-remembered pastime in the lives of most people. True, there are many who boast that they have never taken a holiday in X number of years, but they are more to be pitied than congratulated. A change of air, of scene and perhaps of custom is probably the best of all battery-charges. Glasgow people have the means for enjoying this restorative experience on their doorstep, though it is only in the last two centuries that it has been developed and enjoyed. I refer, of course, to that loveliest of national playgrounds, the Firth of Clyde. An ancient mapmaker, Gordon of Straloch, first gave the opening lower reaches of the river this pleasant-sounding name in 1652, preferring it to the older nomenclature, Dunbryton Fyrth (Dumbarton Firth), thus also removing any parochial claims to its varied loveliness.

Before dealing with those who made a trip 'Doon the Watter', whether on board a steamer for a single day, or to a hotel or a seasonally rented house at the coast, let us consider the main annual summer recreational activity for those who stayed at home in bygone days, the Glasgow Fair.

It began as a market, being unlike the weekly one in that merchants from outside Glasgow could offer their wares for sale. The fair ran for a week, beginning on 7 July, according to Joe Fisher, 'because it was on this day that the Cathedral had been dedicated in 1136'. But this sometimes led to the fair beginning on the Sabbath, an arrangement that was anathema to the pious Reformation burghers; so the

Glasgow Fair in 1825

commencing date was fixed as the Saturday before whenever the 7th fell on a Sunday. Soon, the obvious waste of a day resulted in the fair starting on the following Monday. When in 1752 the Julian Calendar was adopted, eleven days were 'lost', as a result of which the fair began on the third Monday of the month, and has done so ever since. Thus, a right conferred on the city by King William the Lion to the fair's first organizer, Bishop Jocelin, towards the end of the twelfth century, survives into the twenty-first.

The early fairs were held at Wyndhead, near the cathedral. As the city expanded, the fair moved to Stockwell Street. At first, the main events were a horse market and a cattle market, round which entertainments were increasingly established for the benefit of those participating: but after 1810, when a new cattle market was opened, the fair moved to Glasgow Green and became purely an exhibition of such diversions as hobby-horses and other sideshows, together with drinking booths. After 1871, what was left of this old-style fair moved to open ground near Camlachie: but by then its days were numbered. The pleasures of a trip 'Doon the Watter' had become more enticing.

In 1823, the *Literary Reporter* published some verses entitled 'Humours of Glasgow Fair', which no doubt recreate something of the prevailing atmosphere:

Now, every ane, rigged in his best,
 Seems really unco happy;   [very
An' speedily sets out in quest
 O' a drap cheerin' nappy.
Tradesmen, in haste, fling by their tools;
 The Smith leaves his forehammer;
The Labourer his picks an' shools,
 To join the mirthfu' clamour
  An' fun this day.

Wi' bauns o' canty, daunerin' folk [bands; cheerful slow
 Paradin' an' repassin';   walking people
Wi' fiddlers, singers, in each neuk; [corner
 Wi' laddie an' wi' lassie;
Ye'll no get easy through the streets,
 Whan a' move on thegither;
But everybody that ane meets
 Is knockin' on the ither,
  Thump, thump this day.

What was there to see? The poet tells us:

There's Punch, an' cockulorum tricks –
 Ingenious machinery –
Dwarfs, Giants, measurin' seven feet six
 The wild beasts' menagerie . . .

Also:

There's Packmen ranged in twa'–three tiers
 Exposin' their hardware.
'Come, lassie, buy a pair o' shears
 Or caimb to haud your hair.
Come, mister, buy a jocteleg,
 That does for cuttin' a' things,
An' edges on't like razor gleg;
 Nae doubt but different braw things
  You need this day.'

But inevitably:

Now druckenness appeared there,
 In a' its various stages –

To hear focks snorin' on their chair,
    It future woe presages.

But the great day ends:

    Now evenin's sober grey draws near,
        Wise focks are drivin' hame,
    But daft gowks devoid o' fear,
        To wait think it nae blame.
    The kintra lassie kilts her coat,
        An' draws her dearie till her –
    Some are thrang tellin' a' they got,
        Some countin' what's the siller
          They've spent that day.

The fate of 'simple maids' in some cases was warningly celebrated by another Glasgow poet in 1805, George McIndoe, originally a Paisley silk weaver, but latterly a hotel-keeper in Glasgow credited with being the inventor of a machine for figuring muslin:

    Ye simple maids, be tenty a'
        When in ayont the stack,
    For maidenheads, when ance awa'
        Can ne'er be gotten back . . .

Though maidenheads were not threatened in a trip 'Doon the Watter', here, too, however, drunkenness prevailed: so much so that in the latter part of the nineteenth century, one steamer company ran a teetotal vessel, the *Ivanhoe*. McIndoe does not appear to have enjoyed the national drink much:

    Oh, Whisky but *thy* maddenin' heat
        Has risen muckle spore;
    The poets hae ransack'd their wit
        To laud thee an' adore;
    For every ane *thou* dost inspire,
        There is a thousand more
    Driven, through the vehemence of *thy* fire,
        To beg from door to door
          Bread for the day.

SHIPPING NEWS.

Embarkation.
Scene.1st
Voyage of a Steam Boat from Glasgow to Liverpool.
to be continued.

Embarkation for Liverpool in an early paddle-steamer at the Broomielaw

Doubtless so: but one does not blame the internal combustion engine for the high road-toll at the end of the twentieth century. The development of the lower reaches of the Clyde was a direct result of the inventiveness of the *Comet's* owner, Henry Bell (1707–1830). He had been trained in a Bo'ness shipyard and thereafter with a London engineering firm, but settled in Helensburgh in 1807 to run a hotel. Within a year of the *Comet's* first voyage in 1811, and her subsequent passenger runs between Glasgow, Greenock and Helensburgh – '4/s for the best cabin and 3/s for the second' – a rival, the *Elizabeth*, had taken to the water. By the summer of 1814, no fewer than nine paddle-steamers were competing for custom.

Holidays at the coast had occasionally been undertaken before the days of steam by the sort of wealthier folk who would now, perhaps, tour Europe by car. A Glasgow businessman, Robert Reid (1773–1865), a merchant who wrote under the pen-name 'Senex', has left an account of three such trips to the coast which he made as a boy between 1778 and 1782. His voyage to Dunoon was undertaken in 1779. The family hired a wherry, having first made elaborate arrangements to keep themselves in food throughout the summer, since they could put 'no dependance on getting provisions, not even fish, in such an out of the way place'.

Dunoon, 'Senex' tells us, was then considered by Glasgow folk to be 'a Highland wilderness', though it was, in fact, a pleasant little Gaelic-speaking clachan built round the remains of its ancient castle. When the great day of departure came, the Reid family 'had a pretty fair passage down the river till the tide met us at Dunglass; our progress now became slow, and a little below Dumbarton Castle, we fairly stuck fast upon a sandbank. Here we remained for several hours till the tide flowed, when again we got under sail. We did not touch at Gourock, but bore right on to Dunoon, where we arrived the same evening.'

The Reids were at least luckier than another Glasgow gentleman, who, as late as 1817, eschewing the dangerous, new-fangled steamboats, hired a 'fly' (a fast, shallow-draught sailing wherry) to take his family and himself to Gourock for summer quarters. With them, 'all the first day was occupied in making the passage to Bowling Bay, where we cast anchor for the night: weighing anchor next morning, we proceeded down the Clyde, but were so buffeted by wind and waves that, after spending the whole day at sea, we were compelled to return to Bowling Bay. The third day, we succeeded in making Port Glasgow in the afternoon' – suffering, no doubt, from *mal de mer*, for they 'abandoned the fly, hired post-horses, and so reached Gourock', the whole affair having cost the gentleman ('wet, sick and exhausted') seven pounds, fourteen shillings and threepence. He really would have been much wiser to trust himself and his family to the excellent new steamer *Marion*, which would have taken only about four hours to do the journey, and cost him a matter of shillings.

While the Reids and a few other intrepid Glasgow families were venturing thus far abroad, the poorer folk were holiday-making nearer home. Some, indeed, never got farther than the jollities of Glasgow Fair – jollities that became so hearty, it seems, that the fair had to be suppressed. Some went inland to Cambuslang, or Strathaven. Others, content perhaps with occasional day trips, favoured Partick, a former Episcopal residence, though at the end of the eighteenth century more famous for its 'crumpie cake and cheese'; or Govan, another pleasant village celebrated for its Sunday salmon suppers. Both these villages were swept away in the expansion of the shipbuilding industry, which followed the successful development of the steamship, and like so many other once proud separate communities – Gorbals, Calton, Hillhead, Pollokshields, Maryhill, to name only a few – were eventually caught up in the expanding meshes of the Glasgow megalopolis.

So Victorian Glasgow developed a taste for holidays 'Doon the Watter', the more so since the Cowal coast and the islands of Bute and Cumbrae were being opened up by builders. In 1822, for instance, a Glasgow merchant prince took the first large feu at Dunoon, on the west side of the castle. There he built himself a mansion. Other merchants followed his example, and the Highland clachan soon became a little township of 'villas' occupied mainly during the summer months. Strone, Blairmore, Kirn and Innellan all grew suddenly from clachans to sizeable villages dotted about the shores of the Firth. At the height of their glory, these stucco villas, many of them large houses with coachman's quarters attached, must have looked quite impressive, invested as they were with the slow and prosperous air of

Victorian suburbia. Now, their leisured dignity has long since departed. Many of them are panelled off into rooms or flatlets; others are in
a damp and peeling state of disrepair.

The merchant princes, having established their places at the coast,
created a demand for faster and more comfortable steamers. Until the
second half of the century, so rapid was the development of the
steamship, and so keen the competition between owners, many of
them skippers of the 'paddlers' themselves, that within a very few years
a fine new ship could soon be rendered obsolete, and therefore unpop-
ular, by a new rival vessel.

During the 1850s, the issue became one of speed versus comfort. For
a time, speed won. The Clyde steamers of Alexander Smith's day were
mostly lean rakish affairs, designed to paddle themselves over the Firth
with the minimum water resistance, their decks as free as possible of
any luxury structures which might act as impediments in the face of a
wind. An account of these days of cut-price steamer competition, of
dangerous racing in order to snatch away a rival's potential customers,
of steamers banging each other at piers, of captains insulting their
rivals through advertisements printed in local papers, and of the stur-
dy individuality that characterized many of the owner/skippers who
operated through the Iron Years, has been written by Captain James
Williamson, founder of the Williamson Line. Captain Williamson, in
his later years a dandy with a white goatee beard, inherited the business created by his father, one of the earliest steam operators on Loch
Lomond who moved over to the Clyde. Captain Williamson himself
served his apprenticeship as an engineer and then as a ship's master,
qualifications not regarded as essential in the early days of steamboat
operation. His book *Clyde Passenger Steamers* (1904) deals, as might be
expected, with engineering and other technical developments, but also
preserves for us fascinating social glimpses, in the writing of which he
was able to draw on his own memories and those of his family.

Fast but primitive steamers took the workers away for a few hours
from the forges and foundries and the grime of Glasgow to the mountainy loveliness of the Firth of Clyde at a cost of as little as a shilling
for a day's outing. Some of these ships came to an untimely end. Huge
prices were paid for the acquisition of vessels to run the Federal blockade in the American Civil War. Many of these frail paddlers were bat-
tered to pieces in mid-Atlantic before they could reach their new owners. Those that survived made large profits for their unscrupulous operators.

One of the little vessels providing crossing for pedestrians from 1840 to 1977 when
the last ferry was withdrawn from service

The railway companies were slow to appreciate the profitability of
the steamboat business, and at first left the private operators to vie
among themselves for the privilege of running to meet train connections.

Attempts in 1844 and again in the 1850s by the proprietors of the
Greenock Railway (later amalgamated with the Caledonian) and in
1848 by the Wemyss Bay Steamboat Company Limited (ditto) to run
their own steamers failed. To travel by a privately owned steamer connecting with the train meant a more expensive journey than a sail 'all
the way'. Even so, the obvious eventual threat of railway competition
during these peak years of the private owner was clearly one that could
not wisely be disregarded, especially after the North British Railway
built a railhead pier at Craigendoran in 1883 and the Caledonian
Company opened at Gourock in 1889.

One of the reasons for the provision of these increasing travel facilities between Glasgow and the Clyde Coast was the tendency for more
and more wealthy Glaswegians to follow the example of Kirkman

Finlay, for whom David Hamilton had built Castle Toward in 1821, and build holiday houses for themselves along the northern fringe of the estuary, turning little villages like Strone, Kirn and Innellan into water-front clusters of ornate Italianate villas with large gardens. When transporting the owners of these summer villas from their places of leisure to their city offices in the morning and bringing them home again at night, the shorter the travelling time, the better was likely to be the pressure of customers. One of the forms that competition took was steamer racing.

The practice of steamer racing came to a climax on 27 May 1861, when two new paddle-steamers, the *Ruby* and the *Rothesay Castle*, owned by rival companies, were both scheduled to leave Glasgow at 4 p.m. bound for Greenock and Rothesay.

Andrew MacQueen, another historian of the Clyde fleet, has left us an account of this contest in his book *Echoes of Old Clyde Paddle-Wheels* (1924). It had been arranged that the steamers were to change berths at the Broomielaw on alternate days. On Monday 27 May the advantage fell to the *Rothesay Castle*:

> Right well she availed herself of it, for, having the lead, she kept it, travelling as never steamer had travelled on the river before. At twenty past five, the spectators on the Custom House Quay at Greenock saw her race past, with the *Ruby* in close attendance. Keeping up the pace, the *Rothesay Castle* finished at Rothesay Quay two and a half minutes ahead of her rival, having covered the distance in two hours twenty-eight minutes. The feat was suitably recognized, the awards being made the following Monday by Baillie Raeburn at the River-Baillie Court, where Captain Brown of the *Rothesay Castle* was fined a guinea for reckless navigation and Captain Price of the *Ruby*, in view of the reputation he had acquired for similar exploits, double the amount.

But Price, who had no doubt provoked Brown, was not to be cured by a mere two-guinea fine. A few months later, he ran a neck-and-neck race with the *Neptune*, colliding with her twice and missing out Gourock, where he should have called, in order to maintain his lead.

'What right has this man, Price,' thundered the *Glasgow Herald*, 'to entrap people into his vessel for a safe summer-day sail and then subject them to the terror of a violent death by explosion or collision?' This time the River-Baillie Court provided the answer. Price lost his command, and reckless racing came to an end.

The loveliness of the Firth of Clyde, however, is not affected by the manner in which people cross its surface. On the north bank, the scenery is unmistakably Highland. The hills of 'dreaming Cowal' sweep back in a blue haze to the rugged peaks of Argyll. The curves and contours of the south bank are just as markedly Lowland, so rich are the fertile fringes of Renfrewshire and Ayrshire rolling gently away from the river.

To get properly acquainted with the Firth of Clyde, it is necessary to sail down to it from the Broomielaw. It is not enough to arrive at Greenock or Glasgow on an incoming liner or on the Irish boat. For one thing, these deep-water vessels hold too far out from the coast in the lower reaches; for another, they usually arrange to arrive, in obedience either to the state of the tide or to some mystical ritual I have never been able to fathom, in the 'wee sma' hours', when hardly as much as a glimmering shorelight is visible.

In 1857, Alexander Smith in 'A Boy's Poem' described the journey in verse:

> The steamer left the black and oozy wharves,
> And floated down between dank ranks of masts.
> We heard the swarming streets, the noisy mills;
> Saw sooty foundries full of glare and gloom,
> Great bellied chimneys tipped by tongues of flame,
> Quiver in smoky heat. We slowly passed
> Loud building-yards, where every ship contained
> A mighty vessel with a hundred men
> Battering its iron sides . . .
> . . . At length the stream
> Broadened 'tween banks of daisies, and afar
> The shadows flew upon the sunny hills;
> And down the river, 'gainst the pale blue sky
> A town sat in its smoke . . .
> . . . We reached the pier
> Where girls in fluttering dresses, shady hats,
> Smiled rosy welcome. An impatient roar
> Of hasty steam; from the broad paddle rushed
> A flood of pale grey foam, that hissed and wreathed
> Ere it subsided in the quiet sea.
> With a glad foot I leapt upon the shore,
> And, as I went, the frank and lavish winds

Told me about the lilac's mass of bloom,
The slim laburnum showering golden tears,
The roses of the garden where they played . . .

That is still a fairly accurate piece of reportage, even down to the flo-
ral description, for the climate of the coast is relatively frost-free and
mild. Indeed, such foreign exotics as yuccas can be seen in many a garden, though rather self-consciously absurd in their Scots surroundings
and perhaps a little less luxuriant than nature originally intended.

A vivid, slightly later description of a trip 'Doon the Watter' to
Carrick Castle on Loch Goil, comes from the pen of the author of
'Wee MacGreegor', James Joy Bell (1871–1934). He sailed on the paddle steamer *Benmore*, originally the flagship of Captain Bob Campbell
and used on the Glasgow and Kilmun run. Campbell, however, got
into difficulties and had to sell it to Captain William Buchanan, who
ran her out of Glasgow to Dunoon and Rothesay.

Bell, the son of a wealthy factory owner, was brought up in Bank
Street, off Great Western Road by Kelvinbridge, a street originally
called Great Kelvin Terrace. When Bell sailed on the *Benmore*, it was
still under Campbell's captaincy. In *I Remember*, published in 1922,
Bell recalled:

The Glasgow summer holiday was then essentially a family affair. Even
when the children were grown up, they did not go their different ways.
I remember a family of thirteen holidaying together. I knew a family of
eighteen, though I was never in their holiday house. Possibly there
would not have been room for one more. It may seem funny, absurd, but
there it was.

We were not seven then – only four; but there were an infant and a
granny who required much attention, and a West Highland maid who
sat down and wept copiously at frequent intervals, because the granny
reminded her of her own granny, who had departed this life fourteen
years earlier. Fortunately there was also a nursemaid, a Glasgow girl, a
young person who never got ruffled, and who, when things went awry,
sang 'My Grandfather's Clock', and 'Tommy, Make Room for Your
Uncle', and other ditties of the day, at the top of her voice – otherwise
I do not see how my mother could ever have got the packing done. I
have no idea what went into all the trunks and hampers, only that when
the hour came they filled a spring-van.

Luggage apart, it would have been an awkward business to change from train to steamer at Greenock, and the usual method for families like ours was to 'sail all the way', either from the Broomielaw or from Partick Pier, the latter being for us the more convenient point of embarkation. So thither on a fine Friday, about noon, we were rattled over the stony streets in a couple of cabs.

Our ultimate destination was a farmhouse at Carrick Castle, on Loch Goil. My mother had had no opportunity of viewing it in advance, but the place had been warmly recommended to my father by a friend, as one unspoiled by man – or words to that effect.

We arrived at Partick Pier far too early. The sun shone hotly; the tide was low; and it was before the days of the Clyde's purification. Not to be squeamish about it, the Clyde at Glasgow was then a big sewer. We and other families waited and waited. In the heat babies began to 'girn'; small children grew peevish; little girls complained or looked pathetically patient. For boys there was always the entertainment of the shipping-lines, channel and river steamers, cargo vessels, barques, barquentines, brigs and schooners, dredgers, hoppers, ferries.

At last the white funnelled *Benmore* came chunking cannily down the river, already with a fair complement of passengers, for it was the first of the month. She was almost new, the first river steamer to have a 'half-deck' saloon. For some forty years thereafter she led a steady, useful existence, once distinguishing herself – about 1912, I think – by striking, one foggy morning, a sunken rock off Innellan, and lying there for a week or so, submerged to her bridge.

She came alongside; the families were shepherded on board, to find seats where they could, and the luggage was added to the existing mountains. Luggage went free then. Years later, I witnessed the indignation of a family at being charged for their piano's conveyance. The *Benmore* resumed her journey, still cannily, for every now and then appeared on the banks boards bearing the words 'Dead Slow', the warning necessary in order that the wash from steamers should break lightly against the shore of the shipyards or the dredgers at work.

And now the warm air was full of the clangour of shipbuilding. Skeleton frameworks, one after another, and hulls nearing completion rose high above the banks. One could see the riveters, like pigmies, perched aloft, and the glimmer of their fires. 'What an awful noise,' said the ladies, while the men complacently surveyed the tremendous scene of industry – and prosperity. What would not all of us give to hear that hammering again? How merry to our ears it would sound today!

On the other side of the river we called at Govan – where the *Orient*,

of the line of that name, almost completed, lay moored, testing her propeller, churning the murky water into brownish foam – and Renfrew,
where another family or two joined us.

Soon after that it was plainer sailing. Clydebank, as a shipbuilding
town, was not there; the river began to widen between green fields, and
the increased speed meant a current of air, grateful to every passenger.
Lunch baskets and parcels were produced, and the children fed. I dare
say every mother there could have done nicely with a cup of tea, but
there was no tearoom on board – nor was there then such a thing, as we
know it, in all Glasgow.

You would have seen comparatively few fathers on board – impossible, had declared the majority, to get away from business so early; and,
anyway, fathers were not expected to be of much assistance on such an
occasion. Some of those present took advantage of the lull caused by
hunger among their progeny, and went 'down to see the engines'. The
others contented themselves with pipes or cigars – I doubt whether you
would have found a cigarette if you had searched the ship . . . It was a
peaceful enough passage – with a pause at Bowling, and maybe also at
Dumbarton, with its amazingly long pier reaching out from the Rock
over the shallows – to Greenock's Custom House Quay.

There was no space on the deck for 'steering laddies' to run ;about
and get into mischief, so the mothers were free, more or less, to relax.
Some of them may have dozed after the struggles of the morning. But
all, as you might have heard, at one time or another, gave thanks for the
mercy of fine weather. You might have heard also heartrending reminiscences of family journeys to the coast when 'it rained all the time,
and the boat was even more crowded than this one'.

The finest vessel of the river fleet was undoubtedly David
MacBrayne's Royal Mail paddle-steamer *Columba*. Built in 1878 by J
and G Thomson of Clydebank, she made the journey between
Glasgow and Ardrishaig – called the Royal Route, not out of tribute to
its scenic magnificence, but because Queen Victoria once went over it
– daily during the summer months, with very few interruptions, for
sixty-eight years. For her period, she was a model of spacious comfort
below deck; outwardly, she was remarkable for her pleasing combina-
tion of size and grace. Seven o'clock in the morning, and later, eleven
minutes past seven, was the traditional hour for her to cast off her
ropes at the Broomielaw.

I made my first trip 'Doon the Watter' in her a few years before she went the sad way of all old ships, and I can still vividly recall the excitement of that first experience.

We were to set out, I think, on the first day of July; mother and father, four children, dog, cat and goldfish. Although we could depend on being able to purchase rather more than could the Reids, nevertheless a great deal of luggage had to be taken. The packing was done systematically during the last days of June. I do not think I slept much on the night before our departure.

It began early. We got up at five in the morning and had breakfast half an hour later. For some reason, that breakfast had a special quality of its own. Its ingredients were those of many another breakfast eaten since – porridge, bread and butter, and a boiled egg – but I can still remember the extra flavour those comestibles seemed to acquire that morning. (No doubt it was in a similar mood of anticipation that the poet Southey generously praised the excellence of Scottish breakfasts while staying at Old Meldrum.)

After breakfast, we children were expected to keep out of the way of our elders, for a horse-drawn lorry arrived outside the house at six o'clock to cart the luggage down to the quay. I was given the job of guarding the cat while the luggage was being grunted and manoeuvred round the bends of the staircase. The cat, a venerable beast who lived to be eighteen and would then have been about twelve, had the idea that if he managed to escape while the front door stood open to let the carters move freely in and out, he would not have to undergo his annual holiday ordeal of transportation by basket; hence the need for one of the family to stand guard.

At last, the luggage had rumbled away, the cat had been safely basketed, and it was time to prepare ourselves for the arrival of the taxi. That taxi drive itself was something of a novelty. Usually, I went to children's parties in a cab – a musty affair, upholstered in faded green, and driven by a red-nosed, mufflered coachman, whose characteristic smell was almost as strong as that of the horse that pulled the contraption.

Ordinary mortals who go about their affairs during the hours of daylight would do well to take an occasional ride through an industrial city at half-past-six in the morning, if only to remind themselves how large a section of the community has to do 'day labour, light denied' in order to keep essential public services running. The new sun shone out from a clean sky this July morning, glistening the rooftops of the tenements, and lighting up even the drabbest side-street with the promise of a fair day.

MacBrayne's RMS *Columba*. She had sailed for sixty-nine years when she was finally withdrawn from service.

The *Columba* lay on the south side of the river, her two red and black funnels setting off nobly her huge, gilded paddle-boxes. The moment you climbed up her gangway, your nostrils were assailed by a peculiar aroma that was all her own. After some years, I discovered that it was a mixture of engine-oil, good galley cooking and well-scrubbed cleanliness, to which, down the river, the scudding tang of salty spray was added. But, at that time, analysis did not matter. The smell was wholly entrancing.

We were to establish ourselves in the cabin, or the 'saloon' as it was more grandly called. The saloon consisted of a number of seated bays lined with dark red velvet plush, and richly draped with similar hangings. It gave an impression of well-established opulence and time-saturated sea-going. All went well at first. I carried the cat's basket down the companionway, and the cat remained obligingly silent. But at the entrance to the saloon, a liveried steward looked at me and my burden with an unmistakable air of hostility.

'What's in the basket?' he demanded.

'Provisions,' I answered, with a happier promptitude than I have displayed on many a more important occasion since. He grunted and let us past. We chose an empty bay, and comfortably disposed our bits and pieces.

Those final moments of waiting seemed interminable. Above our heads, busy feet tapped out their walking patterns on the deck. In the orange glow of the engine-room, the great gleaming monsters hissed and sizzled quietly to themselves, as if anticipating the moment when the flicker of a dial and the loosening of a lever would send them plunging backward and forward in all their pride of power.

Seven o'clock! Five minutes past! And then the unfortunate happening occurred. A long, thin stream of clear liquid raced down the floor. Its place of origin was unmistakably the basket at my feet.

In a moment the steward was at my side.

'Your provisions seem to be leaking, sir,' he observed acidly. (That 'sir', to one of my tender years, seemed an additional humiliation.) 'You'd better take them on deck.'

I was delighted. I certainly had no desire to spend my first voyage in the feminine confines of the cabin. Now, someone would *have* to stay on deck to see that the cat was not shipped prematurely ashore.

Up there, things were happening. The captain, an impressive and recognizably Highland figure even beneath the disguising weight of his gold braid, was pacing his bridge, which straddled the ship from one paddle-box to the other between the two funnels. (It has always seemed strange to me that, until about 1920, it apparently never occurred to the designers of paddle-steamers that the funnel was a fairly major obstacle in the way of the helmsman's vision.) The captain took one final look at his watch; then he pulled the clanging brass levers at his side. The paddles began to thresh the water, nosing the ship's bow out towards the centre of the river: with a couple of dirty splashes, the ropes were tossed into the water, to be retrieved fussily by puffing steam capstans at bow and stern; and then the long, lean hull, shuddering a little at first, began to slide slowly forward: past close miles of shipyards, resounding with the racket of the riveters welding together the rusty hulks of the ships that would sail tomorrow's seas; past docks, full of towering ocean-going liners and queer-looking tramp ships with foreign characters scrawled across their sterns; past grumphed-up, dirty old dredgers, squatting in the middle of the river, digging away the mud that forever strives to slip back into its ancient bed; past low-built hoppers carrying the mud far down the Firth to be dumped in the deeps around Ailsa Craig;

Dunoon and its castle

past the chain-drawn car ferries at Renfrew and Erskine; past Bowling, with its stone-pencil monument to Henry Bell, and its huge oil port and depot cut back into the hills; past Greenock and Gourock, and over the broad Firth to Dunoon and Innellan.

The salt of the open sea blows in upon Innellan, and the mountainy freshness of the Highland hills creeps down on it from the north. These things I have noticed many times since. But these long years ago, my joy was all at landing at a pier that stuck far out into the water. As I walked up that pier for the first time, I wondered what lay beyond the gates: Glasgow's Highland fringe, to be sure.

Indeed, the sights and sounds and smells of these long-ago holidays meant so much to me that remembered imagery from them has pervaded my poetry ever since – as in *7.11 The Broomielaw*, written half a century after the experience.

> At last the day came, early wakening . . .
> At six o'clock the horse-drawn cart arrived,
> rumbling packed trunks along the cobbled streets
> to reach the Broomielaw as we arrived
> by taxi, climbing up the gangway laid
> across *Columba's* gilded paddle-box,

with led dog, clutching basket-mewing cat,
the chill of early morning shivering
anticipation as, her ropes cast off,
the braided Captain leant along his bridge,
hand resting on the engine-telegraph
clanging departure. Then, the big floats churned,
greening a muddy froth across the Clyde
sizzling as slow, bow-angled, out she sailed,
the thumping paddles picking up their pace,
dividing foam-wash as she cleaved her way
past vessels still in sleep, clanged shipyards spaced
through ever-widening strips of opened fields.
Behind us, office workers slowly stirred;
ahead, the cries of seagulls, beckoning
their fishy hunger distances away,
the salt-edged wind, the scent of holiday.
Thump-thump, thump-thump, thump-thump, the gathered motion
hurried us towards imagination's shores,
the hutted pier, Innellan with its flowers
and nameless pleasures that would soon be ours.

Other youngsters, later among my contemporary fellow-poets, were
having similar experiences: J.F. Hendry (1912–86), for instance, in
'The Broomielaw' remembering:

> A great Trade Fair. A holiday air
> on the lower reaches of the Clyde:
> a floral bandstand in the rain . . .

and Stewart Conn (b.1936) in 'Family Visit':

> . . . off to Innellan, singing, we would go,
> Boarding the steamer at the Broomielaw
> In broad Summer, the bomps-a-daisy
> Days, the ship band playing in a lazy
> Swell, my father steering well clear
> Of the bar, mother making neat
> Packets of note-paper to carry
> To the nearest basket or (more likely)
> All the way back to Cranworth Street.

Until the construction of the riverside walkway, long after the Broomielaw had ceased to function as Glasgow's harbour, it was a scene of noise and bustle, rarely visited by respectable citizens. I remember it as a clatter of horse-drawn carts on the cobbled carriageway, among which lorries soon began to nose their way, ultimately superseding the horses and their flat trundling carts. In *The Clyde, River and Firth*, novelist Neil Munro preserved a picture of it in 1907:

> Come to the harbour by day, and then I grant there is little glamour to be found; come on a wet November day especially, to look for some not very distinguishable shipping-box at the end of some not very distinctive mile-long quay, and before you have found it the melancholy of things will have bitten to your very heart. I do not wonder that to all but those whose business takes them there, the harbour, whose name is known to the uttermost ends of the earth, should be wholly unfamiliar to Glasgow citizens. They may see the upper end of it from the train as they cross the railway bridges morning and afternoon from and to suburban villas or the coast; they may once or twice have ventured down the channel in a 'Clutha', to feel some vague emotion in a scene so strange, but as a rule the harbour, with its vast activities . . . lies wholly beyond their interest or curiosity . . . The harbour life slops over its actual precincts, and the neighbouring streets, as in other parts, bear a marine impress . . . Ship-chandlers' shops, slop shops, shops where binnacle lights, sextants, marlin and nautical almanacks fill the windows . . .'

That scene has changed. The shops have gone. Car-filled streets flood down to the riverside on their way to one or other of the bridges or out towards the west. With respectability has come visual dullness.

IV

Unfortunately, for nineteenth-century trippers the increasing use of the Clyde as a receptacle for industrial waste – and, worse still, for the dumping of raw domestic sewage – must have been an odiferous experience, as at least two local bards recorded. Thus Bass Kennedy in 1888:

Ho! Ye magnates of the city, study this unsavoury ditty,
    For it is a gruesome pity that such words I need inscribe;
But my love was slightly ailing, she desired a little sailing,
    And her wishes all prevailing, we embarked upon the Clyde.
But, alas! our noble river, how it made poor Nannie shiver,
    Loud exclaiming, 'Oh, I never!' as her hanky stopped her nose,
For so fearful bad the stink was, and the water black as ink was,
    Just like Day and Martin's blacking, and as thick as Athole brose.

It cannot always have been 'so fearful bad', when, years earlier, Bass Kennedy had proposed to his future wife aboard a Clyde steamer, as he recalled in 'Doon the Watter at the Fair,' published in 1888.

Ye min yon July morn langsyne,
    A rosy morn like this,
You pledged to be forever mine,
    An' sealed it wi' a kiss.
On board the *Petrel*, near Dunoon,
    Ye yielded to my prayer,
An' sin syne we've managed doon
    The Watter at the Fair . . .

Sae haste ye, Nannie, come awa',
    An' dinna langsome be,
For thrangin' tae the Broomielaw,
    The focks gaun by wi' glee.
A twalmonth's toil in Glesca toun
    Is lichtsome I declare,
Wi' twa-three days' diversion doon
    The Watter at the Fair.

A little later another laureate of the Clyde, Robert D. Jamieson, published 'The Humble Petition of the River Clyde to the Lord Provost'. By April 1904, when the poem was printed, a sail on the river apparently had become a truly odiferous experience. Said the Clyde:

And oh! What joy at Glesca Fair
when, keen to breathe the caller air,
ten thousand toilers wad repair,
    Wi' happy faces,

To Rothesay, Largs, or maybe Ayr,
    And ither places.

What busslin' at the Broomielaw,
The like ye scarcely ever saw,
When manly fellows, ane and a',
    Had one intent
Wi' wives and weans, and lassies braw,
    On pleasure bent.

O' steamers Glesca had the wale;
Ye culdna find a finer sail,
'Neath burnin' sun or moonbeam pale
    Than doon the watter;
Their speed and comfort did avail
    To end the matter.

'Iona' first my glory shared;
The 'Rothesay Castle', built by Caird,
The 'Ruby', 'Eagle', ably ser'ed
    By patrons mony;
MacLean's auld 'Marquis' still is spared
    Could flee wi' ony.

But oh! I'm sair, sair changed noo,
'The glory is departed', true;
My face has taen a deadly hue,
    I'm no mysel';
Wha look at me are like to spew,
    I'm sae polluted.

The smells that frae my surface rise
Micht weel contaminate the skies;
Nae fish in me can live, but dies,
    I needna tell ye;
Sic dreadful odours wald suffice
    To kill a baillie.

My coastin' traffic noo is gane!
It's nae mair steamers, but the train
That whirls the folk wi' micht and main
    To Gourock pier
While I, in sorrow, sigh and grane   [groan
    Wi' mony a tear.

154

There were, of course, other reasons than the state of the river for the transference of traffic to the boat-train services. The 'all-the-way' sail to Innellan from the Broomielaw, for instance, took even the fast *Columba* three hours, whereas the boat-train to Wemyss Bay and the train to Glasgow took one, making daily commuting easily possible. The railway companies, however, were slow to compete with the 'all-the-way' trade, but eventually they did, opening terminals at Greenock, Gourock, Wemyss Bay and Craigendoran.

Even by 1910, Charles J. Kirk could write this 'Ode to the Clyde', composed, apparently, 'in the case of a buoy moored in the Clyde off Cardross'.

> Hail, great black-bosomed mother of our city,
> Whose odiferous breath offends the earth,
> Whose cats and puppy dogs excite our pity,
> As they sail past with aldermanic girth!
> No salmon hast thou in thy jet-black waters,
> Save that which is adhering to the tins.
> Thus thy adorers – Govan's lovely daughters –
> Adorn thy shrine with offerings for their sins.
>
> No sedges check thy flow, nor water-lily;
> Thy banks are unadorned with hip or haw,
> 'Cos why? Now, don't pretend you're *really* silly,
> There ain't no lilies at the Broomielaw.
> MacBrayne defiles thy face with coaly sweepings,
> Into thy lap the tar expectorates;
> The 'Caledonia's' cook his galley heapings
> Casts in thy face as if at one he hates.
>
> Yet art thou great. Though strangers hold their noses
> When sailing down to Rothesay at the Fair,
> Thy exiled sons would barter tons of roses
> To scent thy sweetness on the desert air.

Progress in cleaning up the Clyde accelerated after 1945. Glasgow's sewage was then processed, the residue being taken down to the open sea off Cumbrae for discharge. Sailing on the *Garroch Head* – one of the two sludge boats that, until 1999, carried out this daily task, after which dumping any kind of sewage became illegal under European law – I remarked to the captain that a salmon (they had long since been driven away from the Clyde by pollution) had been seen again as far up as Erskine bridge. 'Mebbe so,' he replied, 'but ye should hae seen the state o' the salmon!'

Today, only one pleasure steamer survives, the *Waverley*, the former London and North Eastern Railway boat, now named after her predecessor lost at Dunkirk. During July and August, she sails from the Broomielaw, or from Ayr, to all the surviving Clyde piers, cruising from ports right round the coast of the United Kingdom during the spring and autumn, as 'the last sea-going paddle-steamer in the world', a great attraction.

The widespread growth of motoring after the Second World War, together with the increasing popularity of holidays abroad, led to the steady withdrawal of most of the Clyde fleet, the friendly paddle-steamers and the elegant turbine steamers that looked like miniature liners being replaced by work-a-day car ferries.

V

Those who stayed at home but still wanted to be out of doors had golf, a game relatively new to Scotland, with which to divert themselves. Golf had been imported to Scotland from Holland and first played on the sandy machairs (or coastal strips) of the East Coast, but by the sixteenth century it had become established in Glasgow. James Arbuckle, a friend of Allan Ramsay, when still a student, in 1721 published a poem 'Glotta', which contains a practical account of golf on Glasgow Green.

> In Winter too, when hoary Frosts o'erspread
> The verdant Turf, and naked lay the Mead
> The vig'rous Youth commence the sporting War,
> And arm'd with Lead, their jointed Clubs prepare;
> The Timber Curve to Leather Orbs apply,
> Compact, Elastic, to pervade the Sky:
> These to the distant Hole direct they drive;
> They claim the Stakes who thither first arrive.
> Intent his Ball the eager Gamester eyes.
> His Muscle strains, and various Postures tries,
> The impelling Blow to strike with greater Force,
> And shape the motive Orb's projectile Course –

If with due Strength the weighty Engine fall
Discharg'd obliquely, and impinge the Ball,
It winding mounts aloft, and sings in Air;
And wond'ring Crowds the Gamester's Skill declare.
But when some luckless wayward Stroke descends,
The Foes triumph, the Club is curs'd in vain;
Spectators scoff; and ev'n Allies complain.
Thus still success is follow'd with Applause;
But ah! How few espouse a vanquish'd Cause!

Golf, as they say, 'took off' in Scotland. A century and a half later, Andrew Lang was moved to observe: 'Golf is a thoroughly national game; it is as Scotch as haggis, cockie-leekie, high cheek-bones or rowanberry jam. Since, as we all know, it never rains on the golf-course, it is a game which does not depend on the seasons.'

Theatre-going seems to be a winter pastime. Early Glasgow stage ventures incurred discouraging verbal bullying by the 'unco guid' clergymen. As early as 1595, the Kirk Session instructed the town drummer to deter all 'persons from going to Ruglen (Rutherglen) to see profane plays on Sundays'. In 1728, the earliest recorded Glasgow theatrical occasion involved Anthony Ashton's company from Edinburgh, which tried to stage John Gay's The Beggars' Opera in the Weigh House, there then being no theatre in Glasgow. However, they were prevented from doing so by the vociferous protests of the clergy, reflecting an anti-theatre prejudice that, albeit secularized, survived into the twentieth century in middle-class circles, which harboured a belief that the theatre fostered 'fallen women' and other nameless sinners.

The first Glasgow theatre was a wooden booth erected in 1752 against the wall of the Bishop's Palace, hard by the cathedral (more or less on the site of Ian Begg's late twentieth-century pastiche castle, which I find delightful, but which many of his fellow-architects deplore). That theatre was, however, a temporary structure, the manager removing the roof at the end of the players' run. As a contemporary noted: 'To this house of the drama came many patrons, who were carried there in sedans, under a strong guard to protect them from the fanatics. This unruly mob gathered round the theatre to threaten those who dared enter "The Devil's Home", not only with the judgement of Heaven, but with, what was worse, summary and immediate violence.'

The next attempt at establishing a theatre was both a disaster and a

The Caledonian Theatre Royal, Dunlop Street

triumph. A group of enthusiasts was refused permission by magistrates to build it within the city boundaries, where no one would sell them ground, so they built it outside at Grahamston, where the Central Station now stands. In the spring of 1764, when the new theatre was to be opened, it was announced that the famous actress Mrs Bellamy would make her first appearance in it. Again, a contemporary account preserves a record of the occasion:

On the previous evening the Revivalists were busy. In the open space at Anderston, a Methodist preacher [George Whitefield] was addressing the crowd . . . 'I dreamed last night that I was in Hell, where a banquet was being held. All the devils in the pit were there, when Lucifer, their chief, gave them a toast: *Here is to the health of John Miller of Westerton, who has sold his ground to build Me a House on*'. The spark had caught fire; the incentive was given . . . With the speed of fanatic wrath the theatre was quickly reached, a light applied to the edifice, and before many hours had elapsed the zealots had succeeded in destroying the stage properties and costumes, as well as a considerable portion of the building. Mrs Bellamy arrived next morning, to find the manager in despair. But she was not so easily daunted:

Rehearsals were held in the Black Bull Inn, where she was lodged. Arrangements were made for repairing the theatre and setting it in order for the same night. Offers of money were made by the city merchants, and the wardrobes of the ladies were placed at her disposal. Dressing at the Black Bull Inn, she was conveyed to the theatre in a sedan chair, appearing that night in *The Citizen*, followed by *The Mock Doctor* . . . A goodly company welcomed her, and remained seated till they saw her safely out of the theatre, the Town Guard being under orders to escort her back to the city . . . Amongst the parts she played during that visit was that of Lady Macbeth, for which she had to borrow a white dress, her own costume having been burned by the religious mob.

The first theatre to become properly established was built on the east side of Dunlop Street, just off Argyle Street, and was run by John Jackson, who was also the licensee of theatres in the other three main Scottish cities. He received the required letters-patent from the magistrates, without which a theatre could not be called 'royal', and Glasgow got its first Theatre Royal, in which, among many other stars of the day, Mrs Siddons appeared in 1795. Jackson was also the manager of the Queen Street theatre, opened in 1805, which took away the fashionable clientele from its predecessor. It became a kind of music hall in 1807, but early in the 1820s was bought by Frank Seymour and again renamed the Caledonian. It survived until 1863, when it accidentally burned down.

John Henry Alexander, described by a contemporary as having had 'a somewhat varied career as tragedian, low comedian, actor and heavy gent,' also wanted to buy the Caledonian, but on being forestalled by Seymour, bought the cellar beneath instead and turned it into a theatre – the Dominion of Fancy, its ceilings so low that 'the boxes and galleries were no more than areas marked off by ropes'.

Great was the rivalry between the two. On the night Seymour opened upstairs with *Macbeth*, downstairs Alexander staged a piece called *The Battle of Inch*. Walter Baynham, in his book *The Glasgow Stage*, wrote of that double opening: '*Macbeth* was nearly acted throughout to the tuneful accompaniment of the shouts of the soldiery, the clanging of dish covers, the clashing of swords, the banging of drums, with the fumes of blue fire every now and then rising thro' the chinks of the planks from the stage below to the stage above. The audience laughed, and this stimulated the wrath of the combating managers.'

An instruction from the magistrates that 'neither party was to annoy the other' led to Seymour's upstairs audience lifting floorboards and pouring water on Alexander's audience beneath, and later to both houses mounting productions of the same piece simultaneously. There was a final flurry when the two theatres offered simultaneous productions of Weber's *Der Freischutz*. On Alexander's first night, Seymour's supporters lifted the stage planks during the incantation scene, grabbed the dragon by the tail, and prevented him from extinguishing his fumes, to the great consternation of the inflamed monster. However, a piece called *Tom and Jerry* ran successfully in both houses for over a month, ending this cat-and-mouse rivalry.

When the Queen Street Theatre went up in flames, fired off by leaky gas, Seymour opened a new Theatre Royal in York Street with *The Merchant of Venice*, billing Edmund Kean as Shylock. J.H. Alexander then acquired the Dunlop Street 'double' theatre and rebuilt it as one establishment in 1840, offering in his first season Diamond's *Royal Oak, or the Days of Charles II*, *Paul Pry*, *Cramond Brig* and *Guy Mannering* (with Mackay as Bailie Nicol Jarvie). Edmund Kean in *Othello* and Charles Kean in *Richard III* were only a few of the varied selection of plays in the ensuing years of his theatrical reign.

Two other places of entertainment further broadened the Glaswegian's choice of theatrical fare. D.P. Miller, a former showman at the Glasgow Fair, made so much money with his penny-a-time Great Gun Trick that in 1842 he was able to open a new theatre, the Adelphi, in the Saltmarket. He was the first to bring another famous Victorian actor, C.J. Phelps, to Glasgow in the title role of *Hamlet* in 1843. The Adelphi went up in flames in 1848. In 1838, Edmund Glover, a member of a famous London theatrical family, opened the Prince's, a converted exhibition hall in West Nile Street, so salubrious that the Western Club booked a box permanently for the convenience of its members. Incidentally, the Prince's was said to have been the first theatre in Scotland to have the stalls separate from the pit.

In 1845, another actor-manager, John Henry Anderson, known as 'The Wizard of the North', built the largely wooden City Theatre at the foot of the Saltmarket, opening with Balfe's opera *The Bohemian Girl*. It went up in spectacular flames in 1845, the embers carrying west to George Square.

Tragedy became all too real at the Dunlop Street Theatre one Saturday in 1849. During the performance of *The Surrender of Calais*, flames flickered around a leaking gas joint in the lower part of the house, but were quickly put out. Panic, however, broke out in the upper gallery and the occupants rushed for the stairs. Although the street doors were open, some of those to reach the bottom first stumbled and fell, and within seconds the whole stairway was a compressed fallen throng.

As the *Glasgow Herald* put it the following Monday: 'The weak were trampled down by the strong – the latter only to be trampled down by the furious crowd in the rear. The noise of the cries and groans, and the struggle for bare life, was most agonising.' Sixty-five people died, causing especial

> grief among the working classes . . . One poor lad in Dunlop Street was the picture of woe. He had taken his sweetheart to the theatre. She was carried away from him in the rush; and in his attempt to save her he had only been able to grasp her bonnet and shawl. With these still in his possession he often exclaimed to the bystanders – 'How can I go home to her parents without her, and tell them of this?'

But the Dunlop Street Theatre really did go up in flames after a performance of the pantomime *Bluebeard* in 1863. We are again indebted to the *Glasgow Herald* for the information that 'the appearance of the conflagration was awfully grand' and that 'sixty thousand gallons of water derived from our noble Highland lochs' were poured into the flames during the course of an hour, providing a spectacle that was eagerly watched by an appreciative crowd, most of whom would probably never have been inside any theatre doors. Patched up after the fire, the Dunlop Street Theatre functioned for a further five years until it was pulled down to make way for part of the approaches to St Enoch's Station.

Some other famous Glasgow theatres of yesteryear included the Britannia Music Hall, which opened in Argyle Street in 1867, occupying the second and third floors of a warehouse building. It offered a variety of entertainments, including Campbell's Music Saloon, Hubner's Cinematograph, Fell's Waxworks and the Iron Cinema, in 1897 showing silent films. During the 1920s, it was taken over by the eccentric but colourful self-publicist and property owner A.E. Pickard and renamed the Panopticon. It functioned as a place of entertainment

until the 1930s, becoming in 1945 a B-listed building and, after the
Theatre Royal in Dumfries, the oldest theatre in Scotland. At the time
of writing it is now a store above an amusement arcade, though its
future is in doubt.

The Apollo, in Anderston, lasted from 1890 to 1960 as a home of
variety, eventually named the Glasgow Gaiety. The Assembly Rooms,
in which Liszt once played, were put up by R. and J. Adams in 1798,
but – one of Glasgow's saddest losses – were demolished in the 1880s
to make way for the Post Office headquarters, now itself threatened
with major change of use.

The Athenaeum, in Buchanan Street, was built by Sir J.J. Burnet in
1893 and was once famous for the rumble of the Underground that
passed beneath it. Part of the Scottish Academy of Music and School
of Drama (as it then was), it was the first venue of James Bridie's
Citizens' Theatre. After the Citizens' had moved to its permanent
home in the Gorbals, from 1946 for just over a year it was the home of
the Unity Theatre Company, though later that company moved to the
Queen's Theatre.

Unlike many of the other theatres built with an eye to West End
audiences, the Queen's Theatre, erected during the 1870s, served the
East End. It had several names before it went up in flames in 1952,
including the Star Music Hall, Shakespeare Music Hall, New Star
Theatre of Varieties, Pringles, Queen's Picture Palace and, finally, the
Queen's Variety Theatre. Scene of a panic caused by a false fire alarm
in 1884, resulting in fourteen deaths and injury to a further eighteen,
it ultimately became famous as the 'home' of the comedians Frank and
Doris Droy. Their Glaswegian dialect turns were so bawdy that alleged-
ly they were only passed by the lord chancellor because nobody outside
Glasgow could understand them.

It was at a performance at the Queen's during 1947 by the Unity
Theatre Company that an amusing debunking incident took place. At
the end of the first part of the Unity Theatre's socially improving,
high-minded play, the actors – stereotyped businessmen, cast as the
exploiters of society – lined up along the front of the stage, chanting
in chorus: 'And where do we go from here?' With a clatter of his
thrown-up seat a wee Glasgow bauchle, obviously more accustomed to
the house's habitual fare than a socially improving drama, leapt to his
feet and left, calling out: 'Hame, as soon as ah can git oot o' here!'

One of the Unity Theatre's greatest successes was *The Gorbals Story*
by Robert MacLeish, an artist on *The Bulletin* newspaper.

The Royal Princess's Theatre, in Main Street, Gorbals, went up as Her Majesty's in 1878. In 1945, it became the home of Glasgow's Citizens' Theatre, a company able and willing in these days (and for some years after) to perform plays in Scots. The theatre was particularly well-loved in Glasgow for its annual traditional thirteen-letter-titled pantomimes, in which the comedian (for many years George West) rather than the principal 'boy' was the lead character.

In the 1920s, the poet Hugh MacDiarmid enriched the revised Scots he used in 'Sangschew', Pennywheep', and 'A Drunk Man Looks at The Thistle' – masterpieces all – with old Scots words taken out of Jamieson's *Dictionary of the Scottish Tongue*. Taking their cue from Burns's lines 'They spak their thocht in guid broad Lallans/like your or me', the group of late 1940 poets (which included Douglas Young, and Sydney Goodsir Smith, and with which I was for a time associated) developed the practice further, provoking an attack in the *Glasgow Herald* (as it was then) by Sir James Fergusson of Kilkèrran and a furious public debate lasting some months. At the height of it, in one of the Princess's Theatre's thirteen-letter pantomimes, one of 'three weird sisters' declaimed the lines

Here's the latest piece of whimsy
From the pen of Maurice Lindsay.

The nearest thing to a rhyme for my name!

Touring repertory companies used the Royalty Theatre in Sauchiehall Street, built in 1879. From 1909 to 1914 it housed the Glasgow Repertory Company. Bought by the YMCA after the 1914–18 War, it was renamed the Lyric and much used by amateur dramatic companies until it was demolished in 1962 to make way for a particularly dull office block.

Almost opposite it, on the site of the Gaiety Theatre, the Empire Theatre was built in 1897, as the Glasgow Empire Palace. It soon became the centre of Glasgow variety, which it remained until destroyed by fire in 1956.

The Scotia Music Hall had previously held that distinction from 1862. Rebuilt after a fire in 1875, it became a centre for the drama of the day, under the title of the Metropole. Sir Harry Lauder trod its boards as a youthful amateur. Eventually, it came into the hands of the Logan family, whose best-known member was the comedian, Jimmy Logan. It, too, went up in flames in 1961, when its title was transferred to the 1913 Empress at St George's Cross. It had begun life as the West End Playhouse. As the new Empress, it was severely damaged by fire in 1956, opened as the Falcon Theatre in 1960 (a serious drama venture that failed) and as the New Metropole by Alex Frutin in 1962. Finally, in 1964, Jimmy Logan had a go at making it work. His venture also failed. Offered to Glasgow Corporation in 1972 and repaired by them, it mouldered emptily until 1989, when it was demolished.

One other of architect Sir John James Burnet's theatres deserves mention: the Alhambra, built in 1910 on the site of the former Waterloo Rooms. It featured music hall and plays and in the 1940s was the home of the popular Wilson Barrett Repertory Company, an annu-al venture killed off by the coming of television. In spite of protests and strenuous efforts to save it, the Alhambra was demolished in 1989.

Another theatre still in use, the Citizens' apart, is the Pavilion, the Palace of Varieties of 1904, still an independent theatre given over to variety, long-running pantomimes and occasional plays with a local slant.

Green's Playhouse, in Renfield Street (1927–87), once the largest cinema in Europe, was also used as a concert hall. The Park Theatre, run by John Stewart from 1940 to 1949 in a Woodside Terrace house, was the precursor for his Pitlochry Festival Theatre. The Mitchell Theatre, part of the Mitchell Library in Granville Street (taken over after St Andrew's Halls, previously on the site, was destroyed by fire), offers a convenient smaller venue. So, too, does the Tron Theatre, opened as a club theatre in 1962. The Tramway Theatre, a converted tramway depot in Albert Drive, stages on occasion large and spectacu-lar productions.

Glasgow's two main theatres, now owned by the local authority, are opulently elegant. The fashionable West End theatre in Bath Street, the King's, went up in 1904. A Grade A-listed building, and the first home of Scottish Opera, it features touring companies, amateur groups and an annual Christmas pantomime.

The Theatre Royal in Hope Street, Cowcaddens, was the Royal Coliseum Theatre and Opera House from 1867 until the closure of the Dunlop Street Theatre Royal in 1869. It was destroyed by fire first in 1879 and again in 1895, its architect being C.J. Phipp. From 1956 to 1974 it was the studios of Scottish Television, being converted back to a theatre by Derek Sugden of Ove Arup and Partners. It has since been home to Scottish Opera and Scottish Theatre Ballet, as well as featuring the productions of major visiting drama companies from time to time.

For those with less exalted tastes there were, for much of the nineteenth century, the Penny Geggies, wooden canvas booths often found around the foot of the Saltmarket and at Glasgow Fair, usually named after their owners. They featured the gorier episodes from Shakespeare's plays and lurid swatches of lesser melodramas.

VI

While variety is a form of entertainment by no means confined to Scotland, it flourished for long with a Scottish flavour, producing a wealth of home-grown talent, from widely-known singing comedians like Sir Harry Lauder and Will Fyffe, to pattermen like Charlie Kemble, Tommy Morgan, Bert Denver, Dave Willis and, especially beloved of Glaswegians, Tommy Lorne (1890–1935), the greatest pantomime dame of them all. By the time I saw him, he had 'graduated' to the Theatre Royal, but he made his name in the Princess.

Tommy Lorne – real name Hugh Corcoran – is generally reckoned to have been one of the greatest Glasgow comics. Though actually born in Kirkintilloch, he grew up in Glasgow, and like many Scots comedians, he was appreciated most in his native land. He died suddenly in 1935 of double pneumonia, at the height of his career – the previous year he had had his own summer show at Dunoon and pantomimes in Inverness, Edinburgh and Glasgow. G.S. Fraser, the Aberdeen-born poet, discussing the people of Glasgow in 1958 in his *Vision of Scotland*, wrote: 'They are affable and talkative with an accent which, while nobody could say it has poetic beauty, lends itself very aptly to the work of the great Glasgow comedians. In such a comedian as Tommy Lorne, Glasgow probably expressed a great deal of itself.'

Writing in *The Glasgow Comedians*, in an essay entitled 'Scotland 1938', the journalist Colm Brogan claimed:

> He was bred in one of the most wretched slums in Europe and he knew Glasgow under the skin. The Clyde for him and his like was the stretch of water which separates the mortuary from the Gorbals. His best days as an artist were spent in the Gorbals. It is not a pretty neighbourhood, nor is it oppressively Scotch. Kosher meat is much in demand, and the pubs have names like Rooney. The local colour is Red.

The Princess pantomime begins in December and it stops in early summer. It doesn't go in much for Tiller Girls or transformation scenes, but it does try to be funny. Tommy gave impersonations there that will still be talked of by senile persons in 1900. He was a tram conductor on an all-night car and a continuous dancer with enormous bandages on his feet . . . Tommy was tall and angular and when he was dressed as a woman he was mostly bones and two mournful and apprehensive eyes. His dame was away daein' working-class woman, with a lot of jerky dignity, determined not to be put on, but finding the world too much for her. She had a beautiful squealing indignation and moments of outraged stillness when she mutely asked Heaven if this or that outrage could be, and only the mobile lips and trembling fingers witnessed the turmoil within.

Tommy's hands were wonderful. In moments of conscious innocence and triumph, they were folded (in white gloves) on his stomach, where they lay like doves asleep. When suspicion of some indignity entered the Dame's mind they stirred, and when shocks of nervous excitement went through her body, every finger had a separate and hysterical life.

Popularity was Tommy's downfall. He went to the Royal in Glasgow and then to Edinburgh, in among the Tiller Girls and the Grand Finales. But he had marvellous moments up to the end. In his last Glasgow pantomime he sat, as Dame, on a log with a lovelorn maiden. The poor Dame described her romance with a gentleman friend many years ago. With coy giggles and nudges she told how they would go to a field and push over a cow to get a warm place. But Fate took the gentleman friend away. As the Dame began to hint at the sad end, her mouth trembled and her fingers shuddered with woe. At last, her face simply melted. It was very delicately done.

There was nobody quite like Tommy. Glasgow could bear the loss of all her MPs and town councillors with Roman fortitude, but the sudden death of Tommy Lorne was a cause of real public grief . . . Life was poorer for everybody.

A useful record, *These Variety Days*, edited by Frank Bruce, Archie Foley and George Gillespie, was published in 1997, tracing the genre down the years:

Scottish variety was from the great tradition of the penny geggies, fitup theatres and concert parties that brought drama, comedy, music and song to the ordinary people of the countryside, villages and small towns. Performers in such entertainments had to be versatile and able to interact with the audiences that often saw themselves as part of the show. Will Fyffe is surely the best-known of the many geggie actor/performers who made the transition to variety and Harry Lauder learned his craft in his early years touring with concert parties the length and breadth of Scotland. It owed something to music-hall and 'pure' variety as played in the Empires and large theatres, but its real strength stemmed from a tradition that found audience and performers in a common popular culture.

That tradition, including the humour of the Scots comedians, both reflected and helped to preserve the kind of Scots spoken by ordinary people; for which reasons I disagreed with the ferocious attacks made on Lauder and his kind by the poet Hugh MacDiarmid in *A Drunk Man Looks at the Thistle* and elsewhere. It is better to have Scots kept alive at the level of the 'Scoatch Coamic' than to die unspoken in the much-glossaried pages of Lallans verse.

Graham Moffat, author of the play *Bunty Pulls the Strings*, recalls in *Join Me in Remembering* (1955) what early Scottish variety was like before it got upgraded to Empire Theatre standard:

After the Theatre Royal had moved to Cowcaddens, an entertainment of a kind still remained in Dunlop Street . . . a friend, whose taste lay that way, took me one night, but one visit . . . was quite enough for me. Yet I am glad that I took the opportunity of seeing what the old-style music-hall was like . . . We enter upon a long, wide hall almost innocent of the gilded grandeur that we associate with theatre. What we call a 'swell' comedian, in immaculate evening dress, is singing a song which for dull insipidity would be hard to equal. The words of the refrain are:

> Riding in a pullman car,
> It is the better way,
> To travel night or day
> Is riding in a pullman car.

The comedian finishes to what I consider very generous applause and there follows an intermission to allow the audience to replenish glasses. My companion orders beer for himself and lemonade for me. I begin now to take in my surroundings. The general atmosphere is that of a smoking concert or a bar parlour. Free and easy jollity prevails as though

members of the audience are mostly bar companions. The chief inspir-
er of this mildly bacchanalian spirit is a figure seated majestically in
front of the orchestra with a drink and a box of cigars on the table. This
is our chairman and he is true to type – a big jovial fellow of ruddy complexion. He is in full evening dress, a flower in his buttonhole, a tile hat
worn jauntily on the back of his head, and a big cigar between his ever-
smiling lips. The pause having served its purpose, the chairman rises in
his place, strikes the table with a wooden mallet which is his insignia of
office and announces the next turn in words something like this: 'Ladies
and gentlemen, you will be delighted to hear that we have with us
tonight your old and tried favourites the accomplished artists The
Sisters Gladley! I know that you will accord these charming ladies the
same generous and rousing welcome as on former visits.'

Enthusiasm thus stimulated, the two ladies – who are not named
Gladley – getting an ovation which their silly songs and gawky dances
are far from justifying. But it must be taken into account that in this
year of grace eighteen eighty – what year actually is this? – we are not
privileged to see shapely female limbs in street or bus, and that 'a wee
drappie o't' may make us uncritically kind.

What, I wonder, half a century on, would Moffat have made of the
inane pop songs – 'music that appeals to the genitals' as a current musical Lord put it – accompanied by pointlessly loose-swinging limbs,
which draw thunderous applause from packed youthful audiences?

Circuses were popular in Victorian Glasgow, the most famous probably being Hengler's, from 1867 to 1883 located in West Nile Street,
from 1885 to 1903 in Wellington Street and from 1904, until its
demise in 1924, in Sauchiehall Street.

Crude and prolonged bouts of fisticuffs also had their following in
the nineteenth century. In one such engagement Deaf Burke actually
killed Simon Byrne in their ninety-ninth round, having previously
killed Sandy MacKay in the forty-seventh round.

VII

The pursuit of music was perhaps more chequered in Glasgow than in
Edinburgh. Andrew Thomson, who organized concerts in Glasgow's
College Hall during the second decade of the nineteenth century,
mounted a performance of Matthew Peter King's work called *The*

Intercession in 1819, according to him: 'the first time an entire oratorio had been attempted' in the city. A music festival was held in Glasgow in 1821 and another in 1823, but the gentlemen's subscription concerts, a late eighteenth-century institution, apparently had to be wound up in 1822 through lack of support. The opening of the City Hall in 1841 (still in use) and the Queen's Rooms in 1857 (now used by a cult religious sect) provided suitably fashionable premises.

The first complete performance of Handel's *Messiah* to be given in Scotland took place in the City Hall in 1844, when one of the soloists was the popular tenor Sims Reeves. A critic of the day recorded that:

Everything turned out favourably; and the ladies and gentlemen of the society composing the chorus, who had been in training for some months previously, assembled in high spirits. At seven o'clock the platform was filled with the performers, 220 in number, each one seemingly anxious that the Oratorio should be done full justice to – so that the people of Glasgow might have the opportunity of proving whether this performance should be the solitary attempt, or the first of a series. All eager to follow the slightest suggestion which might contribute to the desired end – trusting to the skill of Mr M'Farlane, their conductor, they waited for the lifting of his baton to burst out into the mighty chorus. The choristers, amateurs belonging to Glasgow, were placed on the platform erected at the west end of the City Hall, in two compact phalanxes, tier above tier, with the instrumental corps, a number of whom were amateurs, also inhabitants of Glasgow, led by Mr Dewar of Edinburgh, in the centre. One moment's pause, up went the baton of the conductor, and the overture was heard, grave and potent, foreshadowing the coming tide of music – not one jarring note – not a quaver out of place; and the thousands of auditors were hushed as though a spell had begun to operate.

The performance of the 'Pastoral Symphony' [an orchestral interlude in the Oratorio] was not exactly to our taste; there was much twaddle and no simplicity. Here and amongst the instruments we thought we could detect sundry ambitious attempts at adorning the chaste movement by the introduction of the trickery of dextrous manipulation, which with some people is meant to pass current for high art, but which, in such circumstances, in our opinion, is not far removed from impertinent quackery; these fantastic gambollings, which seem to form part of the fashionable taste of the time, only interrupt the even flow of Handel's music, and detract from the solemnity of its movements.

While speaking of the instrumental part of this performance, we may as well state here, that in the accompaniment to all the songs of the Oratorio, the instruments were by far too prominent, in some cases they were so loud as almost to drown the voice of the singer.

The choruses were executed in a manner which proves satisfactorily that there is taste and knowledge sufficient among the amateurs of Glasgow to maintain an efficient choral society.

The performance of the *Messiah* has established the right of Glasgow to the title of one of the music loving cities of Britain, and has proven that the noblest works in musical science only require to be brought forward in like manner, to meet the liberal support and encouragement of the people.

Two music societies – the Glasgow Musical Association, founded in 1843 and the Glasgow Harmonic Society, dating from 1853 – amalgamated in 1855 to become the Glasgow Choral Union, thus encouraging a love of choral-singing applied to serious works.

Glasgow held what was subsequently described as its first festival in the City Hall in 1860, the two previous festivals not counting, it seems, because they did not feature choral works. A second festival was held in the same venue in 1873. It lasted five days. The programmes included Mendelssohn's *Elijah*, Beethoven's *Pastoral* and Schumann's *Spring* symphonies and an oratorio, *Eli*, by the conductor Sir Michael de Costa. The singers included Theresa Tietjens (1831–77) and Charles Santley (1834–1922), both stars of their day. This festival seems to have provided the stimulus for the creation of a new 'permanent' orchestra, proposals for which had been mooted nine years previously.

From 1874 to 1891 the Glasgow Choral Union's orchestra gave concerts all over central Scotland under Sir Arthur Sullivan, Hans von Bulow, Augustus Mann and others less celebrated. A group of music-lovers then engineered a break-away. While the Choral Union continued to give their concerts, the Scottish Orchestra Company Ltd ran a rival series. Eighteen ninety-one is thus the year in which the ancestor of the present Royal Scottish National Orchestra was formed. By 1894 the two bodies had merged, becoming the Choral and Orchestral Union.

A long succession of foreign conductors and foreign orchestra leaders then dominated the musical scene, Glaswegians believing, in common with most British audiences, that a musician who was not a Herr,

James Sellars' St Andrew's Halls, built in 1873, was Glasgow's leading concert venue until it was destroyed by fire in 1962. Only the Granville Street façade remained intact and it is now incorporated in a Mitchell Library extension

a Monsieur or a Signor could not possibly be any good, although a writer in the *Musical Times* for 1914 suggested otherwise. When the composer Max Bruch was appointed conductor to a British orchestra in that year, he protested: 'What becomes of our boasted progress in music if important appointments . . . are not to be filled by native musicians? Cannot we raise the article on our own soil? Are we always to import it? Would such a stigma be tolerated in any other European country?'

The answer to that last question, of course, was no, but tolerated it was in Glasgow. Even the providers of light music for balls and dances had to have names like Monsieur Claude Jacquinot or Herr Wilhelm Iff to be thought 'the real thing'.

The Scottish Orchestra's six-monthly seasons had fallen upon lean times by 1932, when John Barbarolli (later Sir John) took over. Italian in temperament but English in adopted nationality, he eventually left

Scotland to go to the United States, and ultimately returned to raise the fortunes of Manchester's Hallé Orchestra. It was not, however, until Alexander Gibson (also later knighted) took over the Scottish National Orchestra, made permanent from 1950, that the Glasgow musical scene was transformed. Over the years, Sir Alexander fashioned it into an orchestra that both toured abroad and recorded. In addition, Gibson, in partnership with a group of mainly Glasgow enthusiasts, founded Scottish Opera and developed it into a major British opera company. Its early triumphs included a memorable *Ring*, a glittering *Rosenkavalier*, a delicious *Merry Widow* and the finest *Cosi Fan Tutte* I have ever seen anywhere.

Fittingly, his huge achievement is commemorated in the Sir Alexander Gibson Opera School, built against the Royal Scottish Academy of Music and Drama, relocated in Renfrew Street, and opened in 1999.

The Scottish National Orchestra – more lately adding Royal to its title – particularly under Gibson and his successors, from time to time featured contemporary music (including, occasionally, music by living Scottish composers) in their four-city weekly programmes. The public, however, has never shown itself willing to buy tickets for concerts featuring later twentieth-century music, and orchestras such as the Royal Scottish National that have to achieve reasonable box-office receipts cannot afford to risk anything that might reduce the size of its audience. It has therefore been left to some extent to the BBC Scottish Symphony Orchestra, founded by Ian Whyte, to offer more frequent opportunities for indigenous composers to have their works played and audiences to hear new Scottish music. Like the RNSO, the BBC Scottish Symphony Orchestra is based in Glasgow, which also enjoys regular visits from the Edinburgh-based Scottish Chamber Orchestra.

Glasgow has never in the past produced a composer of any significance, but it did nurture a world-class pianist, Frederic Lamond (1868–1946), the son of an impoverished Cambuslang weaver. In his old age, he somewhat resembled portraits of Beethoven, of whose music Lamond was a convincing interpreter.

The revelations made possible by the advent of the compact disc – and the excellent *History of Scottish Music* by John Purser – have, however, done much to reawaken interest in Scotland's music, old and new, from the great polyphonic masses of Robert Carver to the orchestral music of Thomas Wilson, James MacMillan and others in our own day. When one considers the comparative neglect of the music of

English composers like Rutland Boughton, E.J. Moeran and Sir George Dyson, to name but three, perhaps the Scots need not feel uniquely ashamed of themselves in this regard.

From 1906 until 1951, the enormously popular Glasgow Orpheus Choir flourished under Sir Hugh Roberton, for whom mannered choralism, over-emphasized consonants, was more important than the quality of the sung music. Consequently, they specialized in what I once called in a newspaper critique, 'bonnie wee tusheries'.

There are also the products of what is sometimes called the 'folk song' revival, spearheaded by Hamish Henderson (b.1919), a collector of genuine folksong in his academic capacity at the School of Scottish Studies in Edinburgh, and the politician Norman Buchan (1922–90) in the West.

The term used in this context always seemed to me something of a misnomer. Who are, or were, the 'folk'? In days gone by, they were the ordinary people, the peasants of Europe and elsewhere, who fashioned songs that reflected the high points in their lives. Because birth, love (frustrated or otherwise), jealousy, sorrow, death, murder are all features of every society, the subject-matter of the songs of the folk the world over tends to be much the same, though the melodies to which they are fastened usually reflect national music characteristics.

With the passing of the horse as the fastest means of transport, there are now no 'folk' in the civilized world (except in the Scots use of the word as a synonym for people). No group is any longer, so to say, islanded. Since the development of radio, the cinema and television, it is the accents and images of Tin-Pan Alley, Denmark Street or Hollywood, that influence what used to be the once self-contained 'folk' creativity. 'Folk' tunes are now artfully fashioned with commercially orientated sounds in the inner ear of the fashioner. Folk words usually take the form of a simple, direct sort of verse, relatively free of imagery or literary devices that could obscure the immediate communication of the sentiment or emotion. Nevertheless, poetry is sometimes achieved, notably in the works of Bob Dylan, or in our own Adam MacNaughton or Matt MacGinn. But memorable as are some of their pieces, it should properly be described as 'popular' rather than 'folk' art. Folk art is always anonymous, the voice of a necessarily self-contained community denied direct communication by distance and the surrounding silence of the ether; to say which is neither to decry nor deny the achievements of MacNaughton, MacGinn and the others; merely more accurately to define it.

In any case, something in the Scots character seems to make them much more readily appreciative of what might be called the 'private' arts – painting and literature – rather than the 'public' arts – music and drama – where performances inevitably involve exposure before an audience.

VIII

The taste for painting greatly increased during the 1870s. The leaders of 'raw, rich Glasgow . . . in which only engineers prosper', according to the German critic Herman Muthesius, had, in fact, homes with plenty of wall space and money to spend on the pictures they fancied. The work of the Barbizon group and their Dutch followers was much sought after in the 1870s and 1880s, imported to Glasgow by the art dealers John Forbes and Alexander Reid. The *plein-air* method of painting – setting the easel in front of the object and painting direct from nature – had brought home to Glaswegians the excitement of light. The influence of Whistler on young Scots painters was considerable. Revolt was in the international air.

The Glasgow Group of painters (sometimes known as the Glasgow Boys) came together about 1880, much influenced by Whistler – two of them persuaded Glasgow to buy his portrait of Carlyle in 1891. The 'father' of the movement was Finnart-born William York Macgregor (1855–1923), a powerful painter 'glorifying in the quality of the medium for its own sake', as Ian Finlay puts it, 'deriving inspiration from it, in stark contrast to the infilling of colour upon careful drawings which had become the established tradition in the academies'. His masterpiece is generally considered to be *The Vegetable Stall*, from which you can almost smell the produce.

Not all were 'Boys'; there were 'Girls', too, for that matter, including Jessie M. King (1875–1949), Margaret Macdonald, Jessie Newbery and Elizabeth Mary Watt, who gathered in Macgregor's studio. All of them were Scots. Joseph Crawhall (1861–1913) was a Northumbrian hunting man, the delicacy of whose birds and beasts still seems remarkable. Sir James Guthrie (1869–1913), who caught fleeting moments at tennis parties or on the golf course, and whose early portraits abound in character, came from Greenock. Sir John Lavery (1856–1941) of Belfast settled in Glasgow as a landscape painter, but moved to London where like Guthrie he became a sought-after society portrait painter.

Sir John Lavery (1856–1941), the Belfast-born painter who settled in Glasgow, studied at the Glasgow School of Art and became one of the 'Glasgow Boys' group. In later life he was a fashionable portrait painter

E.A. Hornel (1864–1933) an Australian expatriate who studied at the Glasgow School of Art, became a leader of the 'Glasgow Boys' and settled in Kirkcudbright

E.A. Hornel (1864–1933) was influenced by the decorative qualities of Japanese painting, and created his rosy-cheeked children in laid-on daubs of sheer colour. Like Hornel, George Hendry (1858–1943) also visited Japan and produced what has come to be regarded as the key picture of the movement, his *Galloway Landscape*. Others in the group included E.A. Walton, Stuart Park, Alexander Melville and, a younger semi-recruit, D.Y. Cameron.

A show at the Grosvenor Gallery in London, where they were welcomed by the followers of England's rebels against the academies, the New Art Club, brought the Glasgow Group its first major success. Other successes followed in Munich, Dresden and Vienna, where the Secessionists welcomed them.

They were never a 'school' in any unified sense, and the nearest they came to having a manifesto was the short-lived *Scottish Art Review*, which included as fellow contributors characters as diverse as the future playwright James Matthew Barrie, that inverted Calvinist rebel-poet from Greenock, John Davidson, whose later plays hammered home with Knoxian obstinacy his belief that God was dead; and the revolutionary Peter Kropotkin.

All that 'the Boys' had in common was a freshness of approach, a certain emphasis on colour, and chance that brought them enthusiastically together at a moment when rich

175

Glaswegians were ready and eager to buy. By the turn of the century, as always with members of groups, the artists were going their own diverse ways – Hornel to Kirkcudbright, to repeat his coy little-girl pictures so endlessly as almost to suggest a psychological obsession, and Guthrie to become the fashionable portrait-painting president of the Royal Academy. For about twenty years, however, they produced a remark-able range of impressive pictures, as an exhibition of the work of the movement mounted by the Scottish Arts Council in the Kelvingrove Gallery in 1968 clearly demonstrated.

Interest in Art Nouveau perhaps helped to make the work of the Glasgow Boys seem a bit old-fashioned by Edwardian times. Of the Scottish Colourists who succeeded them, S.J. Peploe (1871–1935), and Francis Campbell Boileau Cadell had no real Glasgow links. Only the lyrical Rothesay-born Leslie Hunter (1879–1936) belonged to, and drew inspiration from, Glasgow and the West. Its citizens, on the whole, neglected him during his lifetime.

The father figure of the Colourists, John Duncan Fergusson (1874–1961), was born in Leith. He gave up the study of medicine for painting, which he largely taught himself. As a young man, he painted on small wood panels, which he kept in his pocket. He went to Paris in 1895 and, in a style rather like that of the Fauves, captured the brittle beauty of elegant ladies, fashionably dressed, in the salons, boulevards and music halls of that city, his subtle sense of colour already in evidence. In Paris he met Margaret Morris, who was there with her dance company, and they became known as 'Fergus and Meg'. In her fascinating *Biased Biography* of Fergusson, she quotes his views on the characteristic achieve-ment of the Glasgow Boys. 'By painting I mean using oil paint as a medi-um to express the beauty of light on surfaces . . . quality of paint, with solidity and guts – not drawing a map-like outline and filling in the spaces with an imitation of the colour of the object with the paint.'

Fergusson settled in Paris in 1905, persuading Peploe to join him. Paris in the decade before the First World War was a ferment of artis-tic activity, which included Kathleen Mansfield and Middleton Murray. Fergusson recorded that 'from the start, Peploe and I had been together. When Hunter came back to Scotland from San Francisco after the earthquake', in which he lost all his canvases, 'Alex Reid made the three of us . . . into a group. Les Peintures Ecossasis . . . We went everywhere together, to meet Picasso, to go on painting holidays to Etaples, Paris-Plage, Dunkirk, Delft . . . to Royan, where Peploe's son was born, to Antibes. . . .'

176

Fergusson returned to Scotland during the 1914–18 War – one of his best-known paintings, A *Puff of Smoke near Milngavie*, resulted from this sojourn – but took up residence again in Antibes after the Armistice. He came back again in 1938, settling in Glasgow because it was 'the most Highland city', as opposed to Edinburgh, 'a suburb of London'. Margaret Morris founded her Celtic ballet. Both were associated with the New Art Club, of which Fergusson became president. They lived in 4 Clouston Street, overlooking the Botanic Gardens. A charming old man, he and I together sat on the committee responsible for running the Saltire Club in Wellington Street, for a time managed by my sister Wendy. Whenever some practical issue involving money or menus came up, he used to preface his observations with 'When I was in Paris, freedom was the thing.'

Because of its United Kingdom pre-eminence, several generations of artists have passed through the Glasgow School of Art who were not Scots, let alone Glaswegians, and had nothing further to do with the city, like Clydeside-born William Crozier or Colin Cina who merely claimed to be born there. Of the Glasgow Boys themselves incidentally, Edward Gage, himself a distinguished artist as well as being the author of *The Eye in the Wind: Contemporary Scottish Painting Since 1918*, has written: 'These were no trivial parish-pumpers, but a cosmopolitan band whose work was hailed and recognised across Europe and America.' Incidentally, he remarks that: 'Artists band together for odd reasons because the going is tough, because they share points of view, or simply to further their careers. This gregarious characteristic is often misleading as painters are fundamentally individual and solitary operators, well aware of the lifelong aspect of personal discovery that attends and defines the evolution of their vision. The story of art is one of personal rather than group achievements.' The same holds true, of course, of temporary groupings in any of the arts.

Many of the Glasgow painters from Victorian times to our own day have found their most rewarding subject matter in the Firth of Clyde, particularly the island of Arran, or by Loch Lomond. The Arran painters include John MacWhirter (1839–1911), who favoured Lochranza, and John MacLauchlan Milne (1886–1957), who usually centred on Corrie and Sannox. Mention should be made, too, of Sir William McTaggart of Kintyre (1835–1910) across the Sound.

Of Loch Lomond, H.V. Morton in *In Search of Scotland* enthused: 'Loch Lomond is one of the world's glories. The hills lie against each other fading into the blue distance . . . A man can go out from Glasgow

177

and climb Ben Lomond and see Scotland lying for miles in a chain of dim blue mountains.' George Melville is among those who have most successfully caught these glories on canvas.

John Quinton Pringle (1864–1925) was a solitary painter neglected after his death but now being rediscovered. His *Muslin Street, Bridgeton*, an East End of Glasgow scene, at once captures the attention. It is now in the Edinburgh City Art collection. He was born in the East End, the son of the stationmaster at Langbank. He has a second less enviable distinction in that in 1896 he set up shop at 90 Saltmarket as an optical repairer, 'keeping not only the worst run shop in Glasgow, but the worst run shop in Europe', according to one dissatisfied customer. Pringle's heart was in painting, however, which he accomplished after hours and during weekends, 'applying the paint in a mosaic of small brush strokes', as one critic put it. His other successes included his *Poultry Yard, Gartcosh* of 1906.

The best-known painter of the period (and the wealthiest) was probably Sir D.Y. Cameron (1865–1945), a son of the manse who knew the Glasgow Boys, but was not one of them. He was 'discovered' in an odd way. A wealthy shipbuilder, George Stevenson, dismounted from his home in a side street off Great Western Road to adjust a stirrup, when he noticed Cameron etching in a shop window. This so intrigued him that he subsequently sought out the artist and became his patron. Cameron had attracted public attention with a set of Clyde etchings in the 1880s. He was friendly, too, with a wealthy coach-builder, Archibald McLellan (1796–1854), who collected paintings – Dutch, Flemish and Venetian, for the most part. These he bequeathed to the city, along with money to build the gallery in Sauchiehall Street, named after him, in which to house them. In 1861 the Glasgow Institute of Fine Arts held its first exhibition there, and is still doing so every year.

Sir D.Y. Cameron (1865–1945), painter. He was friendly with, but not of, the 'Glasgow Boys'. He settled in Kippen

Apart from McLellan and numerous lesser patrons, Glasgow

was fortunate in its dealers, two of whom deserve mention: Craibe Angus (1830–99), who opened his gallery in 1874; and Alexander Reid (1854–1928), the first dealer to show the Impressionists to wealthy Glaswegians – which explains why Glasgow is so rich in fine examples of their work. Reid was twice painted by Van Gogh. Some years ago, I found myself chairman of a committee formed to raise money to buy one of these paintings for the civic collection. I have rarely had an easier task.

Other artists that, though not necessarily Glasgow-born, were products of the Glasgow School of Art include Anthony Armstrong. Born in Dundalk, Ireland, in 1935, he came to Glasgow, aged two, on the death of his father, and later became a student of David Donaldson. Armstrong's charming pastel paintings are more numerous than his oils. Bet Low (b.1924) is particularly well-known as a vivid depicter of the Glasgow scene. Her late husband, Tom Macdonald (1914–85), had as one journalist put it 'a natural sympathy for poverty and misfortune, or whatever could not entirely submerge a very typical Glasgow appreciation of the humorous, the odd, or even the grotesque'. He originally trained as a marine engineer at Barclay Curle and went to sea for several years before finding his true painterly vocation.

Edwin Morgan has remarked on the artistic potency of the curious mix of culture and creeds that constitute the late twentieth-century Glasgow scene. This is particularly true as regards post-Second World War art, as in the novels and stories of Kelman and most of his contemporaries and followers, the focus settling on the 'working class' (that hateful categorization again implying patronage by those with no economic need to earn a living, a rapidly disappearing category). Thus it is not so much the handsome Victorian terraces or the between-the-wars suburbs that have attracted the attentions of Joan Eardley, Tom Macdonald, Bet Low and others, but the tenements, often with slogans and graffiti scrawled over them and their frequently deprived inhabitants.

Joan Eardley is probably the most widely regarded of those artists of Glasgow social realism, if one may so describe them. She was born in Horsham, Sussex, in 1921, but came to the Glasgow School of Art in 1939, where she was a brilliant student. Cordelia Oliver, her biographer, records the picture of 'Eardley in the late-afternoon drawing class standing as she invariably did at her easel, feet straddling the floor on either side, her gaze fixed on the model, putting no mark on paper until visual information was absorbed about stance, thrust, weight and balance'.

During her art school years she lived in her mother's house at Bearsden, on the Drymen Road, holidaying at Corrie in Arran. During the war she enrolled at Jordanhill Training College for Teachers, but soon decided that teaching was not for her, and took a job as a labour-er in a boatyard. A further period of study under James Lawrie at Hospitalfield, an art college near Arbroath, followed, and while there she made drawings of the activities around Arbroath harbour. When a selection of her work was displayed at the Glasgow School of Art in 1949, the art critic of the *Glasgow Herald* hailed its 'real power'.

Travel in Europe followed – Florence, Assisi, Venice and Paris – before she settled in her first Glasgow studio, in Cochrane Street. Cordelia Oliver – incidentally a critic who has done more to further the cause of contemporary Scottish art than most – observes that the Glasgow streets gave Eardley her subject-matter in a variety of ways at this time. For example, the coal horses and carts that were still a sight around the city: thus, *The Carter and his Horse* of 1952, which won her the Royal Scottish Academy Award and was bought by the Ministry of Works.

By now she was teaching evening classes at the School of Art. A Gourock friend, Dorothy Steel, introduced her to Port Glasgow, which resulted in such arresting works as *Children, Port Glasgow, Swing Park, Port Glasgow* and *Shipyard with Cranes*. That arresting Van Gogh qual-ity, whereby the viewer feels that he is being looked at by the picture, is apparent in all these works.

During the Edinburgh Festival of 1957, Eardley's work was part of a 'Six Young Scottish Painters' Exhibition, at once drawing the atten-tion of the wider art world to her singular qualities.

She moved her studio to St James Road, Townhead, and, like her friend the photographer Oscar Mazarolli, found fresh inspiration in the life around her. Invited to show her work in London in 1954, a year later she had her first one-woman show in the St George's Gallery in Cork Street, London. At this exhibition her first Catterline pictures appeared. But it was the Glasgow pictures that most impressed the *Glasgow Herald*'s critic Alick Sturrock, who declared: 'This artist . . . is interpreting Glasgow to the world with an authenticity not achieved, perhaps since Sir Muirhead Bone (1876–1941) who, in his own very different manner, brought the shipyards and the city streets alive in line . . . Her preoccupation with the seedier streets, the pavements and

The front entrance to The Glasgow School of Art

the tenement walls' shows that 'the main emphasis is on the children of no mean city.'

She became friendly with Audrey Walker, the violinist wife of Allan Walker (later, sheriff principal of Glasgow and Lanarkshire). Music was Joan Eardley's second passion after painting, and in the Walkers' holiday cottage near Selkirk, she concentrated on interiors, like *The Music Stand.*

She had discovered Catterline, south of Stonehaven, during a visit to Aberdeen in 1951, when her work was on show in the Gaumont Cinema. While there she contracted mumps, and while convalescing was driven along the coast through Catterline by a friend, Annette Stephen, wife of a Stonehaven fisherman. She first went back to Catterline on holiday, then acquired a studio in the Watch House, spending an increasing amount of her time there. We are not here concerned with the fine paintings that emanated from her Catterline period, often inspired by sea and snow, the elemental forces of nature, resulting in her being judged not only a great Scottish, but a great British artist. We must focus instead on such Glasgow work (in which, it seems, drawing was always the essential material for studio paintings) as *Glasgow Tenement with Blue Sky, Three Children at a Tenement Window, Sweet Shop, Rottenrow* and *Little Girl with Squint.*

Elected an academician of the Royal Scottish Academy in 1963, she died in Killearn Hospital on 16 August of that year, of a neglected breast cancer that had spread to her brain.

'The common man is my work and will always be my work,' Peter Howson (b. 1938) has declared. In his book on this artist, Robert Heller tells us that Howson (who spent his childhood in Ayrshire) 'believes that when, at a very young age he was frightened on the beach by some thugs in Ayr,' the incident 'destroyed a kind of innocence I had about people.' It has been said of his muscled, louring portraits – though he has also produced a number of excellent 'academic' portraits – that 'the way in which he draws and paints people flays them alive'. It must be said that he has applied the technique more than once to himself in his self-portraits. He states his aim as being to achieve 'the greatest possible resemblance to the whole of the person portrayed . . . disproportionally increasing and emphasising the depths of the features, so that the portrait as a whole appears to be the sitter himself while its elements are all transparent'. He says that what he is after is 'not politics, but an artistic vision created from the social realities of violence and squalor,' leading Heller to suggest that in Yeats's words 'a terrible beauty is born'. Howson first exhibited at Flowers Gallery in London in 1987.

Some of his pictures are huge in scale and powerful in implied comment, like *The Fools of God* (1989), which shows 'the road-sweepers of Glasgow, brown-uniformed, armed with vast brushes, marching in quasi-military formation'. *Gallowgate Girls* is a study in slightly menacing unsexual attraction, while *Conferences 1 and 2* provides a comment on pomposity and perhaps futility. We are never allowed to forget that, in his own words, 'violence is, alas, endemic below the surface of both men and manners'.

Also with strong Glasgow connections were R. Henderson Blyth (1919–70), a product of the Glasgow School of Art and of Hospitalfield, who became an RSA in 1954; William Burns (1921–72), from Newton Mearns, an RSA in 1970 who died prematurely making a solo flight from Dundee to Aberdeen; Glasgow-born Ian McCulloch (b. 1935), one of the founders of the artists who have called themselves the Glasgow Group, and who now lectures at Strathclyde University; that closely-linked Ayrshire pair Robert Colquhoun (1914–62) and Robert MacBride (1913–60); perhaps above all, David Donaldson (1916–96)

Donaldson, born in Coatbridge, just outside Glasgow, claims that at 'fifteen and some months his childhood was interrupted . . . on my arrival at the Glasgow School of Art . . . in January 1932, long before being a Charles Rennie Mackintosh enthusiast was a recognised way to the top'. He was to become head of the Department of Painting there, and one of Scotland's most distinguished portrait painters, whose sitters included HM Queen Elizabeth. As one critic put it: 'He has consistently been able to prove that a portrait may be a work of art as well as a study of character – He works in a bold style, using a direct approach and enjoying the handling of paint with a bravura and verve that are almost operatic.'

Apart, perhaps, from Fergusson's protégée Louise Rachel Annand (b. 1959) and James Morrison (b. 1932), whose early admirable studies of Glasgow tenements and street scenes have given place to landscapes, some of them Canadian, the younger Glasgow artists are too numerous to mention here, showing that the Glasgow School of Art, in British, if not European, terms, continues to excel.

Just as in the literary department light verse has its place, so with the arts of painting and drawing does the cartoon. Most cartoons relate so strongly to passing news stories, however, that their interest is

The Glasgow School of Art library, 1961. It was once said by a fanciful anonymous writer to resemble the slow movement of a late Beethoven quartet

ephemeral. Not so the range of cartoons of famous Scots and celebrities visiting Scotland that provided the subject-matter for the sharp eye of Emilio Coia (1911–97).

Coia, the son of a Glasgow ice-cream parlour owner, Giovanni Coia, came from the Dennistoun/Townhead area of Glasgow, was schooled at St Mungo's Academy and afterwards went to the School of Art. He made his name in London in the 1930s. During the war, he was a manager in an armaments firm and after, in a Kilmarnock shoe manufacturing firm. On his return to Glasgow, Coia worked for the *Evening Times* and the *Scotsman*. He quickly became famous in Scotland with 'those bold characterisations, whose outsize heads and foreshortened bodies echoed his own physique of leonine head on a short, dapper figure,' as Lesley Duncan put it in her *Herald* obituary.

The great violinist Lord Menuhin once declared: 'Coia is every musician's favourite caricaturist. A good caricaturist needs more than a brilliant sense of humour; like a clown, he must have a great sense of compassion, tragedy and concern. Coia had all these qualities in addition to his wonderful draftsmanship.'

Coia was a president of the Glasgow Art Club. The Scottish National Gallery in Edinburgh houses several of his works.

Memorable, too, are the cartoons of Bud Neill (1911–97), whose Lobey Dosser character is commemorated by a statue in Glasgow's Woodlands Road.

Of Glasgow sculptors, by far the most distinguished was the Estonian-born Benno Schotz (1891–1984), who came to Glasgow in 1912 to study engineering at the Royal Technical College (now part of Strathclyde University). He spent nine years working by day in John Brown's shipyard. Learning his art by night, he became a professional sculptor – and one of the most distinguished in Europe – in 1923. He held his first one-man show in Glasgow in 1926. The Scottish Arts Council mounted a large retrospective exhibition of his work in 1978.

In 1920, he was already president of the Society of Painters and Sculptors, and was elected a member of the Royal Scottish Academy in 1937. From 1939 to 1961 he held the post of head of the Sculpture and Ceramic Departments of the Glasgow School of Art. Of the many honours that subsequently came his way, there was an LLD from Strathclyde University and an honorary fellowship of the Hebrew University of Jerusalem, as well as being awarded the freedom of the city by Glasgow City Council in 1981.

Hugh MacDiarmid (1892–1978), Scotland's leading twentieth-century poet, who made his home in Glasgow during the 1940s and 1950s

His subjects, caught with unmistakable verve and strength, included Golda Meir, Hugh MacDiarmid, William Soutar, Duncan Macrae as Harry MacGog (in Bridie's play *Gog and MacGog*) and several fine statues of his wife.

He modelled his head of MacDiarmid during a television programme that I introduced. It was in the earliest days of television in Scotland, and two of the three cameras went down seconds before the programme began. As a result, the whole half-hour was devoted to Schotz shaping the head of MacDiarmid while I talked to both of them. A visit to his studio was always a memorable experience. He had great charm and, like all the few other great men I have encountered in my lifetime, an extraordinary modesty. *Bronze in My Blood: The Memoirs of Benno Schotz*, which appeared in 1981, contains much that is interesting about MacDiarmid, Dr Tom Honeyman and other figures on the between-the-wars Glasgow cultural scene.

In some ways the Scottish sculptor (if that is the correct term) who has made most imprint on the consciousness of the Glaswegian in recent years has been George Wylie (b. 1921). Wylie startles, shocks even, his viewers; but they do not forget his work. As one critic (or, rather, three, writing in a combined study of Wylie) put it:

> To see his works only in terms of issues, is too limited a view. It misses their essential strangeness and inherent simplicity . . . *The Paper Boat* provoked fresh interpretations in each of the cities it visited – Glasgow, London, Antwerp, New York – questioning the ideals and values of its temporary surroundings, from the shipyards of the Clyde to the Houses of Parliament and the World Financial Centre. Conversely, *The Straw Locomotive*'s primary relationship to a specific place and history seems

inseparable from its wider significance. No other work of art has entered so quickly and so deeply into the mythology of Glasgow.

Wylie, who saw war service in the Royal Navy, now lives in Gourock. *The Straw Locomotive* was a 'full-scale, skeletal locomotive of heavy steel wire filled with straw and suspended from the marine hammerhead crane that used to load the great North British locomotives into the ships that took them all over the world.'

IX

In fiction, the latter part of the Victorian era in Scotland was dominated by Robert Louis Stevenson (1850–94) and James Matthew Barrie (1860–1937), the novelist who, so to say, preceded the playwright with such things as *Auld Licht Idylls* (1888) and *The Little Minister* (1891), part of which is set in Glasgow. Neither of these men had Glasgow connections, any more than had the Kailyaird (or backgreen cabbage-patch) school of Gallovidian S.R. Crockett (1860–1914) and the Reverend John Watson, 'Ian MacLaren' (1850–1907), whose novels *The Lilac Sunbonnet* (1894) and *Beside the Bonnie Briar Bush* (1895) showed a coy archness of sugar-sweet sentimentality never before achieved, though doubtless devoured avidly by many Glasgow readers. The novel that realistically jerked fashionable validity out of such saccharine literary pietism was Ayrshire-born George Douglas Brown's (1869–1902) *The House with the Green Shutters*, which must have come as a disagreeable shock to many gentle readers.

The darling of the circulating libraries throughout the 1870s and 80s, however, was undoubtedly Trongate-born William Black (1841–98), who took the journalist's road to London. After two false starts he produced *The Daughter of Heth* (1871), a love story painting the contrast of manners and conventions through the arrival of a French girl at a prim country manse in the West.

In almost all his novels, Black contrived to introduce his native city. Thus in *The Daughter of Heth*, Coquette, the French heroine of the book, who captures the fancy of the minister of Airlie's eldest son (known by his nickname of 'the Whaup'), comes up from Ayrshire by train to see him, chaperoned by Lady Drum, one of the minister's aristocratic parishioners.

As Coquette and Lady Drum drew near Glasgow, the impatience of the girl increased. Her thoughts flew on more swiftly than the train; and they were all directed towards the Whaup whom she was now about to see.

'Will he be at the station? Does he know we are coming? Or shall we see him as we go along the streets?' she asked. 'Dear me,' said Lady Drum, 'Ye seem to think that Glasgow is no bigger than Saltcoats. Meet him in the streets? We should scarce see him in the streets if he were dressed in scaurlet.'

It was growing towards dusk when the two ladies arrived. Lady Drum's carriage was waiting at the station; and presently Coquette found herself in the midst of the roar and turmoil of the great city. The lamps on the bridges were burning yellow in the grey coldness of the twilight; and she got a glimpse of the masses of shipping down the dusky bed of the river. Then up through the busy streets – where the windows were bright with gas, and dense crowds of people were hurrying to and fro', and the carts, and wagons, and carriages were raising a din that was strange to ears grown accustomed to the stillness of Airlie.

'Alas!' said Coquette, 'I cannot see him in this crowd. It is impossible.' Lady Drum laughed and said nothing.

And so they drove on in the high, old-fashioned chariot which ought to have been kept for state purposes down at Castle Cawmill, swinging gently on its springs – up to the north-western districts of the city.

For those who really cannot bear not to know what happened, Coquette never married the Whaup, for she fell in love with a dashing earl who perished when his yacht *Caroline* was run down by a steamer bound for Ireland. Coquette, after visiting the spot where his body had been washed ashore, fell ill with one of these fatal 'fevers' that Victorian doctors could not accurately diagnose and for which they knew no cure.

Black's other successes included *The Strange Adventures of a Phaeton* (1872) and *MacLeod of Dare* (1878), after which, as J.H. Millar put it, he merely repeated his stock effects, 'impulsive tomboys, Highland seas, polychromatic sunsets'. There is perhaps an air of contrivance about all his tales, which has no doubt militated against their revival. Nevertheless, *The Daughter of Heth* could well bear reprinting as a period piece.

Nor was the output of the verse department in Glasgow much more distinguished. Throughout the 1870s and 1880s, Robert Buchanan

(1841–1901), Staffordshire-born but brought up and educated in Glasgow, was thought by some to be the equal of Browning; but the rhetoric of such pieces as *Judas Iscariot* has worn decidedly thin. He is really better remembered now for his onslaught on Rosetti and his friends, of the so-called 'Fleshly School of Poetry', and for thus providing W.S. Gilbert with the theme for the Gilbert and Sullivan opera *Patience*, than for anything he achieved during his London career as a somewhat pugnacious man of letters.

Glasgow-born Sir James George Frazer (1854–1941) produced between 1890 and 1914 *The Golden Bough*, his enormous Spencerian attempt to unify life through the interpretation of myth and legend. It aroused considerable interest and was still spoken of in tones of hushed awe by *savants* when I was a boy, though more recent scientific enquiry has discredited some of its conclusions. Bret Harte, the American writer, was American consul in Glasgow for four years from 1880, during which time he lived at 113 West Regent Street, where he wrote his Glasgow tale *Young Robin Gray*.

Edwardian prose-writing was dominated by the remarkable popularity of *Wee MacGregor* (1902) and *Wee MacGregor Again* (1904) by James Joy Bell (1871–1934), which began to appear in the *Evening Times* in 1901. Its humorous portrayal of Glasgow working-class life won it a popularity that spread even to the United States. The novelist who best captured the atmosphere of Edwardian Glasgow was Frederick Niven (1874–1944) with *The Staff at Simsons*, though there is also real merit in *The Seatons* by Anna Buchan (1877–1948). Neil Munro (1864–1930) succeeded to the Stevenson tradition with romantic historical novels like *John Splendid* (1898), *Doom Castle* (1901) and many others still popular. He became editor of Glasgow's *Evening News*, lived latterly in the house next to the building that had once been Henry Bell's hotel in Helensburgh, and especially endeared himself to Glaswegians and many others with his *Para Handy* tales about the West Highland skipper of a Clyde 'puffer' or coal boat and his pawky crew – tales that subsequently achieved a wider popularity through television, even if becoming over-extended and temporarily devalued in the process. Munro's autobiographical reminiscence *The Brave Days* does for middle-class Edwardian Glasgow life what Bell's *I Remember* did for life in the late Victorian city.

The *fin de siècle* 1890s and most of the first Edwardian decade knew of John Davidson (1857–1909), the Barrhead-born, Greenock-bred writer, as the Glasgow representative in the London *Yellow Book* coterie, of which the young Yeats was also a member. He taught in various schools, including Kelvinside Academy, before going south, where he battled with the usual odds against making a living as a poet and essayist – odds stacked higher by depressions stemming from the strain of insanity in his family. His novels are now not read, though he is increasingly remembered for his poetry.

His best poem 'Thirty Bob a Week' (which powerfully influenced T.S. Eliot and Hugh MacDiarmid) is couched in Cockney terms, but the hopeless position of the struggling London clerk he depicts was probably little different from that of his Glasgow counterpart.

> And it's often very cold and very wet,
> And my missis stitches towels for hunks;
> And the Pillar'd Halls is half of it to let –
> Three rooms about the size of travelling trunks.
> And we cough, my wife and I, to dislocate a sigh,
> When the noisy little kids are in their bunks.
>
> But you never hear her do a growl or whine,
> For she's made of flint and roses, very odd,
> And I've got to cut my meaning rather fine,
> Or I'd blubber, for I'm made of greens and sod;
> So p'r'aps we are in Hell for all that I can tell,
> And lost and damn'd and served up hot to God.

Hugh MacDiarmid took many a poetic pot-shot at Glasgow, usually 'improving' upon Davidson's 'in Hell' line, notably in the 1925 'In Glasgow'.

> How can I be fearful
> Who know not what I do
> More than did they whose labours
> We owe this chaos to?
>
> I'd rather cease from singing
> Than make my singing wrong
> An ultimate Cowcaddens
> Or Gorbals in a song.
>
> I'd call myself a poet
> And know that I am fit

When my eyes make glass of Glasgow
And foresee the end of it.

Two of the most powerful novels in which Glasgow features are by
Highlanders. In their émigré eyes at least, Glasgow, as Moira Burgess
puts it in *Imagine a City*, is 'not merely dirty, crowded, unhealthy – conditions explicable, and curable in practical terms – but independently
evil, a malevolent force.' In *Gillespie*, by John Dougal Hay
(1881–1919), 'Glasgow itself becomes some sort of creeping malady, an
affliction of the body or soul – its significance shifts from the general
to the personal; Glasgow becomes part of ourselves . . . What we see
developing in the thirties . . . is a sensibility that projects Glasgow as
the detritus of industrialism, some awful cesspit of human depravity
and as a terrifying personal view of hell.'

In another Highlander's view, Murdo, hero of *The Albanach* by
Fionn MacColla (1906–75), one is 'suffocatingly aware of the fact that
in the city of Glasgow there were at least a million people deformed,
malformed, idiot-faced, loose at the mouth with pendant ears . . .'

Admittedly, this is the view of a man who has just discovered that
he has contracted a sexual disease by going with a Glasgow prostitute:
but in similar circumstances, would London, Liverpool, Manchester or
Leeds have seemed significantly otherwise?

Native novelists, on the whole, have taken a kinder view, yet most
of the novels of the so-called Glasgow School of the 1920s have sunk
without much trace. John Cockburn, John Carruthers, George Woden
and John Macnair Reid are now hardly even remembered names.
Catherine Carswell (1879–1946) and Dot Allen (1892–1964), however, certainly deserve to be read.

Allan, a prolific journalist with a tendency to whimsy, was a keen
observer of people and social affairs, from *The Syrens* (1921) – which
won somewhat grudging approval from Hugh MacDiarmid – through
The Deans (1929), in which Moira Burgess claims that the author 'has
observed, but not experienced, tenement life'; to *Hunger March*
(1923), her best novel and a candidate for reprinting in some future
series of key Scottish novels, should any publisher ever feel far-sighted
enough to embark upon such a worthwhile enterprise.

Glasgow-born Carswell is perhaps best remembered for her semi-
fictional study of *The Life of Robert Burns*, but *Open the Door!*
(1920), according to Moira Burgess (whose *Imagine a City! Glasgow
in Fiction* is now the standard reference work on the Glasgow novel),

is based on her own family and surroundings in 'turn-of-the-century middle-class, West End Glasgow'. It won considerable acclaim, no less a person than D.H. Lawrence telling her in a letter: 'It's like Jane Austen at a deeper level.' She followed it up with *The Camomile* (1922).

Mary Cleland (real name Margot Wells), brought up in Pollokshields, produced *The Two Widows* (1922) and *The Sure Traveller* (1928). These are no more read today than is *Tenement* (1925) by John Cockburn, nor even *Mince Collops Close* by George Blake (1893–1961), the Glasgow journalist who succeeded novelist and poet Neil Munro as literary editor of the *Evening News*.

Blake went on to write his compelling series of Garvel novels, based on Greenock, as well as *Young Malcolm* (1926), the story of a Greenock boy become a doctor in Glasgow. Edwin Morgan has opined that 'Blake is likely to endure as an acute social commentator and historian rather than as a novelist.' But to get the social comment, you have to read the novels!

In any case, with *The Shipbuilder* (1935), for all the criticisms levelled against it – 'excruciating sentimentality'; 'pseudo proletarians'; 'insistence upon people knowing their place in a universe where status is something fixed'; 'failure to get inside the skin of the workers'; and so on – Blake made an undoubtedly major contribution to the Scottish novel. 'Taken on its own terms', as one critic put it more sympathetically, '*The Shipbuilder* is perhaps the most perfect novel of its decade, a noble threnody on the collapse of the shipbuilding industry.

'Yard after yard passed by, the berths empty, the grass growing about the sinking keel-blocks . . . A tradition, a skill, a passion, was visibly in decay and all the acquired loveliness of artistry rotting along the banks of the stream.'

In *The Scottish Novel* (1978), the critic Francis Russell Hart calls it 'too long . . . at times verbose and offensive in its propaganda,' summing up his verdict with: 'The book is schematic, didactic, doctrinaire.' It has, of course, its defenders, one critic finding it 'a heroic attempt to lay, almost single-handed, the foundations for the proletarian socialist-realist novel in Scotland.'

Blake suffered a good deal of unwarranted criticism from Hugh MacDiarmid, who was not over-kind to many of his contemporaries. Nevertheless, Blake was widely read in his day and his Garvel sequence makes a substantial and worthy contribution to twentieth-century Scottish fiction. It has always seemed strange to me that it has not yet been 'discovered' as possible material for an absorbing television serial.

In his final Garvel novel, *The Westering Sun* (1946), Blake brings the last of the Oliphants, whose preceding generations the series chronicles, to run a city tea-room, movingly contrasting middle-class women patrons with the workless outside. It is a fine piece of social criticism.

The Shipbuilder was one of the first of what one might call the proletarian Glasgow novel. The other was James Barke's *Major Operation* (1936). Barke (1905–58) went on to produce a series of novels on the story of Robert Burns that were again widely read in their day, but that – to me at least – seemed somehow to cheapen the life of a genius who had so much adversity with which to contend, by over-stressing the salacious aspects of his dealings with women and interpreting his social aspirations in terms of modern left-wing propaganda. As television has made clear to us in recent years, fiction and documentary simply do not mix well.

One should not allow oneself to be influenced by the personality of an author in judging his books, but to one then young newcomer to the Scottish literary scene, 'Beefy Blake', as MacDiarmid unkindly dubbed him, was genial and encouraging, while Barke was gruff and discouraging. Towards the end of his life he thought it a great joke to keep a concealed tape-recorder in his car, encouraging his passengers to make indiscreet observations and assessments never intended to be public.

I have already quoted from *No Mean City* (1935). Its begetter, the unemployed Alexander MacArthur (1901–47), lived in the Gorbals, scribbled novel after novel, but was not, it seems, either very skilful at delineating character or structuring a story.

In June of the previous year, 1934, the publisher Longman tells us in his preface to the published book that he had received from MacArthur two short novels in an unpublishable state.

'Mr H Kingsley Long, a London journalist, whom we had asked to read MacArthur's manuscript, visited Glasgow,' and called on MacArthur. MacArthur was then summoned to London to enable the publisher to satisfy himself as to the truth of his account of slum life. After several encounters, Long decided to collaborate with MacArthur and the result was *No Mean City*.

It was lavishly praised on publication, but has subsequently fallen out of favour with most critics for being melodramatic. Critically perceptive as always, however, Edwin Morgan observes that 'crude and melodramatic' though it was, 'it had a certain archetypal power about it'. No doubt that is what made it first sell, and keeps it selling into our own day, whatever its formal shortcomings may be.

Of the many novelists whose best works a civilized society should see kept in print, none would be a more obvious candidate than Frederick Niven (1878–1944). Though born in Valparaiso, and, for the last twenty or so years of his life, resident in Canada, he spent his years as a boy and as a young man in Glasgow. *Justice of the Peace* (1914) is a close study of a Glasgow businessman. In my view even finer is *The Staff at Simsons* (1937), a recollection of Niven's own apprentice days in a Glasgow store. *Mrs Barry* (1935) is the vividly portrayed story of a widow in reduced circumstances. It won encomiums from both R.B. Cunninghame Graham and Compton Mackenzie.

The other runaway best-seller Glasgow novel of the period was *Wax Fruit* (1947) by Guy F. McCrone (1899–1975), followed by his sequels *Aunt Bel* (1950) and *The Hayburn Family* (1952).

Wax Fruit is a middle-class family saga, tracing the fortunes of the Moorhouses and the Hayburns, prosperous merchants and engineers, respectively, from 1870. The changing period atmosphere over the decades was carefully researched and is painstakingly recreated. Family life fascinated McCrone, as did the changing 'feel' of Glasgow. In an article in the *Scottish Field* of March 1952, McCrone explained: 'I found myself in a city that was my own, and yet was oddly strange to me. Where people with the same kind of mind to mine met their very different problems in a very different way. Where standards were less flexible, yet where emotional needs were much the same.'

Was Fruit was translated into French and is still in print and selling well. The vivid evocation of middle-class Glasgow and the book's easy narrative flow are surely the secrets of its continuing success. McCrone, a man of great charm, was the unlikely Aeneas in the first ever British production of Berlioz's great opera *The Trojans* mounted by the Glasgow Grand Opera Society in 1935.

Nancy Brysson Morrison (1907–86), one of a writing family – her sister (d. 1973) wrote under the name of March Cost, producing *The Dark Class* (1935) and *The Bespoken Mile* (1953) – achieved appreciative recognition, particularly for *The Gowk Storm* (1933). Edwin Muir, author of a never-to-be-finished Glasgow novel – his *Poor Tom* (1932) is more or less undisguised autobiography – praised Morrison's 'original gift'.

Until Barke's *Major Operation*, the production of Glasgow fiction tended to be a middle-class occupation. In a sense the mere business of successful writing propels an author (economically at least) into the middle-class category, whether he likes it or not. So it was with Barke, despite his relentless left-wing propagandizing.

Moira Burgess is certainly aware of 'Dot Allan's uneasiness about the role of the middle-class in "Depression Glasgow" '. It was perhaps a kind of double unease, because as well as being an author, she had private means. It is an uneasiness that, as a teenager (without private means), I, too, shared.

The first post-war 'working-class' novel of real distinction was *Dance of the Apprentices* (1948) by the distinguished short-story writer Edward Gaitens (1897–1966).

Gaitens's novel was the precursor of change: novels like Hugh Munro's *The Clydesiders* (1961) dealing with west of Scotland religious confrontation; Cliff Hanley's *The Taste of Too Much* (1960), authentic in its colloquial humour; Alexander Trocchi's *Young Adam* (1962) and *Cain's Book* (1963); and Hugh Rae's *Night Pillow* (1967), set in the new jungle of high-rise flats, where people were 'like a rabbit in the side of a hill; no, even less individual than a rabbit; a bee in a box hive, a bee in its cell'. All surveyed the wider Glasgow scene – the majority scene, in fact.

The two novels that really set the pace of subsequent social change in Glasgow fiction, however, were Archie Hind's (b. 1928) *The Dear Green Place* (1966) and Alan Sharp's *A Green Tree in Gedde* (1965), the latter set in Greenock, though some of the action takes place in Glasgow's Kelvingrove Street.

Robin Jenkins (b. 1912), though not primarily a Glasgow novelist, has dealt with Glasgow circumstances in several of his books: with evacuated children in *Guests of War* (1956); with the country-versus-city syndrome in *The Changeling* (1958) and, above all, with the stultifying effects of environment in *A Very Scottish Affair* (1968). Set in a Bridgeton regarded by its inhabitants as 'a ghetto', this is one of Jenkins's most penetrating and powerful successes. Kilmarnock-born, William McIlvaney's (b. 1936) *Remedy is None* (1966) was the first of a series of novels that has included *A Gift from Nessus* (1968), *Laidlaw* (1977), a quasi-detective novel with powerful images of Glasgow, *Docherty* (1975), *The Papers of Tony Veitch* (1983) and *The Kiln* (1988), among others.

Reading McIlvaney, I sometimes feel that I am hearing the tone of the clever author's voice through that of his characters, though more so in the earlier than the later books. His fascination with Glasgow has produced such memorable aphorisms as (in *Laidlaw*): 'Glasgow people have to be nice people. Otherwise they would have burned the place down years ago,' and, in *The Papers of Tony Veitch*: 'When Glasgow gave up the world could call it a day.'

Neil M. Gunn (1891–1973) leaves his traditional Highland scene to include something of Glasgow in *The Serpent* (1943), but seems perhaps a trifle ill at ease there, reflecting the usual *émigré* bewilderment.

Passing over for lack of space the many novels of George Friel (1910–75), including the masterpiece that was his fourth novel *Mr Alfred MA* (1970); the prolific Margaret Thomson Davis's (b. 1927) *The Breadmakers* (1970) and *The Prince and the Tobacco Lords* (1976) in particular; and the brilliant short-story writer Alan Spence's (b. 1947) only novel so far, *The Magic Flute* (1990) – though with a recommendation to read them all – we come to what might be called the post-Glasgow group, most notably, Alasdair Gray (b. 1934), James Kelman (b. 1946) and Janice Galloway (b. 1956).

Gray's *Lanark* appeared in 1981, an enormous work in four books. It somehow manages to contain something of the several Glasgows that exist concurrently. It has had its critics. It is inordinately long. His place, Unthank, has been said to reflect 'a skewed, wrong Glasgow'. The fate of the hero of the earlier part of the book, Duncan Thaw, the sinister lad at odds with himself and the world around him, is left unclear. But there are numerous swatches of marvellously atmospheric Glasgow word-painting.

I must confess that I found *Lanark* difficult to read – or rather, difficult to keep on reading. A novelist has to draw in the reader and hold him with a kind of more-than-real conviction that the author's world is, for the time being, the 'real' world around him. That *Lanark* failed to do for me what some of Gray's later novels certainly succeeded in doing – for example, *Poor Things* (1992) – is probably a defect in my appreciative faculty. My personal reaction, however, does not lessen the force of the appeal the book has made to such critics as Brian McCabe, who found that '*Lanark*'s importance consists in the fact that it has opened a very large door in the windowless little room of Scottish fiction, a door we did not know to be there, and only now can we begin to realise how much scope there is.'

Lanark, incidentally, is illustrated by Gray's own drawings, for he has led a double life as author and highly original artist (though I have to confess that his portraits of the 'famous' rarely seem to me to capture a recognizable likeness of the originals, at least of those sitters known to me). He also designs the typography for his novels.

Glasgow features similarly in Carl MacDougal's (b. 1941) novel, *The Light Below* (1993) and in Jeff Torrington's (b. 1935) angry yet funny novel *Swing Hammer Swing* (1992), a winner of the Whitbread Prize.

By far the most successfully convincing author of short stories and novels dealing with 'ordinary people in ordinary situations' is James Kelman (b. 1946) with *The Busconductor Hines* (1984), *Greyhound for Breakfast* (1987) and the 1994 Booker Prize-winning *How Late It Was, How Late.*

The Busconductor Hines has been described as 'the most depressingly fair and sophisticated picture of Glasgow life, at one of its most significant levels, that has yet been written'. *A Disaffection* (1989), shortlisted for the Booker Prize, movingly reflects the thoughts and disillusionment of Patrick Doyle, a school teacher. *How Late It Was, How Late*, Kelman's fourth novel, achieved the Booker Prize, despite the objections of one of the judges, an English critic. True, it accurately reflects the darkest and dreariest end of Glasgow's social life, foul language and all. By any standards it is undoubtedly well done, even if, in the end, it is apt to make wearisome reading, such a stream of bloodys and fuckings grating on the ear. But life is life; and Glasgow, or at least one side of Glasgow, is like that. (I can almost hear the virulently class-conscious voice of Valda Grieve, wife of the poet MacDiarmid, hissing at me: 'Just your bloody middle-class upbringing!')

Ayrshire-born Janice Galloway (b. 1956) is in a sense a Kelman protégée. Both have social validity and a forceful personal style. I do not, however, find in the related and hugely popular writings of Irvine Welsh (b. 1943), whose *Trainspotting* (1993) struck a chord with the young, much of such quality.

To those unfamiliar with Glasgow Scots (or patois, depending on your point of view) and as an aid to reading some of the novels referred to above, Michael Munro's *The Patter* should prove an invaluable guide.

It is usually a mistake in such a survey as this to proclaim too much achievement in young writers, lest in years to come, picking up the book in some secondhand shop, a later reader may say, 'Who?' I would not have the slightest hesitation in stating that the novels so far published by Dundee-born A.L. Kennedy (b. 1965) – also a brilliant short-story writer 'in love with Glasgow', where she now lives – *Looking For The Possible Dance* (1998) and *So I am Glad* (1995), reveal a realism illuminated by convincing magic in such a manner as to suggest that, by the early years of the next century, she will have established herself as the current Glasgow novelist who most matters, were it not for one thing. As I finish writing this page, I read in the issue of the *Observer* of 24 October 1999 that she contemplated suicide on experiencing 'writer's block' in fiction, only releasing it by becoming an *aficionado* of bullfighting, resulting in her *On Bullfighting (1999)*.

X

Leaving aside a reference to the city in Blind Harry's (1450–91) *The Wallace* and the Latinist Arthur Johnstone's *Glasgow* (c. 1650), of which Robert Barclay made a passable translation in 1685, Glasgow poetry probably begins with the effusions of that one-time minister of Glasgow Cathedral, the Reverend Zachary Boyd (1589–1653). He it was who preached such an offensive anti-Roundhead sermon when Oliver Cromwell was in the congregation on a Sunday in 1650 that Secretary Thurloe asked permission to 'pistol' him. Cromwell forbade him to do so, but instead invited Zachary to supper that evening, then engaged the worthy preacher in a two-hour prayer session, which must surely have taxed even his theological stamina.

Whatever he was like as a preacher, Zachary Boyd was hardly much of a poet, as these lines from 'Zion's Flowers', dealing with Potiphar's wife, show:

> **Potiphar's Wife**
> Now time is come. My heart it springs for haste,
> About his neck my milk-white arms to cast.
> I'll hold him, hug him, saying Welcome mine!
> Dear mine thou art, and I am also thine!
> Here's fair occasion; why desire we thus
> To sport in love? None is to hinder us.
> While we have time now let us do with speed.
> Lovers must dare, and for no dangers dread.
> Why burn we daylight? We have time and place –
> My dearest Heart, now let me thee embrace!
>
> **Joseph**
> Madam, madam! How far misled ye are!
> Think that ye are the wife of Potiphar,

My noble lord, who doth us all command.
He would not look to get this from your hand.
Sith as ye hear the matters so and so,
Now loose your grips, and quickly let me go.
If from you I this favour cannot find,
I'll rather choose to leave my cloak behind.

Potiphar's Wife
O dule! O dule! Help! O dule, O dule!
I am abused by a slave – a fool!

On his death, Boyd left a not inconsiderable sum of money to Glasgow University, on condition that they would publish a collected edition of his works. The University sat on the money for a considerable time, and in the end got away with erecting a small memorial bust instead.

Allan Ramsay's friend James Arbuckle wrote 'Glotta' a poem in Augustan couplets, whose lines on golf have been previously quoted (see p.156), published in 1721. Much more celebrated in its day was another poem in Augustan couplets, 'Clyde: A Poem', by schoolmaster John Wilson (1720–89), published in 1764. He, poor chap, had to promise to abandon 'the profane and unprofitable act of poem-making' in order to secure his final promotion to Greenock Grammar School. He anticipates by a couple of decades Burns's famous lines on the ultimate necessity of solitude for the poet:

Tho' oft the Muse to lone recesses flies;
And much she walks alone who would be wise:
Yet both the sage and poet are allowed
To catch instruction in the busiest crowd,
And those of both have ever brightest shone
Who much conversed, and often thought alone,
For in the pop'lous town we best may see
Of human life the strange variety.

At a different level, more famous in his day than either Arbuckle or Wilson, was hump-backed Dougal Graham (1721–79), the last Glasgow Bellman, the Skellet bell being the lighter-toned bell with which he proclaimed news items, as opposed to the less frequently used deep-toned mort bell, rung when he was announcing a death. His 'uniform' was 'a cocked hat, scarlet coat, blue breeches and white stock-ings'.

Graham collected local stories which he then rewrote, often in verse. They were issued as chapbooks, many of which he sold himself. Some were printed by the Paisley publisher, George Caldwell, who declared: 'A' his warks took weel. I never had a history of Dougal's that stuck in the sale yet, and we were aye fain to get haud o' some new piece frae him.'

There was, of course, a sniffier view of Graham's achievements, one superior fellow declaring: 'To refined taste Dougal had no pre-tentions. His coarsenesses were an abomination, but they are charac-teristic of the class for whom he wrote.' But he had a ready wit. One night, in a Glasgow pub, when some officers of the 42nd Highlanders, recently defeated in the American War of Independence, were making merry, one of them called out: 'What's that you've got on your back?' Dougal replied: 'It's Bunker's Hill. Do you choose to mount?'

He was possibly the first recorded Lowland poet to make fun of the dialect of the Highlands. Here is a sample of his numerous stanzas:

> Her nainsel into Glasgow went,
> An erran there to see't,
> And she never saw a ponnier town
> Standing on her feet.

> For a' the houses that be there,
> Was thicket wi' blue stanes;
> And a stane ladder to gang up,
> No fa' to prack her banes . . .

> I gang upon a staney wood,
> A street they do him ca',
> And when me seek the chapman's hoose,
> Her name pe on the wa' . . .

And so on: a kind of Lowlander's patronizing of Gaelic culture that Highlanders no doubt found as offensive then as they still do its mod-ern equivalent.

John Mayne's 'Glasgow', already quoted from (p.43), persuaded Sir Walter Scott that it was a better poem than the productions of Ramsay or Fergusson – Scotland's first town poets – and, indeed, almost as good as Burns.

Vincenzio Lunardi (1751–1806) made five Scottish ascents by hydrogen balloon, two from Glasgow, landing the first time at Hawick and the second time at Campsie. The second ascent was celebrated in Scots verse by Robert Galloway, in Burnsian style. In 1788 Galloway published his *Poems, Epistles and Songs. Chiefly in the Scottish Dialect*, even echoing the title of Burns's Kilmarnock Poems of 1786.

The most frequently anthologized Glasgow poem of the early nineteenth century, which first appeared in *Blackwood's Magazine* for September 1819, is undoubtedly John Gibson Lockhart's 'Captain Paton's Lament', an elegy upon a deceased eccentric dandy who made a daily habit of parading on the plainstones at Glasgow Cross. Lockhart had seen him there as a boy, noting:

> . . . The blue strip in his stocking
>   Round his neat slim leg did go,
> And his ruffles of the cambric fine,
>   They were whiter than the snow.
> Oh! We ne'er shall see the like of Captain Paton no mo'e!

> In dirty days he picked well
>   His footsteps with his rattan
> Oh! You ne'er could see the least speck
>   On the shoes of Captain Paton.
> And on entering the coffee-room
>   About two, all men did know
> They would see him with his *Courier*
>   In the middle of the row.
> Oh! We ne'er shall see the like of Captain Paton no mo'e!

James McIndoe, a Pollokshaws man writing under the pseudonym Jamie Blue, raised the class issue in 'Queer Folk at the Shaws'. He died in 1837, having been soldier, pedlar and sometime temporary town crier. Others have laid claim to these verses, but no matter. The radical flavour is the thing.

> The folks are green, it's oft been said,
>   Of that you'll find no trace:
> There's seasoned word in every head,
>   And brass in every face.

Look smart, and keep your eyes about,
Their tricks will make you grin;
The Barrhead coach will take you out,
The folks will take you in!

Francis George Scott (1880–1958), the songwriter, who spent the last forty years of his life in Glasgow

Passing over the lively, if Burnsian, 'Saturday in Glasgow' by William Watt, a handloom weaver whose poems were printed posthumously in 1860, we come to Thomas Campbell (1777–1844), whose statue stands in George Square. He was the youngest of the eleven children of a Virginia tobacco merchant. He graduated at Glasgow University, of which he was to become three times lord rector, defeating Sir Walter Scott. To his contemporaries, Campbell was famous mainly for his long poem 'The Pleasures of Hope', from which today, if we remember anything, it is only that "Tis distance lends enchantment to the view'. To my generation, from Campbell we learnt by heart at school 'The Battle of the Baltic', 'Hohenlinden' and 'Lord Ullin's Daughter'. 'Ye Mariners of England' preserves his wider fame: but there is one lovely lyric, 'Florine' not too well known, beautifully set to music by Francis George Scott, and certainly worth quoting here.

Could I bring back lost youth again
    And be what I have been,
I'd court you in a gallant strain,
    My young and fair Florine.

But mine's the chilling age that chides
    Devoted rapture's glow,
And love – that conquers all besides –
    Finds Time a conquering foe.

Farewell! we're severed from our fate
As far as night from noon;
You came into the world too late,
And I depart so soon

Campbell was fairly scathing about the polluted state of the Clyde, fondly remembered from his youth, when he revisited it in 1847.

And call they this improvement? – to have changed
My native Clyde, thy once romantic shore,
Where nature's face is banish'd and estranged,
And heaven reflected in thy wave no more;
Whose banks, that sweeten'd May-day's breath before,
Lie sere and leafless now in summer's beam
With sooty exhalations cover'd o'er;
And for the daisied green-sward, down thy stream,
Unsightly brick-lanes smoke and clanking engines gleam . . .

There are, of course, numerous radical Glasgow poems about work – the enormously lively 'The Weaver's Saturday: A Political Poem', which Hamish Whyte, in his anthology *Mungo's Tongues*, attributed to the weaver George Donald (1801–51); and, in the same anthology, poems such as 'St Rollox Lum's Address to its Brethren' by John Mitchell, a Paisley shoemaker. It echoes Burns's professed scorn for noblemen, though here the target is 'some pampered pensioned sot/With haughty air,' who 'slides down pleasures' stream triumphant flood/unscathed by care.'

In similar vein, though with a different Burnsian echo (the 'Address to the Haggis' in this case), is wretched Ellen Johnston's 1867 'Address to the Factory of Messers J. and W. Scott and Co'. She died in the poorhouse. There are the socially interesting effusions of Bass Kennedy, from which I have already twice quoted. Other minor nine-teenth-century Glasgow versifiers may be met with in George Eyre-Todd's *The Glasgow Poets: Their Lives and Poems* (1903).

There has been a great outburst of Glasgow poetry during the present century, particularly in the post-war years. I myself vividly remember sitting in an early 1943 English billet during the war after walking through a London square in the gloaming, and experiencing an almost unbearable sense of longing for Glasgow, which the war and my youth

42 Miller Street, which was built in 1775 by the architect John Craig for his own use. At first the houses in this street would not sell, being considered too far out of town. It was acquired as the headquarters of The Scottish Civic Trust in 1997

had left behind. The resulting poem, 'The Exiled Heart', subsequently found its way into the *Oxford Book of Scottish Verse*. My memories were, of course, of the Glasgow of the thirties.

> Two purple pigeons circle a London square
> as darkness blurs and smudges the shadowless light
> of a winter evening. I pause on the pavement and stare
> at the restless flutter of wings as they gather flight,
> like rustling silk, and move out to meet the night.
>
> And my restless thoughts migrate to a Northern city –
> fat pigeons stalking the dirty, cobbled quays,
> where a sluggish river carries the cold self-pity
> of those for whom life has never flowed with ease,
> from a granite bridge to the green Atlantic seas;

the bristling, rough-haired texture of Scottish manners;
the jostling clatter of crowded shopping streets
where lumbering tramcars squeal as they take sharp corners;
the boozy smell from lounging pubs that cheats
the penniless drunkard's thirst with its stale deceits:

where my heart first jigged to the harsh and steady sorrow
of those for whom mostly the world is seldom glad,
who are dogged by the flat-heeled, footpad steps of to-morrow;
for whom hope is a dangerous drug, an expensive fad
of the distant rich, or the young and lovesick mad:

where chattering women in tearooms, swaddled with furs,
pass knife-edged gossip like cakes, and another's skirt
is unstitched with sharp words, and delicate, ladylike slurs
are slashed on the not-quite-nice or the over smart
till smoke to the eyes is a hazy, prickled hurt.

I remember Glasgow, where sordid and trivial breed
from the same indifferent father; his children side
with the mother whose sour breasts taught them first to feed
on her hot, caressing hates that sear and divide,
or swell the itching, distended bladder of pride.

Yet my guilty sneers are the tossed-down beggar's penny
which the goaded heart throws out, in vain, to procure
the comfortable forgetfulness of the many
who lie in content's soft arms, and are safe and sure
in the fabled Grecian wanderers' lotus-lure;

who forget the sullen glare of the wet, grey skies,
and the lashing Northern wind that flicks the skin
like a whip, where poverty's dull and listless eyes
are pressed to the window, hearing the friendly din
of the party, watching the lights and laughter within.

But oh, I cannot forget! So I wait and wonder,
how long will the thinly dividing window hold,
how long will the dancing drown the terrible anger
of those, the unwanted, who peddle their grief in the cold,
wrapped in their own despair's thick and unkindly fold?

Yet evil is no pattern of places
varied, like terraces from town to town;
a city's charms and individual graces
are but the sculpter's bleak and basic stone,
the photographic face without a frown.

The wound is in this bewildered generation,
tossed on the swollen, analytic mood,
its compass-point no longer veneration
of that lost God who rewarded the simple and good,
vivid and real, now, only in childhood.

For we, the children of this uncertain age,
breathing its huge disasters and sad airs,
have seen that our warm, humanitarian rage
is impotent to soothe war's animal fears,
can never quell the lonely exile's tears.

So the heart, like a wounded seabird, hungers home
to muffled memories on faintly beating wings
which once climbed over history's clouded foam
to that clear sky where each new hero flings
the careful stone that fades in slow, concentric rings.

Many of the highly sensitive poems of Steward Conn (b. 1936) reflect
the same period and similar social circumstances.

In the years after the Second World War, Edwin Morgan (b. 1920)
has been, among other things, a kind of poetic Kelman, as part of his
fine poem 'Glasgow Green' exemplifies:

Clammy midnight, moonless mist.
A cigarette glows and fades on a cough.
Meth-men mutter on benches,
pawed by river fog. Monteith Row
sweats coldly, crumples, dies
slowly. All shadows are alive.
Somewhere a shout's forced out – 'No!' –
It leads to nothing but silence,
except the whisper of the grass
and the other whispers that fill the shadows . . .

Marvellously evocative! I consider Morgan to be the most variedly talented poet Glasgow has produced; indeed, in the overall Scottish context, not so very far behind MacDiarmid himself. As I write, it is announced that he is to be Glasgow's first poet laureate for the next three years. How he will deploy his talents in matters civic is, to say the least, intriguing.

Tom Leonard (b. 1944) catches the Glasgow sound, though no doubt he baffles some non-Glasgow readers, as in 'The Good Thief' which begins thus:

> heh jimmy
> yawright ih
> stull wayis urryi
>
> heh jimmy
> ma right insane yiira pape
> ma right insane yirrwanny uz jimmy
> see it nyir eyes
> wanny uz
>
> heh . . .

Other poets include Stephen Mulrine (b. 1937) – 'The Coming of the Wee Malkies' – Liz Lochhead (b. 1947), something of a cult symbol with the young and perhaps more memorable as a playwright than a poet; Frank Kuppner (b. 1951) – author of the amusing 'A Node' – and, among younger writers, David Kinloch (b. 1959).

While poets, like all artists, must ultimately stand or fall on their own, there have been two very different literature 'schools' or groups, both roughly based in Glasgow, in the reassurance of which some young writers first found their feet. In the nineteenth century, there was the Whistlebinkie school of rather sentimental or 'Kailyaird' (cabbage-patch) verse, reflected in a series of anthologies bearing its name. It produced two enduring gems, 'Wee Willie Winkie' by William Miller (1810–72), beloved of all Scots children; and 'Behave Yourself afore Folk' by Alexander Rodger (1784–1846), a splendid take-off of fake gentility.

The mid twentieth-century Scottish Renaissance Movement, so named by a Frenchman, Dennis Saurat, was grouped around C.M. Grieve (Hugh MacDiarmid). While he did live in Glasgow during and, for a time, after the Second World War years, he was a Borderer. Of the 'second wind' poets of the movement (as Eric Linklater dubbed them in *Poetry Scotland*), I suppose I was almost the only native Glaswegian.

Some Glasgow light verse implies social comment. There is, for example, James Bridie's witty serenade 'The West End Perk' with its take-off of the extreme Kelvinside accent, written when he was a student at Glasgow University.

It's long pest midnight, there's no one in the street,
The consteble is sleeping at the corner of his beat.
The cold white erc-lemps fizz like gingerade,
And I'm below your window with this cherming serenade.

Open your window, the night is beastly derk
The phentoms are dencing in the West-End Perk,
Open your window, your lover brave to see,
I'm here all alone, and there's no one here but me!

Over the Cowkeddens a gentle stillness spreads,
All good little Redskins are tucked up in their beds.
A deep and holy stillness broods the Gorbals o'er,
And softly blow the zephyrs down on Goven's peaceful shore.

(*As if with a cold in the head.*)
Still do bovebed frob your lofty widdow-sill?
Well, I bust be boving off, I fear I've got a chill,
Do tibe for eddy bore pethetic sighs or such,
So suffice it to assure you I adbire you very buch.

Opedd your widdow, the dight is beastly derk,
The phedtops are dedsig id the West-End Perk.
Opedd your widdow, your lover brave to see,
I'd here all alode, ad there's do wudd here . . . atishee!'

In contrast to refined Kelvinside comes the humorous protest song, 'The Jeely Piece Song' (1967), about the inconveniences of life in a high-rise flat (as compared to a traditional tenement) by Matt McGinn (1928–77):

I'm a skyscraper wean; I live on the nineteenth flair,
But I'm no' gaun tae play ony mair

'Cause since we moved to Castlemilk, I'm wastin' away
'Cause I'm getting' wan meal less every day.

O ye cannae fling pieces oot a twenty-storey flat,
Seven hundred weans'll testify to that.
If it's butter, cheese or jeely, if the breid's plain or pan,
The odds against it reaching earth are ninety-nine tae wan.

No survey of Glasgow verse could be complete without cartoonist Bud Neill's 'Perishin' Poem', which first appeared in the *Evening Times* on 1 December 1952:

Winter's came,
The snow has fell,
Wee Josie's nosis frozis well,
Wee Josie's frozis nosis skintit
Winter's diabolic – intit?

XI

The Scots came late to the native stage. James Bridie (1881–1951), in real life Dr O.H. Mavor, has been by far our most distinguished Scottish dramatist, with *The Anatomist* (1931), *Mr Bolfry* (1942) and *Mr Gillie* (1950) among many other, beautifully crafted plays of strong character-development and witty argument. Amusing and rumbustious, too, are the plays of Liz Lochhead (b. 1947), particularly *Mary Queen of Scots got her Head Chopped Off* (1992) and *Britannia Rules* (1999).

Among the Citizen's Theatre's Scots triumphs were Robert MacLellan's (1907–85) *Jamie the Saxt* (1937), perhaps the most successful play in Scots during the twentieth century, and Alexander Scott's *Right Royal* (1954). MacLellan followed up his success with *Jeddart Justice* (1934) and *Toom Byres* (1936), *The Laird o' Torwattlie* (1946) and *The Flowers o' Edinburgh* (1947). The Citizens' also presented *The Warld's Wonder* (1953) and *The Lass wi' the Muckle Mou* (1950) by Alexander Reid (b. 1914), while Roddie MacMillan's (1923–79) *All in Good Faith* and Bill Bryden's (b. 1942) *Willie Rough* provided the Citizens' with good Scots fare.

Poet Alexander Scott (1920–89) also wrote several radio plays in

Scots, and founded the Department of Scottish Literature at Glasgow University, though – much to that august body's disgrace, in the opinion of many – he remained reader in Scottish Literature, the distinction of occupying the first Chair in the subject eventually going to one of his students.

Light verse is, as I am never tired of insisting, a genre in which Glasgow has excelled.

Having regard to the propensity of some Glaswegians for strong drink as an aspect of holiday – and before anyone writes to me protestingly via the publishers, it should be noted that to this day, passengers boarding the last surviving Clyde pleasure-steamer, the paddler *Waverley*, are not allowed to carry alcohol on their person! – there is surely well-observed humour in 'Waitin' on the Glesca' Train' by Andrew Lang (1844–1912):

> When the holidays come roun',
> And on pleasure ye are boun',
> For the Trossachs, Brig' o' Allan or Dunblane;
> You'll be sometimes keepit waitin',
> When ye hear the porter statin'
> That ye're waitin' on the Glesca' train.
> Tak' yer time – tak' yer time,
> With indifference sublime,
> Ye may watch the people hurry micht an' main;
> Just tak' a seat an' wait,
> For ye canna be ower late,
> When ye're waitin' on the Glesca' train.

> It's attended wi' expense;
> For a lad o' ony sense,
> If it's het or cauld or looks like rain,
> The interval maun fill
> Wi' a mutchkin or a gill,
> When he's waitin' for the Glesca' train.

> There's a frien' o' mine, Mackay,
> Constitutionally dry,
> Thocht that he had just got time to tak' a drain,
> But he somehow lost his way,
> An' he's no' foun' to this day,
> A' wi' waitin' on the Glesca' train.

I was ettlin' at Kinross,
Where the train is kin' o' cross,
And Bradshaw's no' that easy to explain;
And what was left o' me,
Was jist coupit at Dundee,   [turned out
A' wi' waitin' on the Glesca' train

But the ploy has merit whiles,
For a sonsie lassie's smiles   [plump
Had entrappid aince ma frien' Maclean;
But Maclean has clean got off it,
For the lass was lost at Moffat,
A' wi' waitin' on the Glesca' train.

There's occasions when I think
That the interests o' drink
Is a notion that Directors entertain;
And that's maybe why ye're waitin',
When ye hear the porter statin',
That ye're waitin' on the Glesca' train.

Perhaps the greatest Scots actor of all time was Duncan Macrae
(1905–67), who for many years delighted television audiences on
Hogmanay with a rendition of his own improved version of Edinburgh
lawyer Hugh Frater's 'The Wee Cock Sparra'. Since it, too, is hard to
come by in print, here it is again:

A wee cock sparra sat on a tree,
A wee cock sparra sat on a tree,
A wee cock sparra sat on a tree
Chirpin awa as blithe as can be.

Alang came a boy wi' a bow and an arra,
Alang came a boy wi' a bow and an arra,
Alang came a boy wi' a bow and an arra
And he said, 'I'll get ye, ye wee cock sparra.'

The boy wi' the arra let fly at the sparra,
The boy wi' the arra let fly at the sparra,
The boy wi' the arra let fly at the sparra
And he hit a man that was hurlin' a barra.

The man wi' the barra cam owre wi' the arra,
The man wi' the barra cam owre wi' the arra,
The man wi' the barra cam owre wi' the arra,
And said, 'Ye take me for a wee cock sparra?'

The man hit the boy, tho he wasne his farra,
The man hit the boy, tho he wasne his farra,
The man hit the boy, tho he wasne his farra
And the boy stood and glowered; he was hurt tae the marra.

And a' this time the wee cock sparra,
And a' this time the wee cock sparra,
And a' this time the wee cock sparra
Was chirpin awa on the shank o' the barra.

XII

A major source of diversion for Glaswegians was its five major exhibitions, the first of which, inspired by the success of London's Great
Exhibition of 1851, was the Glasgow International Exhibition, held in
the West End Park in 1888.

While celebrating the high point of Glasgow's commercial success,
it aimed to promote the arts and sciences, stimulate further commercial enterprise and raise money towards the cost of a new art gallery,
museum and school of art. James Sellars was the architect. This exhibition had an Oriental flavour, because Sellars thought such a style
particularly amenable to construction in wood. It was opened on 8
May 1888 by the Prince and Princess of Wales.

The exhibition was, in fact, contained under one roof, and featured
a machine section, which contained a splendid display of Macfarlane's
decorative ironworks, some of which still adorn our public places; a
marine engineering display; a section devoted to 'women's industries' –
arts and crafts; an extensive fine arts section that included murals by
some of the Glasgow Boys, and the red terracotta Doulton fountain re-
erected in 1890 on Glasgow Green by its donor, Sir Henry Doulton. It
also had an electrically illuminated fairy fountain. Across the river
there was an amusement section, which included a switch-back railway. It was twice visited by Queen Victoria, the second time privately,
and by the time it closed on 10 November, it had attracted nearly 5½
million visitors, making a profit of £46,000.

A building from the 1888 exhibition

The Illustrated London News of 1 September waxed lyrical about the reception given to the Queen on her first official visit to the Exhibition.

The city of Glasgow, the greatest in population of the provincial cities of the United Kingdom, and one of the greatest in trade and industry, was honoured by Her Majesty the Queen, on Wednesday, August 22, with a gracious visit which was performed under the most gratifying conditions, favoured by fine summer weather.

St Enoch Station was reached at ten minutes past four o'clock. Here elaborate preparations had been made for the reception. The station is the terminus of the Glasgow and South-Western Railway, and the spacious interior and also the extensive square readily lend themselves to the art of the decorator. The immense arch of the station was draped with flowing curtains and enlivened with wreaths of evergreens and flowers. The ornate fronts of the station and hotel were brilliant with colour.

Headed by an escort of the 15th Hussars, the Royal pageant departed from the station, and proceeded amidst the hearty cheers of the people to the new Municipal Buildings, going by way of St Enoch Square, up Buchanan Street, along St Vincent Place, to the front of the Municipal Buildings in George Square.

On this part of the route the decorations were very fine. The opening from St Enoch Square into Argyle Street was spanned by the first triumphal arch, shaped and painted so as to imitate a structure of freestone. It was surmounted by a royal crown. The somewhat sombre appearance of the arch itself was relieved by flowing draperies of rich crimson, looped with orange. Looking up Buchanan Street, the eye was almost dazzled by the profusion of gorgeous colours . . .

Because of the recent death of the Queen, the celebrations attending the opening by the Duke and Duchess of Fife of the 1901 International Exhibition, also in the West End Park, were somewhat muted, at least in the matter of fashion, as the *Evening News* of 3 May reported:

Our first gathering in our splendid Art Galleries, inaugurated only yesterday by the King's eldest daughter, must needs be a memorable one. The long corridors, in a blaze of light, the great halls of statuary were to be seen under the happiest of auspices, with music playing and a gay crowd of citizens in uniform and brightly coloured gowns moving among the palms and statues and making the scene brilliant and picturesque. The walls were, it must be confessed, only of interest to the passing eye, and the treasures they displayed were for the time being glanced at casually with good intentions of learning to know them another day. The scene from the windows that looked on the lively grounds of the Exhibition was for the moment more to our taste at the end of an important and exciting day when our great venture had been so happily launched.

Without perhaps any intention of retaining mourning except in cases of domestic bereavement, the majority of the ladies were in black. One or two notable gowns there were of scarlet, others of rose and many shades of pink, some of blue, and many of heliotrope and white, but certainly the greater number of the guests did not wear colours . . .

A striking gown of white and pink chiffon was worn by Miss Macdonald, the clever Glasgow artist.

Miss Macdonald was one of the sisters associated with Charles Rennie Mackintosh, Glasgow's greatest architect and designer of the Glasgow School of Art. Opened in December 1899 by Sir James King, it was described by the *Evening Times* as 'a structure which will long remain as a monument to the strong originality and artistic conception of Glasgow designers'.

The 1901 Exhibition was accommodated in two separate buildings, one being, of course, the recently built museum and art gallery of J.W. Simpson and Miller Allan (facing inwards towards the heart of the exhibition and giving rise to the subsequent myth that the architect had built it the wrong way round and committed suicide on having his error pointed out to him!) The other building, the machinery hall, was on the site of what later became the Kelvin Hall. There were several foreign exhibits, including a spectacular Russian one, and a grand court hall. It also featured a 'quick-silver fountain, using three tons of mercury illuminated by coloured electric light and a golden obelisk'.

By the time it closed on 9 November, just under 11½ million visitors had passed through its turnstiles, one of them Tsar Nicholas II of Russia; another, the author J.J. Bell, commented in verse on the exhibition's royal bungalow restaurant.

The Great Hall, the centrepiece of the 1901 exhibition

Oh my, I'm thankful that it's by –
That dreidfu' exhibition, my temper it did try,
For every time our Jock gaed there
He cam' hame roarin' fu',
And he always blamed it on the tea
He got at the Bungaloo.

The exhibition made a profit of £40,000.

The exhibition of 1911 was a Scottish affair, designed to fund a Chair of Scottish History and Literature at Glasgow University. As Persila and Juliet Kinchen put it: 'Devolution was the order of the day ... with nearly one third of the Cabinet Scots, independence seemed within reach. Political motivation was complemented by a cultural renaissance, and Gaelic, for so long suppressed, had become fashionable.'

The exhibition had a palace of history and literature, a costume-populated Auld Toon, and an auld tartan shop, a fake Palace of Falkland, an olde toffee shop, and An Clachan, a Highland village on the banks of Caol Abhain (River Kelvin).

It also had a fine arts palace, a less prominent palace of industry and an extended amusement section, which included an aerial railway across the Kelvin. Model ships, including the *Victory* and the latest dreadnought, HMS *Resolution*, sailed in daily pageant on the river. For this exhibition, Charles Rennie Mackintosh designed a tearoom for Miss Cranston, the 'White Cockade.'

Nearly 9,400,000 visitors checked through the turnstiles, and £15,000 went to endow the History Chair.

There were also several industrial exhibitions. A small one was held at 99 Argyle Street, but the East End Industrial Exhibition of Manufacturers, Science and Art of 1890–1 was held in buildings in Duke Street, its object being to raise money towards the construction of the People's Palace, on Glasgow Green. Money towards this building also came from the Caledonia Railway Company and from the sale of ground at Bridgeton, the total cost of £32,000 being made up by the

A local scene in the 1911 exhibition

Corporation. The People's Palace was opened by Lord Roseberry in 1898, and housed many exhibits recalling Glasgow's social history, including a Roman samian-ware bowl, the five-gallon pottery punch bowl from one of Glasgow's most famous inns, the Saracen's Head, and a painting of the tobacco lord John Glassford, as well as some recon- structions of Glasgow scenes in earlier times and a considerable col- lection of paintings of Glasgow and its inhabitants.

Other smaller exhibitions on the same site took place in 1895/6 and 1896/7, but the next major exhibition, the Empire Exhibition, was mounted in 1938, the fiftieth anniversary of the 1888 Exhibition. The site at Bellahouston Park stretched over 150 acres, at a cost of £10 mil- lion. Thomas Smith Tait was the architect. It was a bravura gesture as Glasgow emerged out of a huge depression under the clouds of an impending war.

The exhibition had three categories, together containing more than 200 pavilions. One represented the soon-to-be-dispersed empire, dominions and colonies; another, British affairs with a prominent Scottish representation including a Highland clachan; while the third reaffirmed the 'United Kingdom's industrial and manufacturing tri- umphs,' as one observer wrote. The palaces and avenues circled the hill on which stood Tait's Tower, a striking shaft of a building with an observation platform reached by a lift. The Empire Exhibition was opened by King George V on 3 May and closed on 28 October, a sum- mer of persistent windy rain, however, keeping the attendance figures down to 12½ million instead of the expected 20 million. There was, of course, anxiety in the air, the summer of 1938 being shadowed by the betrayal of Czechoslovakia, the false peace of Munich and closely gath- ering war clouds. Three buildings from the Exhibition survived – the palace of arts, now used by the Education Authority; the palace of engineering, which was dismantled and re-erected at Prestwick International Airport; and Tait's Tower, though hurriedly taken down, in spite of much protest, shortly before the outbreak of the 1939–45 war, lest it should become a marker for enemy aircraft. In addition, the memorial slab unveiled by the King survives, as does the Peace Cairn.

Having a student's season ticket for the exhibition, I was a frequent attender, my strongest image being of a high-hatted and powdery-look- ing Queen Mary, driving through the lined-up crowds on a wet day, looking out of the window of her car and giving a gloved wave, half- rising in her seat, as if the rear axle of her car lifted her up every time it turned.

Tait's Tower, the 1938 exhibition

'Argos' of the *Evening Citizen* reported his experiences on 5 May,
two days after the opening:

Everywhere were gadgets for turning you upside down, rolling you round
and round, shaking your liver, in short, putting you in any position

other than the normal one. Here man (and that means woman too) is twisted, thrown, bumped and shaken, and he likes it. If you doubt me, go and see for yourself. Watch him come off the most fearsome-looking machine smiling and happy, and asking for more and getting it. No wonder that poets sing of the wonderful Spirit of Man.

Come with me into the Stratoship, a cigar-shaped 'aeroplane' that seats about six or seven. It is attached to a long arm and has a propeller. When you are securely strapped into a cage arrangement, off you go, the motion being something like a plane beginning to rise. It's all very pleasant – and then your plane suddenly rolls right over, and before you know where you are you're sitting up gasping – and then over you go again.

The subtlety of this thing is that it doesn't turn over with unfailing regularity. You are all prepared for a roll and it doesn't come. You go round smoothly again and decide that there are to be no more rolls, and at that moment over you go again. And everybody loves it.

If the Stratoship is a thrill, the Rocket Railway is even more thrilling. I'm not sure whether the more exciting thing is to travel on this railway or watch it go round. It goes round in a deep pit. You've probably seen that act known as the Wall of Death in which a motorcyclist goes round a 'well' at tremendous speed. This is the Rocket Railway on a smaller scale.

As the train gathers speed it climbs higher and higher up the side of the wall or pit until the passengers are all sitting sides-up. It doesn't seem possible, I know, but believe me it does happen. I could not help wondering what the driver of the train feels about it. You go on once or twice but, remember, he goes on all the time. Does he end the season with a lop-sided view of life, and find the ordinary method of train travelling flat, stale and unprofitable?

After the Rocket Railway I felt the need for something less exciting, so I went in to see the giraffe-necked ladies, who sat in a comfortable cabin on the floor of which a baby played. The neck rings I was told were never removed.

Then I made for the Octopus via the crooked house. No, I didn't go into the house. A laughing sailor (a most realistic dummy) sits above the door and rocks with laughter. Little Audrey had nothing on him. She merely laughed and laughed and laughed, but he laughs and laughs and laughs *ad lib*. And everybody also laughs. I tried not to but it was impossible. Soon I was holding myself, and I decided not to go into the house yesterday for I had laughed my fill, and any more might have been dangerous.

Now for the Octopus. It is a machine with long steel arms reaching into the air. On the end of each arm or tentacle – there must be about 20 of them – is a chair that holds two. The passengers are carefully fastened in, and the Octopus begins to waggle its tentacles. Up they go, down they go, and all the time the seat is revolving. It may not be your form of enjoyment, but you are in the minority, for it was highly popular yesterday. As one man came off, after several rounds, his eyes were sparkling and he said, simply, 'It's a wow!'

The Exhibition of 1988 took the form of the Glasgow Garden Festival, on both banks of the Clyde, linked by Bell's Bridge which survives as a memorial. It was the United Kingdom's biggest single consumer event of the year, designed to 'match the great Empire Exhibition held fifty years ago . . . to boost the local and regional economy,' as the guide book put it. But the catalogue added: 'The days are past when magnificent buildings can be run up for six months' use in the manner seen in earlier Exhibitions. Landscaping and planting fulfil comparatively many functions of the Exhibition building . . . Grandeur is no longer part of the brief.

XIII

A walk in the park was one of the most popular forms of recreation in less sophisticated times: sometimes to listen to military bands in the bandstands or sail model boats in the pond.

Glasgow is more fortunate than many other large cities in that it is generously provided with parks. Some of these were originally common lands that a cash-short town council sold off, then bought back again bit by bit in the late seventeenth and early eighteenth centuries. It was in this fashion that Glasgow's oldest public park came into being. It runs on the north bank of the Clyde from the foot of the Saltmarket towards Bridgeton, bounded on the north side by the former village of Calton. A mere fifty-nine acres in 1730, it reached its present size of 136 acres in 1894. Glasgow Green, the city's most historic park, on which was once held the annual Glasgow Fair, is used by preacher ranters, politicians and the like who in London sound off at Hyde Park Corner.

In 1852, the town council bought sixty-nine acres of land on the east side of the Kelvin, engaging Sir Joseph Paxton to lay out this West End Park. It was extended by seventy-three acres on the west side

Glasgow University, Gilmorehill, by Sir Giles Gilbert Scott in 1870, just after it was completed. The gate of the Old College and the 'heraldic' beast staircase were later incorporated in the new building. Scott described the style as being 'of his own invention'

when in 1870 the university moved to Gilmorehill, overlooking the Kelvin. It was then that it first became known as Kelvingrove Park, the site of the International Exhibitions of 1888 and 1901 and the Scottish National Exhibition of 1911. Its Stewart Memorial Fountain, built in 1872, commemorates Lord Provost Robert Stewart of Murdostoun, who, in the teeth of opposition, got the Loch Katrine Act passed, thus ensuring that expanding Glasgow had an adequate supply of pure water.

It has fine statues of Lord Lister, Lord Kelvin and Thomas Carlyle with on the eastern heights a monument to Lord Robert of Kandahar. Copies of workers' cottages at Port

William Thomson, Lord Kelvin (1824–1901), physicist, university professor and the man behind the laying of the first transatlantic cable

Sunlight, designed by James Miller, still survive the 1901 Exhibition, sloped on the right bank. Framed, as it is, by the art galleries, Glasgow University and the outstanding conservation area of Park Circus, it is a remarkable example of urban landscaping.

Queen's Park was the next to be created, on the lands of Pathhead Farm – 143 acres, costing £30,000, Paxton again being the landscape architect. The queen commemorated is Mary, Queen of Scots, whose army was defeated at the Battle of Langside, on the southern side of the park, in 1560. The Camphill Estate was added in 1894, Camphill House becoming a museum two years later. It is now a museum of costume.

Next came Alexandra Park, bought by the City Improvement Trust in 1869, an additional five acres being gifted to add to the original thirty by Alexander Dennistoun, who now has a district named after him. Near the entrance is the fountain made in Walter Macfarlane's Saracen Foundry – he specialized in cannon when not making decorative park furniture! – for the 1901 exhibition.

Next came Cathkin Braes Park in 1886, seventy-two acres gifted by James Dick, one of two brothers who pioneered the use of gutta-percha, or rubber, for the soles of boots, a practice which made them rich. When opened, it then lay five miles outside the city boundary. From its heights, I am told, may still be seen (on a very good day) Arthur's Seat in Edinburgh, Goatfell on Arran, Ben Lomond and Ben Ledi to the north.

Maxwell Park was gifted to the burgh of Pollokshields by Sir John Stirling-Maxwell in 1878 and came into Glasgow by boundary extension in 1891. Similarly, Victoria Park was gifted to Partick in 1886 by Gordon Oswald of Scotstoun, becoming Glasgow's again through boundary extension in 1912. Part of it, unfortunately, was lost to provide an access road to the Clyde Tunnel in 1967.

The original purpose of the Botanic Gardens, off Great Western Road, was to provide a more extensive third botanical garden, the previous two having been on a small patch off the High Street, then an eight-acre site at Sandyford. The extension of the city westwards led to the purchase of twenty-two acres between Great Western Road and the Kelvin in 1839, laid out and opened in 1842 as the new Botanic Gardens. Access was free to members of the Royal Botanic Society and their friends, and admission cost one penny to everyone else. It was opened as a park in 1891.

The Kibble Palace is its most striking adornment. It was built at his Coulport, Loch Long, home by John Kibble (1818–94), son of the owner of a Paisley wire warehouse. Probably an engineer, Kibble once 'cycled' across Loch Long on a bicycle fitted with floats, and in 1858 built what was then the world's largest camera, mounted on wheels and horse-drawn, with a lens diameter of thirteen inches and negative plates weighing forty-four pounds.

His palace, an iron-framed conservatory designed by the Glasgow architects Boucher and Cousland and built by the Paisley firm of James Boyd and Sons, had a large circular dome connected by a short passage to a smaller one.

In 1871, he offered it to the Corporation for re-erection in Queen's Park. Kibble was to pay the cost of removal and re-erection, estimated at £1,500, and would contribute a further sum towards increasing the diameter of the main dome, retaining the lease for twenty-one years. The Corporation declined the offer.

Kibble then offered it to the Royal Botanical Society of Glasgow, which accepted. In 1871 it was dismantled and towed on rafts down Loch Long, up the Clyde and into the Kelvin. Re-erected, it now had an area of 23,000 square feet, one of the largest glasshouses in the United Kingdom. A promenade concert with an audience of 2,000 marked its opening in June 1873.

It became a venue for concerts, political meetings and for the inauguration of university rectors such as Disraeli in 1873 and Gladstone in 1879.

None of this public use improved the health of the plants, so in 1881, with a Corporation loan, the Botanic Society bought out the remainder of Kibble's lease, installing a heating system and returning the vast greenhouse to its original purpose. The result, however, was bankruptcy, so the Corporation, as the major creditor, took possession of the building and the grounds in 1887, the Botanic Gardens being handed out to the trustees for public use.

Later parks include Dawsholm (seventy-two acres, 1921), Hogganfield (144 acres, 1920), King's (ninety-eight acres, 1930) and Toryglen (forty-one acres, 1965).

I still remember my early impressions of the Kibble Palace, which, to a small boy, seemed a kind of cosy wonderland.

> Holding my uncle's hand, in the Kibble Palace
> we left coat-buttoned coldness sealed outside,
> as if it were some kind of fatal malice
> that statues, plants and goldfish can't abide.

The marble statues fixed unlikely poses,
caught blind-eyed in some ancient secret act
beyond what any six-year-old supposes;
topped high above the ferny bric-a-brac.

That islanded the pond where goldfish darted,
trees hung bananas underneath the roof;
glimpsed oranges and lemons, too, half-parted
their sheltered leafy branches, offering proof

fruit didn't grow in boxes. Left and right,
past KEEP SHUT signs, hothouses reached out arms,
and I was dazzled by the scent and sight
of coloured orchids kissing open charms.

Outside again where, meanwhile, Winter mouldered
the footprints of besmirching snow, the real
world moved about its dailyness, hunch-shouldered,
chilled by what flowers and statues never feel.

The City's finest park is surely Pollok (361 acres), gifted by Mrs
Anne Maxwell Macdonald from the Pollok Estate, which includes
Pollok House, built by William Adam in 1752 and still rich in fur-
nishings, decorations and paintings, especially of the Spanish
School. The magnificent art collection of shipowner Sir William
Burrell was gifted to the Corporation in 1944 and is located in
the prize-winning, custom-built Burrell Gallery on the estate, the
work of Barry Gasson.

XIV

I have left to the last the most widely popular of all Glasgow, indeed
Scottish, pastimes. Rugby, in which the Scots often distinguished
themselves, only made its entry into Scotland through the boarding
schools, mostly in Edinburgh, modelled on Dr Arnold's Rugby, while
cricket, though an ancient game, tended to be popular among the better off. Football, by contrast, became in the nineteenth century almost
the religion of the workers. It seems to have been a rough game from
the start, as an anonymous quatrain, 'The Bewties of the Futeball', collected in the Maitland Manuscript (1570–85), testifies:

Brissit brawnis and broken banes   [crushed muscles
Strife, discord, and wastit wanes   [children
Crookit in eild, syne halt withal   [age, lame
These are the bewties of the fute-ball.

By the time these lines were written, muscles must have become accustomed to the strain, for, in 1590, the city council, arranging a match, asked one John Neill to provide 'six guid and sufficient fut balles' for the same.

It has been suggested that there were three reasons for the growth of football in nineteenth-century Glasgow: first, the enormous increase in the working-class population in the city; second, the gradual reduction in working hours as the decades advanced, and third, the growth of cheap transport across the city, enabling fans to travel to 'away' matches. Football manager Bill Shankly (1913–81) perhaps summed up the Glaswegian's enthusiasm for the game when he quipped: 'Some people think football is a matter of life and death. I don't like that attitude. I can assure them it is much more serious than that.'

The oldest Glasgow club is Queen's Park, founded in 1867 by members of the Glasgow YMCA. A letter dated 29 July from Robert Gardner of Queen's Park, in reference to a challenge from a club called Thistle (not, however, Partick Thistle, which was not founded until 1876), suggested the tentative nature of what has been called (by Alan Bold) 'the first big Scottish match'.

> I have been requested by the Committee, on behalf of our club, to accept the challenge you kindly sent, for which we have to thank you, to play us a friendly Match at Football on our Ground, Queen's Park, at the hour you mentioned, on Saturday, first proxime, with Twenty players on each side. We consider, however, that Two hours is quite long enough to play in weather such as the present . . . Would you also be good enough to bring your ball with you in case of any break down, and thus prevent interruption.

On 13 March 1873, a group of local clubs, headed by Queen's Park, met in Dewar's Temperance Hall, Bridge Street, and formed the Scottish Football Association. Most of the others participating on that historic occasion have long since disappeared, but the Challenge Cup Trophy they established is still played for, though now called the Scottish Cup.

The Rangers were formed by a group of young men on Glasgow Green in 1872, while a Catholic priest, eager to provide an interest for the poor in the East End of the city, formed a team he called Celtic in 1887. Three years later, thirty-five clubs were registered in Glasgow.

Despite opposition from Queen's Park, Scottish football turned professional with the setting-up of a Scottish Football League in 1890, finally legally acknowledged by the Scottish Football Association in 1893. Rangers and Celtic first confronted each other on the field the following year, and quickly established themselves as Glasgow's most famous teams.

Unfortunately, religious connotations soon attached themselves to these two teams, Celtic's Catholic origins confirming the support of believers in that religion, while Rangers adopted Protestant blue as their colour and, until 1989, would not employ a Catholic player. Their annual game together on New Year's Day thus took on a totally irrelevant quasi-religious significance, on more than one occasion leading to crowd disorder.

The internationalizing of football in the post-war years has weakened local ties somewhat, but added pace and *élan* to the game. Rangers (Ibrox Stadium) tend to be the dominant Glasgow club, though Celtic (at Celtic Park) is never off its heels, so to say. As well as Queen's Park, other Glasgow Clubs include Clyde FC and Partick Thistle (who share Firhill Park). Third Lanark, the first club to turn professional, was wound up by order of the Court of Session in 1967.

Among the worst football disasters occurred at Ibrox in April 1902, when, during an England versus Scotland match, a wooden stand gave way before the pressure of a surging crowd. Twenty-four people were killed, twenty-four others seriously injured and nearly 500 suffered minor injuries.

Ibrox was the scene of an even worse disaster on 2 January 1971, during an Auld Firm match, when a late Rangers goal led to another crowd surge, resulting in sixty-six deaths and hundreds injured.

It was, however, the Hillsborough disaster in England that resulted in the Taylor Inquiry and the mandatory provision of seated accommodation for all spectators. No more can there be a repeat of the experience of my brother, among the standing spectators at a football match some years ago, when a wee Glasgow bauchle next to him, overcome by the need to pee, unzipped his trousers and let fly. Understandably, my brother, surprised, drew back. Said the bauchle, zipping himself up again, 'Whit's wrang wi' youse? Shoes leakin' or somethin'?'

To end on a more positive note, perhaps the last word should go to Sir Walter Scott, who, in 'Lines on the Lifting of the Banner at the House of Buccleugh, at a great football match at Carterhaugh' (1815), wrote:

> Then strip, lads and to it, though sharp be the weather,
> And if, by mischance, you should happen to fall,
> There are worse things in life than a tumble on heather,
> And life is itself but a game of football.

4   As Ithers See Us

I

PEOPLE TRAVEL FOR various reasons, though nowadays, I suppose, mostly to do business or go on holiday. Sometimes, however, in days gone by travel was taken for more sinister reasons.

John Hardying, for instance, spent three-and-a-half years in Scotland during the reign of James I (1406–37), having been sent north by Henry V and again by Henry VI to establish the distances between the most important places in Scotland and the conditions that a subduing army could expect to meet while moving, as it were, through enemy territory. On the whole, he reported a greater degree of prosperity than many of the historians who wrote of Scotland during the earlier part of the fifteenth century, finding the countryside around Glasgow 'replenished well with all commodities'.

One of the first tourists who came to Scotland was a thirty-year-old Cheshire nobleman and future parliamentary general in the English Civil War, Sir William Brereton (1604–66), known for his 'aversion to Church government'. He kept notes while he travelled and wrote up an account of his journey on the way home.

He reached Scotland from Berwick-upon-Tweed, crossing the border on 24 June 1634. In due course he rode on to Edinburgh, where he arrived at nine o'clock on Friday 26 June. There he greatly admired the 'very high and substantially built of stone' houses in the High Street, 'the most graceful street that ever I saw in my life'. While he thought the city 'placed in a dainty, healthful pure air and doubtless were a most healthful place to live in,' he thought the good burghers of Edinburgh 'slutish, nasty and slothful people . . . their houses and halls and kitchens have such a noisesome taste, and savour, and that so strong, as it doth offend you as soon as you come within the wall . . .'

On 1 July, he entered Glasgow by way of Kirkintilloch, Falkirk and Stirling. He thought Glasgow 'a brave and ancient place', observing that it had 'two streets like a cross, in the middle of both of which the Cross is placed, which looks four ways into four streets'. He viewed the city from the top of the Tolbooth tower, then only nine years old, admiring 'the Archbishop of Glasgow's Palace', on the site of what is now the Royal Infirmary; the old bridge over the Clyde, which, built around 1245, was to do duty for almost 600 years; and the Faculty of Arts, one side of which had been built. From Glasgow, Brereton journeyed to Irvine, admiring the view of Arran and Ailsa Craig on the way.

Thomas Tucker, whose birth and death dates are no longer known, in 1655 was the registrar to the commissioners for the Excise in England. In August of that year he was instructed to proceed to Scotland 'to give his assistance in setting the excise and customs there'. A conscientious civil servant, he tended to compare Scotland with England, usually to the latter's advantage. While he thought Scotland:

> naturally commodious for commerce and traffique, yet the barrenness of the county, poverty of the people, generally affected with slothe and a lazy vagrancy of attending and following theyr heards up and down in theyr pastorage, rather than any dextrous improvement of theyr time, hath quite banished all trade from the inland parts, and drove her down to the very sea-side, where the little is still remayning . . . lives pent and shutt up in a very small compasse.

The 'small compasse' he found to be the east coast and the Clyde, or 'Dunbryton Fyrth', as he called it.

Duly inspecting all the Scottish ports, he was impressed by the situation of Glasgow, in spite of the fact that 'no vessels of any burden' could come nearer than fourteen miles, noting that it was at Newark (now Port Glasgow) where 'all vessels doe ride, unlode, and send theyr goods up the river to Glasgow in small boates'.

Tucker's fellow Cromwellian Richard Frank (?1624–1708) while in Cromwell's army had also visited the Scottish ports five years earlier and had written rather fulsomely of the city, commenting on:

> the splendour and gaiety of this city of Glasgow, which surpasseth most, if not all the corporations in Scotland. Here it is you may observe four

large fair streets, modell'd, as it were, into a spacious quadrant; in the centre whereof their market-place is fix'd; near unto which stands a stately tolbooth, a very sumptious, regulated uniform fabrick, large and lofty, most industriously and artificially carved from the very foundation to the superstructure . . . infinitely excelling the model, and usual build of town-halls . . . without exception, the paragon of beauty in the west.

He noted that Glasgow was, even then, already a commercial city, writing of 'the merchants and traders . . . where store-houses and ware-houses are stuft with merchandize, as their shops swell big with foreign commodities, and returns from France and other remote parts . . . The staple of their country consists of linens, friezes, furs, tartans, pelts . . . They generally exceed in good French wines, as they naturally super-bound with fish and fowl.'

The first naturalist to visit Scotland was John Ray (1627–1705), an Essex man who graduated at Cambridge in 1649, was appointed to a minor fellowship, appointed lecturer in Greek in 1651, lecturer in Mathematics in 1653, reader in Humanity (Latin) in 1655, Praelector in 1657, Junior Dean in 1658 and a college steward in 1659. A year later he was ordained. In 1662, however, misfortune struck this multi-talented man, when he was deprived of his fellowship by the Act of Uniformity. Nothing daunted, he developed his gifts as a naturalist, making a botanical tour of the Midlands and North Wales. By the time he entered Scotland from the garrison town of Berwick-upon-Tweed on 17 August, he had already published *Catalogus plantarum circa Cantabrijum*, which listed and described 626 Cambridge plants, the first catalogue of the plants of a district to be issued in England. No wonder that when he died in 1705 he was dubbed 'the father of English naturalists'.

He had much to say about Dunbar, Leith, where one of Cromwell's forts then stood, Edinburgh, Linlithgow and Stirling, before he arrived in Glasgow on 22 August, finding it 'fair, large and well built, cross-wise, somewhat like unto Oxford, the streets very broad and pleasant'.

He noted that the cathedral was now called 'the High Kirk, and they have made two preaching places, one in the choir, and the other in the body of the church', apparently not noticing the third division. He admired the college, which he thought 'a pretty stone building, and not inferiour to Waltham and All Souls in Oxon', the Tolbooth, 'where courts are kept and sessions held', several 'fair hospitals' and the 'very long bridge of eight arches', before departing for Hamilton en route for Dumfries. He commented on the fact that the country abounded with 'poor people and beggars' and calculated that 'a shilling scotch (that is six bodels) equalled a penny sterling'.

Daniel Defoe (c. 1659–1731) of *Robinson Crusoe* fame, first came to Scotland as a spy, calling himself Alexander Goldsmith, the agent of Robert Harley, one of Queen Anne's most important ministers. He came to promote the Union, his instructions being 'to write constantly the true state of how you find things, at least once a week, and you need not subscribe any name . . .'. Defoe had by then been arrested, pilloried and put in prison for publishing a pamphlet against 'high flying Churchmen', *The Shortest Way with Dissenters*. Thanks to Harley, also a Whig dissenter, Defoe spent only five months in Newgate out of a seven-year sentence. He therefore had little option but to do Harley's subsequent bidding. A 'middle-sized spare man about forty years old, of a brown complexion and brown-coloured hair' with 'a hooked nose, a sharp chin, grey eyes, and a large mole near his mouth', he arrived on horseback in Edinburgh, by way of Leicester and Newcastle, on 6 October 1706.

Defoe described to Harley the way in which he set about his business:

> I converse with Presbyterian, Episcopal-Dissenter, Papist and Non-Juror, and, I hope, with equal circumspection. I flatter myself you will have no complaints about my conduct. I have faithful emissaries in every company, and I talk to everyone in their own way. To the merchants, I am about to settle here in trade, building ships, etc. With the lawyers, I want to purchase a house and land to bring my family and live upon it (God knows where the money is to pay for it). Today, I am going into partnership with a member of Parliament in a glass house, tomorrow with another in a salt work. With the Glasgow mutineers, I am to be a fish merchant, with Aberdeen men, a woollen and with the Perth and Western men, a linen manufacturer. And still at the end of all discourse, the Union is the essential, and I am still to everyone that I may gain some advantage.

When Defoe came back to Scotland as himself, he published a record of his four short visits between 1724 and 1726 in the third volume of his *Travels Through Great Britain*. Like most early travellers he entered Scotland from Berwick-upon-Tweed, though his itinerary included Ayrshire, Fife and the Borders.

He first came to Glasgow from Irvine, 'one of the most agreeable places in Scotland', crossing the Clyde 'dry-footed without the bridge', presumably at low tide, a reminder of the magnitude of the task undertaken by John Golborne of Chester in deepening the upper reaches of that river. On a subsequent visit, however, he crossed the bridge put up by Bishop Rae and Lady Lochow in 1345. Defoe noticed that the river not only 'filled up all the arches of the bridge, but running about the end of it, had filled the streets of all that part of the city next to the bridge, to the infinite damage of the inhabitants'.

Defoe obviously felt very much at home among Glaswegians, and the description that this shrewd man of business and observant journalist left of the place, a generation or two before the Industrial Revolution destroyed its beauty and utterly transformed it, is therefore especially interesting.

He noted that Glasgow was the only city in Scotland where both home and foreign trade were increasing, a fact he attributed to the Union, which 'the rabble of Glasgow made the most formidable attempt to prevent'. He visited 'sugar-baking houses' (refineries), a large distillery that made 'Glasgow brandy' from sugar molasses, a manufactory of tartan or plaiding, 'a stuff cross-striped with yellow and red, and other mixtures, for the plaids or vails which the ladies wear in Scotland'. He also inspected 'muslins of quality' destined for the English market.

He confirmed the beauty of Glasgow:

> The four principal streets are the finest for breadth and the finest built that I have ever seen in one city together. The houses are all of stone; and generally equal and uniform in height, as well as in front; the lower story generally stands on vast square Dorick columns, not round pillars and arches, which give passage to the shops adding to the strength as well as the beauty of the building. In a word, 'tis the cleanest and beautifullest and best built city in Britain, London excepted.

He admired the divided cathedral, and particularly the university, 'a very spacious building' containing 'two large squares, or courts, and the lodgings for the scholars, and for the professors . . . very handsome; the whole building is of freestone, very high and very august'.

He also envisaged linking the Forth and Clyde with a canal, so that Glasgow merchants could send their tobacco and sugar to Alloa by water, a project that was to be realized with the opening of John Smeaton's Forth and Clyde Canal in 1790.

It was with his friend John Golborne that Flintshire-born Thomas Pennant (1716–98) visited Loch Lomond from Glasgow in 1772. Oxford graduate, correspondent with the Swedish naturalist Linnaeus and elected a member of the Royal Society of Upsala, Pennant paid several visits, after being struck with the reflection, in 1769, of 'never having seen Scotland'.

He travelled widely in the north and east of Scotland, reaching as far as Caithness, on the Pentland Firth, where he had 'a full view of Orkney and Stroma'. He then came down the west coast via Inverary and Dumbarton, 'a small, but good old town' with a 'church with a small spire steeple' and its castle on 'a two-headed rock of stupendous size'. He crossed the River Kelvin at Partick on 8 September and so reached Glasgow:

> the best-built of any modern second-rate city I ever saw: the houses of stone, and in good taste. The principal street runs east and west and is near a mle and a half long; but unfortunately it is not strait. The Tolbooth is large and handsome. Next to that is the Exchange . . . Many of the houses are built over piazzas, but too narrow to be of much service to walkers. Numbers of other streets cross this at right angles.

This, indeed, is possibly the earliest reference to Glasgow's grid-street pattern, later copied in the United States.

Tobias Smollett (1721–71), a Dunbartonshire man, must have known Glasgow well. In his finest novel, *The Expedition of Humphry Clinker*, young Jerry Melford writes to an Oxford friend, and Matthew Bramble (his uncle and travelling companion) writes to his family doctor. Jerry Melford reports:

> Glasgow is the pride of Scotland, and, indeed, it might very well pass for an elegant and flourishing city in any part of Christendom . . . Considering the trade and opulence of the place, it cannot but abound in gaiety and diversions. Here is a number of young fellows that will rival the youth of the capital in spirit and expense; and I was soon convinced that all the female beauties of Scotland were not assembled at the hunters' ball in Edinburgh. The town of Glasgow flourishes in learning as well as in commerce. Here is an university with professors in all the different branches of science liberally endowed, and judiciously chosen . . . Their mode of education is certainly preferable to ours in

17–27 High Street, 1868, showing lodgings for those who could not afford the Tontine Hotel

some respects. The students are not left to the private instruction of tutors, but taught in public schools or classes, each science by its particular professor or regent. My uncle is in raptures with Glasgow . . .

Indeed he was, declaring:

I am so far happy as to have seen Glasgow, to the best of my recollection and judgement, it is one of the prettiest towns in Europe; and without all doubt, it is one of the most flourishing in Great Britain. In short, it is a perfect bee-hive of industry.

It stands partly on a gentle declivity; but the greatest part of it is plain, watered by the River Clyde. The streets are straight, open, airy, and well paved; and the houses lofty and well-built, of hewn stone. At the upper end of the town, there is a venerable cathedral, that may be compared with Yorkminster or Westminster; and, about the middle of the descent from this to the Cross, is the college, a respectable pile of building, with all manner of accommodation for the professors and students, including an elegant library and an observatory well provided with astronomical instruments.

The number of inhabitants is said to amount to thirty thousand; and marks of opulency and independency appear in every quarter of this commercial city, which, however, is not without its inconveniences and defects. The water of their public pumps is generally hard and brackish,* an imperfection the less excusable, as the River Clyde runs by their doors, in the lower part of the town; and there are rivulets and springs above the cathedral, sufficient to fill a large reservoir with excellent water, which might be thence distributed to all the different parts of the city. It is of more consequence to consult the health of the inhabitants in this article than to employ so much attention to beautifying their town with new streets, squares and churches.

Another defect, not easily remarked, is the shallowness of the river, which will not float vessels of any burden within ten or twelve miles of the city; so that the merchants are obliged to load and unload their ships at Greenock and Port-Glasgow, situated about fourteen miles nearer the mouth of the firth, where it is about two miles broad. The people of Glasgow have a noble spirit of enterprise.

There is an interesting early reference to Glasgow in the *Travel Diary*, published in 1732, of John Loveday, from the English Midlands. He was full of the then traditional praise for the city and its environs, calling it:

the chief city of the kingdom next to Edinburgh, delightfully situated in a plain and (for Scotland) fruitful country, is also a perfectly well-built city, divided into four parts by cross streets of a noble width, the houses of stone, most of them five stories high. These for a good way have very handsome piazzas of stone before the lower story, under which you may walk, free from rain or sunshine, but not more than two abreast . . .

The streets of the city are kept very clean. The houses discover a very different face from that you see without: they are contrived thus: the shops front the street; to get into the main house, go in at a narrow

* Prior, of course, to the inauguration of the Loch Katrine scheme, providing Glasgow with water noted for its softness.

entry, and there is a stone staircase on the right or left, such a staircase as you have in a church tower. This is the only one in the house: as it is therefore in common to all the families that live in the respective stories, you can't expect it very clean.

The era of Glasgow as the 'beautifullest little city', a description first bestowed on it in 1732 by John Mackay, ended with the turn of the century. The first *Statistical Account* of Sir John Sinclair, published in 1790, pointed to the inevitability of environmental change:

The variety of manufactures now carried on in Glasgow, which have extended in almost every branch, are very great; but that which seems, for some years past, to have excited the most general attention, is the manufacture of cotton cloths of various kinds, together with the arts depending on it. For this purpose cotton mills, bleachfields, and printfields, have been erected on almost all the streams in the neighbourhood, affording water sufficient to move the machinery, besides many erected at a very considerable distance; and though the number of these mills have increased greatly of late, yet they are still unable to supply the necessary quantity of yarn, required by the increased manufactures, as a considerable quantity is still daily brought from England. This trade not only employs a great number of persons in Glasgow, but is extended over a very large tract of country in the neighbourhood, many weavers being employed by the Glasgow manufacturers twenty and thirty miles from the city. In 1791, it was computed that they emloyed 15,000 looms; that each loom gave employment to nine persons at an average, including women and children, in the different stages of manufacture, from picking the cotton wool, until the goods were brought to market, making in all 135,000 persons; and that each loom at an average produced goods to the value of £100 *per ann*, making £1,500,000. The increase, since that calculation was made, has been very great; but to what extent it is at present carried on, cannot be said with any precision, for want of sufficient data.

About the year 1760, a very extensive brewery was erected near Anderston, from which large quantities of ale and porter were exported to Ireland and to America. Since that time, a number of others of the same kind have been erected in the city, and so great is the additional increase in the use of malt liquors, that most part of what they now manufacture, is consumed at home. As porter brewed in the city, and its vicinity, is now much more drunk in public houses by tradesmen, than formerly, it has consequently diminished the consumption of whisky, that article so destructive to the health and morals of the people, though still it is to be lamented, that so much of it is yet made use of.

The increased population of the city, arising from the various branches of manufactures established in it, has necessarily occasioned a greater dissoluteness of manners and more crimes; and hence the necessity of a bridewell, or workhouse, for the punishment and correction of lesser offences, became evident. This institution was begun in the year 1789, when, in order to try the effects of a plan of solitary confinement and labour, some buildings belonging to the city and formerly used as granaries, were fitted up as separate cells, for the confinement of persons guilty of crimes meriting such punishment. These have been gradually increased to the number of 64, where the prisoners are kept separate from one another, and employed in such labour as they can perform, under the management of a keeper, and under the inspection of a committee of council, who enquire into the keeper's management, etc. The members of the town council, also, in rotation are appointed to visit, not only this, but the prison and cells near the hospital, once every week, and report whatever appears to them proper, either to be rectified or altered. The keeper has a record of the sentences, on which each prisoner is confined – keeps an exact account of the wages of their labour, and after defraying the expense of their maintenance, the surplus is paid to them, when the period of their confinement expires; and some have received £5 to £7. Experience in this and other great towns, where this institution has been established, has demonstrated, that of all the species of punishment for offenders of a certain description, solitary confinement and labour is not only the most humane, but the best calculated to answer one great end of punishment, the amendment of the offender.

As to the manners of the people in general, they are, for the most part, industrious, and *still* economical. They are in general contented and happy in their situation. They grumble at taxes, and the high price of provisions; and some of the more ambitious wish for some more political consequence, than they at present enjoy, under the laws of the Scottish burghs; which they consider as confining the presentation of ministers, and the power of election and offices to a few, in exclusion of the rest, and these they wish to have put on a broader bottom. As they are getting rich, this desire will increase among the people; yet, notwithstanding, there is at present much difficulty to get proper per-

sons, of the merchant rank, to accept the offices of councillors and magistrates, almost every year furnishing instances of their paying a fine
rather than serve.

The American War, followed by the Napoleonic Wars, did, indeed,
put a strain on Glasgow's economic structure, several of the banks having to suspend dealings. But recovery was relatively swift, the process
of expansion, which was to last for three-quarters or so of the nineteenth century, being already under way and attracting immigrants
from the Highlands (fuelled to some extent by the cruel Highland
Clearances) and from Ireland, especially during the years of the potato famine.

The most famous hotel was, of course, the Tontine, which opened
in 1783. There stayed the Revd John Lettice (1737–1832), a Sussex
vicar, later chaplain to the Duke of Hamilton, as he recorded in his
Letters on a Tour through various parts of Scotland in the year 1789 (1794):

We entered the Tontine Hotel . . . a house of public accommodation,
worthy of this magnificent city. Its name imparts that it was built by
subscription, raised on the modern scheme of survivorship; and no small
sum must have sufficed to carry this establishment to its present state;
although the new stables and some other of its appendages, are yet
incomplete, or remain to be added. Several apartments, consisting of
large dining-rooms, bed-chambers, etc. neatly finished, and fit for the
reception of the most distinguished travellers, occupy a considerable
portion of a large court; removed backward from the noise of the street.
The rest of the house branches out in different directions; and contains
an infinity of rooms and offices on the several stories. But all were nearly full, or else previously engaged on our arrival, yesterday afternoon,
and we were uncertain for some hours whether beds could be found for
us within the precincts of the hotel. But an unexpected departure, or
two, toward the evening, fortunately made room.

We had time this morning to examine at leisure an important member of our hotel, which had, yesterday evening excited our curiosity, as
we contemplated it from our dining-room window opposite. A grand
bow, lighted by fine lofty sashes, projects into the court of the hotel: all
we could then perceive through them, was space apparently considerable, with a number of figures sitting, standing or walking about. On
entering we found a room of seventy or eighty feet in length, with cor-
responding dimensions of height and breadth; having another vast win-

dow on one of its sides, mingling its auxiliary light with those of the bow. This was no other than the great subscription coffee-room; supported by certain annual contributions of more than six hundred of the principal citizens of Glasgow and members of the university. Half the newspapers of London, the Gazettes from Ireland, Holland, France, and a number of provincial journals, and chronicles of Scotland and England, besides reviews, magazines, and other periodical publications, were objects of the Subscription. At the daily arrival of the post, a more stirring, lively, and anxious scene can hardly be imagined. But no part of the day passes without some concourse of subscribers, or of strangers at the hotel, whom their liberality permits freely to partake the benefit of the room. At those hours, when the news of the morning may be said to have grown cold, the monthly publications claim attention in their turn; people meet for the sake of looking up their acquaintance, or of engaging in casual parties of conversation.

The Tontine Hotel, incidentally, stood until 1912, when it was destroyed by fire.

Two of the most celebrated visitors to Glasgow were that extraordinary pair James Boswell (1740–95) and Dr Samuel Johnson (1709–84), who arrived in the city on 25 October 1773 on their way north. Boswell's *Journal of a Tour of the Hebrides* (1785) was his account of their adventures. Boswell's *Letters* were edited in 1924 and his *Notebook, 1776* the following year. About this time a considerable quantity of unpublished diaries and papers was discovered at his great-grandson's seat, Malahide Castle, in Ireland, several volumes of which have subsequently appeared.

In his *Journal of a Tour in the Hebrides*, Boswell records that 'The Professors of the University' – Johnson apparently found the conversation of both Thomas Reid and John Anderson, who held, respectively, the chair of moral philosophy and natural philosophy, disappointing –

Dr Stevenson, Dr Reid and Mr Anderson breakfasted with us. Mr Anderson accompanied us while Dr Johnson viewed this beautiful city. He had told me that one day in London, when Dr Adam Smith, then lecturing at the university on Rhetoric and Belles Lettres, was boasting of it, he turned to him and said, 'Pray, sir, have you ever seen Brentford?' This was surely a strong instance of his impatience and spirit of contradiction. I put him in mind of it today, while he expressed his admiration of the elegant buildings and whispered to him, 'Don't you feel some remorse?'

The Tontine Hotel, Glasgow's leading hotel for many years

In June 1787, Robert Burns stayed at the Black Bull Inn, in Argyle Street – a plaque on the wall of Marks and Spencer commemorates the occasion – where he met up with a Glasgow medical man, George Grierson. Grierson had been by far the largest Glasgow subscriber for the Kilmarnock edition of Burns's poems, taking thirty-six copies in all. Grierson accompanied Burns on his subsequent Highland trip, left an account of it and became a regular correspondent. Unfortunately, the letters were lost while in the possession of one John Reid of Kingston, being destroyed by flood waters when the Clyde rose alarmingly in 1831.

Burns is reputed to have bought some bolts of black silk to be sent to his mother and sisters for 'a bonnet and a cloak to each'. He also received an order from John Smith, the bookseller, for fifty copies of the second edition of his poems, which he sent to Creech, his Edinburgh publisher to have fulfilled.

He had several further, mostly overnight, stays in the city, on one occasion in 1788 apologizing to his friend Captain Richard Brown for having failed to get him a copy of a directory of Glasgow; on another, picking up from the booksellers Dunlop and Wilson in the Trongate a parcel of books for his Edinburgh mistress, Nancy Maclehose. He did, however, dispatch by carrier a supply of cocoa to another friend, William Cruickshank, and order a further fifteen yards of black lustre silk from Robert McIndoe's establishment at Horn's Land, off Virginia Street, this time for his wife.

Burns's other connections with Glasgow were indirect. Elizabeth, 'Dearbought Bess', his illegitimate daughter by Anna Park, married John Thomson, a Pollokshaws weaver, and died a widow in 1873, when she was buried alongside her husband in the Old Vennel Burying Ground. Nancy 'Clarinda' Maclehose (1759–1841), the daughter of a Glasgow surgeon, after her desertion by her husband (just before she met Burns), was dependent on two Glasgow annuities, one from the Royal Faculty of Physicians and the other from the Royal Faculty of Procurators.

Sir Walter Scott (1771–1832) knew Glasgow and its ways, being frequently there on legal business, attending the old Court House in Jail Square. He liked to stay at 'a quaint hostelry' in King Street, according to Lockhart, 'the Institution, where the Sheriff met, ate a chop and drank wine' with the prototypes of Baillie Nicol Jarvie, MacVittie and MacFinn.

He frequently visited Ross Priory on the shores of Loch Lomond. It was considerably enlarged by Hector Macdonald Buchanan, an Edinburgh Writer to the Signet – the posh Edinburgh term for a lawyer – and a friend of Scott. It is said that he stayed there when researching the setting for his poem *The Lady of the Lake*, and that in 1817 he wrote part of *Rob Roy* also at the priory. It is in that novel that Baillie Nicol Jarvie makes a splendid defence of Scotland's ability to trade, over a bowl of punch.

When the cloth was removed, Mr Jarvie compounded with his own hands a very small bowl of brandy-punch, the first of which I had ever the fortune to see.

'The berries,' he assured us, were from his 'own little farm yonder-awa' (indicating the West Indies with a knowing shrug of his shoulders), and he had learned the art of composing the liquor from 'auld Captain Coffinkey, who acquired it,' he added in a whisper, 'as maist folk thought, among the buccaneers. But it's excellent liquore,' said he, helping us round; 'and good ware has aften come frae a wicked market . . .'

We found the liquor exceedingly palatable, and it led to a long con-versation between Owen and our host, on the opening which the Union afforded to trade between Glasgow and the British colonies in America and the West Indies and on the facilities which Glasgow pos-sessed of making up sortable cargoes for that market. Mr Jarvie answered some objection which Owen made on the difficulty of sorting a cargo for America, without buying from England, with vehemence and volu-bility.

'Na, na, sir, we stand on our ane bottom – we pickle our ain pock neuk – we hae our Stirling serges, Musselburgh stuffs, Aberdeen hose, Edinburgh shalloons and the like, for our woollen or worsted goods – and we hae linens of a' kinds better and cheaper than you hae in Lunnon itsel – and we can buy your north o' England wares, or Manchester wares, Sheffield wares, and Newcastle earthenware, as cheap as you can at Liverpool – and we are making a fair spell at cot-tons and muslins. – Na, na! Let every herring hing by its ain head, and every sheep by its ain shank, and ye'll find, sir, us Glasgow folk no sae far ahint but what we may follow.'

It was an account of Staffa by the president of the Royal Society, Sir Joseph Banks, which Thomas Pennant had included in his *Tour of Scotland*, that stimulated one of the liveliest and most likeable of French diarists to visit the Hebrides. Bartholemy Faujas de Saint Fond (1741–1809) was born in the old town of Montelemart, in the valley of the Rhône. His family owned the lands of Saint Fond, in Dauphine, from which he took the territorial part of his name.

From the Jesuit College of Lyons, where he received his early schooling, he went to Grenoble, where he studied law, in due course qualifying as an advocate. When still only twenty-four, he became president of the Seneschal Court.

Law, however, was not to be his ultimate career. He came strongly under the influence of Buffon, the outstanding French naturalist of his day. Buffon was no doubt in part responsible for Saint Fond's appoint-ment as assistant naturalist at the Museé d'Histoire Naturelle in Paris, with a yearly salary of 6,000 francs (then worth about £240), later aug-mented by a further 4,000 francs when he was appointed royal com-missionaire of mines. He eventually became professor of geology at the museum.

In 1778, he published a treatise setting out his views on the volcanic nature of hills. His curiosity aroused by Banks's description of the columnar structure of Staffa, he set out for Scotland.

Having been down a coal mine when in Newcastle, Saint Fond travelled by way of Wooler, entering Scotland through Cornhill; on reaching Edinburgh he settled into Dunn's Hotel, 29 St Andrew's Square. He published his account of his Scottish journey as *Travels in England, Scotland and the Hebrides* in 1799.

As a geologist he collected specimens wherever he went. 'The environs of Glasgow,' he observed, 'present a fertile field of observation, by assemblages of pitcoal, freestone, calcareous stones and volcanic productions within a very short distance of each other'.

Two diarizing travellers arrived in Scotland in 1803: Dorothy Wordsworth, with her brother William, originally came to Scotland to do homage at the grave of Robert Burns, in Dumfries; and the St Andrews-educated Revd James Hall (later chaplain to the Earl of Caithness), who travelled round the coast, publishing his observations in his *Travels in Scotland* (1807).

Dorothy Wordsworth's *Recollections of a Tour Made in Scotland A.D. 1803* was first published in 1874, but, reprinted in our own day, has become something of a classic of its kind. She had a sharp eye, both for people and places. Travelling in a jaunting car, they reached Glasgow on 23 August – actually, the poet's second visit, for he had come to Glasgow briefly two years earlier to attend a friend's wedding.

Dorothy chronicled their joint arrival:

The suburbs of Glasgow extend very far, houses on each side of the highway – all ugly, and the inhabitants dirty. The roads are very wide; and everything seems to tell of the neighbourhood of a large town. We were annoyed by carts and dirt, and the road was full of people, who all noticed our car in one way or another and the children often sent a hooting after us.

Wearied completely, we at last reached the town, and were glad to walk, leading the car to the first decent inn, which was luckily not far from the end of the town. William, who gained most of his road-knowledge from ostlers, had been informed of this house by the ostler at Hamilton; it proved quiet and tolerably cheap, a new building, the Saracen's Head. I shall never forget how glad I was to be landed in a little quiet back-parlour, for my head was beating with the noise of the carts which we had left, and the wearisomeness of the disagreeable objects near the highway; but with my first pleasant sensations also came the feeling that we were not in an English inn – partly from its half-furnished appearance, which is common on Scotland, for in general the deal wainscots and doors are unpainted, and partly from the dirtiness of the floors. Having dined, William and I walked to the post-office, and after much seeking found out a quiet timber-yard wherein to sit down and read our letter. We then walked a considerable time in the streets, which are perhaps as handsome as streets can be, which derive no particular effect from their situation in connection with natural advantages, such as rivers, sea or hills. The Trongate, an old street, is very picturesque – high houses, with a mixture of gable fronts towards the street. The New Town is built of fine stone in the very best style of the very best London streets at the west end of the town, but not being of brick, they are greatly superior. One thing must strike every stranger in his first walk through Glasgow – an appearance of business and bustle, but no coaches or gentlemen's carriages; during all the time we walked in the streets I saw only three carriages, and these were travelling chaises. I also could not but observe a want of cleanliness in the dress and outside of the whole mass, as they moved along. We returned to the inn before it was dark. I had a bad headache, and was tired, and we all went to bed soon.

Next day, duly refreshed, they explored further, beginning with Glasgow Green.

A cold morning. Walked to the bleaching-ground, a large field bordering on the Clyde, the banks of which were perfectly flat, and the general face of the country is nearly so in the neighbourhood of Glasgow. This field, the whole summer through, is covered with women of all ages, children, and young girls spreading out their linen, and watching it while it bleaches. The scene must be very cheerful on a fine day, but it rained when we were there, and though there was linen spread out in all parts, and great numbers of women and girls were at work, yet there would have been many more on a fine day, and they would have appeared happy, instead of stupid and cheerless. In the middle of the field is a wash-house, whither the inhabitants of this large town, rich and poor, send or carry their linen to be washed. There are two very large rooms, with each a cistern in the middle for hot water; and all round the rooms are benches for the women to set their tubs upon. Both the rooms were crowded with washers; there might be a hundred, or two, or even three; for it is not easy to form an accurate notion of so great a number; however, the rooms were large and they were both full. It was amusing to see so many women, arms, head, and face all in motion, all busy in an ordinary household employment, in which we are accustomed to see, at the most, only three or four women employed in one place. The women were very civil. I learned from them the regula- tions of the house; but I have forgotten the particulars. The substance of them is, that 'so much' is to be paid for each tub of water, 'so much' for a tub, and the privilege of washing for a day, and, 'so much' to the general overlookers of the linen, when it is left to be bleached. An old man and woman have this office, who were walking about, two melan- choly figures.

The shops at Glasgow are large, and like London shops, and we passed by the largest coffee-room I ever saw. You look across the piazza of the Exchange, and see to the end of the coffee-room, where there is a circular window, the width of the room. Perhaps there might be thir- ty gentlemen sitting on the circular bench of the window, each reading a newspaper. They had the appearance of figures in a fantocine, or men seen at the extremity of the opera-house, diminished into puppets.

I am sorry I did not see the High Church: both William and I were tired, and it rained very hard after we had left the bleaching-ground; besides, I am less eager to walk in a large town than anywhere else; so we put it off, and I have since repented of my resolution.

Dined, and left Glasgow at about three o'clock, in a heavy rain.

Some schoolboys were fascinated by the unusual sight of the Wordsworths' jaunting car and longed to jump aboard as it drove out westwards through the city.

At last, though we were seated, they made several attempts to get on behind; and they looked so pretty and wild, and at the same time so modest, that we wished to give them a ride, and there being a little hill near the end of the town, we got off, and four of them who still remained, the rest having dropped into their homes by the way, took our places, and indeed I would have walked two miles willingly, to have had the pleasure of seeing them so happy. When they were to ride no longer, they scampered away, laughing and rejoicing.

From Glasgow they drove to Dumbarton, admiring Lord Blantyre's Erskine House, across the Clyde, and finding Dumbarton Rock 'not grand, but curiously wild'. They travelled on the next day through the Vale of Leven paying tribute while there to the monument to the novelist Tobias Smollett, to Luss on Loch Lomond, and then on to the Trossachs and the Highlands.

Revd James Hall, who admitted to 'a propensity to prattle', though determined to observe 'the notions, customs and follies of the people', lacked both Dorothy's acuteness of perception and her easy literary style. It is perhaps odd that Hall, being a churchman, should land at Glasgow on a Sunday, but at least he could gratify his professional propensities, because:

> on one side of the street, almost in every house, I heard psalms singing and fervent prayers ascending to the father of the universe, while, on the other, there was nothing to be heard but swearing, blaspheming, and the most obscene and abusive language. In short, the one side of the street, if appearances were not false, might be called the temples of the Holy Ghost; the other . . . the hotbeds of the devil. And it was astonishing to see in some places a set of drunkards and debauchers reeling from the bagnios and, at others, numbers going leisurely home with their Bible under their arm . . .

The good divine is perhaps more convincing when he records the changing circumstances of Glasgow:

> The prosperity of Glasgow is truly astonishing, and shews what industry can do . . . But commerce and manufacturers have their inconveniences, and there is two good reasons to conclude, that though the external circumstances of the common people are considerably bettered by them, yet their morals are not. The manners of the common people here were certainly never so profligate; and their high wages but serve to furnish too many of them with the means of becoming more wicked . . . Nay, so abandoned are some of the lower orders about Glasgow, that, on a Sunday afternoon, in the Green, which is a large meadow, with public walks, belonging to the citizens at large, and where hundreds are assembled, after having, for the special purpose, formed a ring, only a few yards diameter, one of the inhabitants, with an abandoned woman that had agreed to it, while his companions and those forming the ring continued to shout and applaud him, did what, even cats, elephants, and many other of the inferior animals avoid in public, for a scotch pint of gin.

Nay, indeed! Whatever would Dorothy Wordsworth have said? In the year that she and William made their Scottish tour, one of the earliest writers of guide books about Scotland, the Honourable Mrs Murray of Kensington, published the second edition of her remarkably titled, *A Companion and Useful Guide to the Beauties of Scotland, to the Lakes of Westmorland, Cumberland and Lancashire: and to the Curiosities of the District of Craven in the West Riding of Yorkshire, to which is added, a more particular Description of Scotland, especially that part of it called the Highlands.* The first edition had appeared in 1799 and a third edition, which came out in 1810, the year before her death, also contained a survey of new and recent roads.

Born in 1744, Sarah Murray married, first, the Honourable William Murray, younger brother of the Earl of Dunmore. After his death in 1768, she married George Aust but kept her aristocratic name for literary purposes.

Of her qualifications as an authoress she declared: 'I have no wings to soar the heights, no talents to tread the wild path of imagination; but having a little of *ce gros bon sens qui court les rues*, I am able to relate in my own fashion, what my eyes have seen.'

She travelled in a specially equipped chaise, entering Scotland through Longtown and driving along the Border Esk to Langholm, 'a drive that must give pleasure and satisfaction to anyone who has a taste for natural beauty'. Hawick and Selkirk were visited on the way to Edinburgh, where she heard Burns's pompous mentor, Dr Hugh Blair, preach at the age of eighty-one.

After exploring Edinburgh thoroughly, she crossed the Forth at Queensferry, driving along the foot of the Ochils, to inspect the ruins of Castle Campbell at Dollar. Stirling, Doune, Callandar, the Trossachs, Loch Katrine (on which she got a boatman to row her), Comrie, Crieff, Perth, Scone, Blair Atholl, Aviemore, Fort George and Inverness were all on her itinerary. She made the return journey by Inverary and Loch Lomond – the drive down which was 'superbly beautiful' – to Dumbarton, where she had to yield up her sketch book before being allowed up to the castle; and so on to Glasgow.

'Glasgow is amazingly large,' she recorded. 'I was there eleven years previous to this tour, and I could hardly believe it possible for a town to be so altered and enlarged as I found it to be in 1791. Its situation is very fine; but the town is like all other great manufacturing towns; with inhabitants very rich, saucy and wicked.'

The entrance to the Old College, regarded as one of the city's finest buildings

Born in 1751, Thomas Thornton, of Thornville Royal in Yorkshire, was the son of a soldier and member of parliament for York. Young Thornton left Charterhouse to finish his education at Glasgow College. Twenty-seven years after his birth, he returned as a sportsman, afterwards publishing *A Sporting Tour Through the Northern Parts of England and Great Part of the Highlands of Scotland*, when it was rather unfavourably reviewed by the then Mr Walter Scott:

> The performance is termed a Sporting Tour, not because it conveys to the reader any information, new or old, upon the habits of the animals unfortunate enough to be distinguished as *game*, nor even upon the modes to be adopted in destroying them *secundem artem*; but because it contains a long, minute and prolix account of every grouse or blackcock which had the honour to fall by the gun of our literary sportsman – of every pike which gorged his bait – of every bird which was pounced by his hawks – of every blunder which was made by his servants – and of every bottle which was drunk by his friends.

Hardly a review likely to sell many copies: but happily, Thornton's account of his visit to Glasgow is rather more lively than his usual manner, which so aroused Scott's ire.

Thornton arrived in Glasgow on 17 June, along the road from Edinburgh via Kirk o' Shotts, noting how the city was bounded by 'the delightful hills of Campsey'. He admired 'the villas, whimsically built according to the taste of their respective proprietors', making 'the approach to that magnificent city truly noble'.

His first day in Glasgow was spent in inspecting with his companions 'the regularity of the streets and universal magnificence of the buildings' In the evening they were invited to a ball. 'The ballroom was elegantly fitted up, and my companions agreed that handsomer women, or, in general, better dressed, were not to be met with; their style of dancing, however, quite astonished these *southrons*, scarce able to keep sight of their fair partners.'

The ladies retired at three in the morning, but the gentlemen stayed on 'to pay the proper compliment of toasting their respective partners'. Thornton was 'detained', against his wishes, 'till six in the morning, and then got away, leaving the majority by no means disposed to retire'.

Another day was spent taking a walk around Glasgow Green:

a large spacious piece of ground, not unlike a park, being walled in, except to the west, which is girded by the river Clyde. This piece of ground has a very excellent walk in it, and is the mall to the town. In the centre stands a very useful square building, inclosing a court, where the washer-women reside, and dress and dry their linen.

The soil of this green is very rich, and affords excellent pasturage for large herds of cows, and here the gentlemen resort to follow their favourite amusement, the game of golf, which is universal throughout Scotland, as well as Holland . . . It is a wholesome exercise for those who do not think such gentle sports too trivial for men, being performed with light sticks and small balls, and is by no means so violent an exertion as cricket, trapball or tennis.

After breakfast, he visited the college, 'a piece of architecture in no respect extraordinary.' (One must allow for the predilections of Georgian taste, together with the feelings for his *alma mater*, of one who may not have been a notable scholar, though Thornton claimed to have spent 'many, many happy hours' within its walls.) He then went to see the 'High Church', as he dubbed the cathedral, 'that great, stupendous, and inelegant pile of building'. This day was rounded off attending a private dinner at the newly opened Tontine Hotel, in Argyle Street. Thornton thought the famous coffee-room 'very elegant indeed, but much too large for the company likely to resort to it' – he was wrong in this verdict, for it became the most fashionable resort of its kind in the city – but was full of praise for a meal which included 'turtle and every other luxury in provisions'.

A day or two was spent fishing for pike and perch in Bardowie Loch, a few miles north west of Glasgow – he caught ten pike and two perch at one session. Then, on 27 June, the party set out for Luss. Even this short journey in these days was not without its hazards, for, Thornton recalls, they:

came to Kelvin, but found the bridge over the river had been broken down, and, though newly repaired, was scarcely passable: we had the prudence under these circumstances, to get out of the carriage, and by that means probably saved our lives, as the shaft-horse swerved, when half-across, in such a manner that it was impossible but that, with our additional weight, he would, otherwise, have gone over, and we must have been dashed to pieces in the torrent below, foaming at a tremendous distance with the agitations occasioned by the preceding heavy rains.

In due course they reached Dumbarton, which they had expected to reach before a gathering shower broke:

> But we were mistaken, for, at the distance of about half a mile, a sudden jerk broke the traces, owing to the neglect of the groom, who had not sufficiently attended to my constant orders to examine every part of the carriage, harness, etc., most minutely, and particularly so when entering the Highlands, where no assistance could be expected but from our own ingenuity.
>
> We inquired for a cobbler, as the likeliest person to assist us, and having found one, in quarter of an hour the damage was repaired. It now rained pretty freely, but we went on at a good trot, and got to Dumbarton tolerably wet, but were nevertheless much pleased with the indistinct view of the castle, Clyde, etc., seen through the heavy vapours that surrounded them.

On his way back South it 'blew a hurricane' as Thornton arrived at Tarbet on Loch Lomond, giving him 'an opportunity of admiring the dreadful magnificence of the lake, the waves ran mountains high, and from freshwater waves breaking so much shorter than salt, they were infinitely more dangerous.'

Calling on Sir James Colquhoun at Luss and, after crossing the Clyde by ferry, the Earl of Glencairn at Finlaystone House, Thornton then made leisurely progress homewards, through Hamilton, where the Duke of Hamilton entertained him, Lanark, Edinburgh, Kelso and Hawick. He crossed back into England at Gretna.

Another Laker, Robert Southey (1774–1843), visited Glasgow in 1819, when he undertook a tour in the company of the great engineer Thomas Telford (1757–1834), who was inspecting his works in person, the principal one being the construction of the Caledonian Canal. On their return journey they travelled by Loch Long, Loch Lomond and Dumbarton where Southey saw 'several steamboats . . . plying on the Clyde' having previously seen one 'smoking before the window' at Arrochar, on Loch Long.

'A city like Glasgow,' Southey wrote, 'is a hateful place for a stranger, unless he is reconciled to it by the comforts of hospitality and society. In every case the best way is to reconnoitre it, so as to know the outline and outside, and to be contented with such other information as books can supply.' He thought Argyle Street 'a mixture of old and new buildings, but long enough and lofty enough to be one of the

A typical crowd of shoppers in busy Argyle Street, *c.* 1930

best streets in Great Britain'. Southey also admired the cathedral, which he wrongly thought 'the only edifice of its kind in Scotland which received no exterior injury at the Reformation'.

Inside, he thought the seats 'so closely packed that any person who could remain there during the time of service, must have an invincible nose'.

The Hungarian composer Franz Liszt was a world-famous musician who in 1814 played in Glasgow, when he was twenty-nine. He had played in Dublin with a group of musicians. The Ireland and Scotland trips had been organized by the impresario John Orlando Parry, himself a composer and instrumentalist.

They crossed from Donoghadee in the packet boat *St Patrick*. After a good deal of pitching and heaving, the little steamer bumped up the Galloway beach. A number of Irish immigrants, who also had been ill on the voyage, staggered ashore, followed by 'Four Englishmen, a Welshman, and a foreigner', the foreigner being Franz Liszt. The harbour-master was waiting with planks for their carriage to be rolled ashore, but such was the state of the waves crashing up the beach that the musicians decided to leave its disembarkation till the following day.

They repaired to Gordon's Hotel, which stood above the harbour, and signed the visitor's book, Liszt's signature scrawling over most of a newly-turned page.

Liszt had been living in semi-retirement from the piano virtuoso round (although he was still composing) in Switzerland with one of his mistresses. He was now said by those who had known him to be handsomer than ever before.

Next day, 18 January, a sleety gale greeted him when they looked out of the hotel – but whisky for breakfast cheered up the party and they decided to set out for Glasgow.

By midday, however, their safely disembarked carriage had slowly struggled through snowy mud on the road to Stranraer. At Cairnryan, the horses were too exhausted to attempt the hilly haul up to Ballantrae and no fresh horses were available. 'Liszt in a passion', Parry recorded in his diary, but there was nothing for it but to go back to Stranraer in the hope of getting another sailing to Ayr.

Liszt fell asleep in the carriage and rather than risk his anger again, the others left him sleeping when the carriage was parked in the stables at Stranraer.

In the middle of the night they were told that the *Sir William Wallis* (as Parry misspelt it) was loading for Ayr. With Liszt still asleep inside, the others pushed the carriage aboard her, there being no other help available. It was a further three hours before the boat could sail. Liszt, now awake, huddled under the funnel for warmth.

When they arrived at Ayr, the Glasgow train was just steaming out. As they were supposed to be giving a concert in Glasgow that afternoon, the journey over Fenwick Moor by coach would have taken too long, so Parry arranged for them to travel on a cattle train leaving at 11 a.m., to which a few third-class coaches were added – in these early railway days, open wagons with planks.

Even so, the Glasgow concert had to be postponed. The party travelled in their coach overnight to Edinburgh, arriving at the Royal Hotel in Prince's Street at 5 a.m. They gave an afternoon concert in Edinburgh, returning to Glasgow for the postponed concert there. It was back to Edinburgh next day for a third concert, then a trek over to Glasgow again for a fourth – unpleasant journeys with rain and sleet so violent that they feared the carriage windows might break.

Robert Adam's Assembly Rooms, the Ingram Street frontage

The Edinburgh concerts were given in the Assembly Rooms in George Street, the Glasgow ones in Adam's Assembly Rooms in George Square, later demolished to make way for the General Post Office (itself, at the moment of writing, about to be redeveloped or replaced).

The musicians, it seemed, liked Glasgow's George Hotel, where the late-night snacks of toasted cheese met with their particular approval.

When in Edinburgh, Liszt visited the Calton Hill and the castle esplanade and gave his farewell concert in the Hopetoun Rooms before an audience of 400 – the largest of the Scottish tour. Afterwards, he had dinner with one Miss Steele and her mother.

The Scottish tour ended with a final departure from Edinburgh on 23 January, their carriage leaving the George Hotel at 2 a.m. in a snowstorm.

A crowd gathered to see him and the others off when their coach, drawn by four white horses, set out next morning down the Great Post Road for Newcastle and London. Promising to return, though he never did, the composer set off to the strains of 'Auld Lang Syne' from the crowd.

The twenty-year-old composer Felix Mendelssohn (1809–47), in company with his closest friend Karl Klingeman (1798–1862) came to Scotland in the late spring of 1829. Klingeman, then twenty-seven years old, the son of a minor dramatist who provided the composer

Marschner with the libretto for his opera *Das Schloss an Aetna*, later became a diplomat. On their Scottish tour he chronicled their trip in a series of letters, while Mendelssohn filled a sketchbook.

They left London on 28 July on the post coach, arriving in Edinburgh a week later. Edinburgh delighted them both, although they just missed seeing Sir Walter Scott when they visited Abbotsford. They went to the Highlands, visiting Blair Atholl, Inverness, Staffa, Mull and Iona. It was on this trip that Mendelssohn had the germ idea for his *Hebrides*, or *Fingal's Cave* overture (as it is sometimes named). On the return trip, through Inverary, they sailed down Loch Eck and in another steamer arrived by boat in Glasgow, which they reached on 10 August. Klingeman wrote:

> Sitting as we are now, in the best hotel of a commercial town, which has a university and common manufacturers, and coffee and sugar at first hand, we look back with equanimity on past distance. The Highlands, however, and the sea brew nothing but whisky and bad weather. Here, it is different and smooth, but comfortable. With a blue sky overhead and a good sofa underneath, palatable victuals before and ministering spirits around us, we brave all dangers, particularly the past ones.
>
> In Glasgow, there are seventy steam-boats, forty of which start every day, and many long chimneys smoking. An excellent inn refreshes us. The waiters minister to us with two hands and as many feet, as steam-service in hotels has not yet been invented.

Later he added:

> We have seen and admired Glasgow. This morning we were in a stupendous cotton mill as full of maddening noise as the divine waterfall of Monass. What is the difference to the ear?
>
> One old wash-woman wore a wreathe of cotton, another had tied up her aching tooth with it. Hundreds of little girls toil there from their earliest days, and look yellow.

Next day, Mendelssohn related, they made an excursion of a few days to Loch Lomond, where they had:

> weather to make the trees and rocks crash. The day before yesterday on Loch Lomond, we were sitting in deep twilight in a small rowing boat and were going to cross to the opposite shore, invited by a gleaming

light, when there came a sudden tremendous gust of wind from the mountains. The boat began to see-saw so fearfully that I caught up my cloak and got ready to swim. All our things were thrown topsy-turvy and Klingeman anxiously called to me, 'Look sharp, look sharp', but with our usual good luck we got safely through.

Just before they 'flew away from Glasgow on the top of the mail, ten miles an hour, past steaming meadows and smoking chimneys to the Cumberland Lakes,' Mendelssohn gave his verdict on their Scottish tour:

It is no wonder that the Highlands have been called melancholy. But two fellows have wandered merrily about them, laughed at every opportunity, rhymed and sketched together, growled at one another and at the world when they happened to be vexed or did not find anything to eat, devoured everything eatable when they did find it, and slept twelve hours every night. These two were we, who will not forget it as long as we live.

Hans Anderson (1805–75) stayed briefly in Glasgow, as did Queen Victoria, on one of her earliest visits north. On her first visit she sailed into Glasgow Harbour in August 1849, aboard the royal steam yacht *Fairy*. She visited the cathedral and the university and knighted the provost before departing from Queen Street Station for Balmoral. On her first visit she had thought Glasgow 'handsome . . . with fine streets built in stone, and many fine buildings and churches. We passed over a bridge commanding an extensive view down two quays, which Albert said were very like Paris. There are many large shops and warehouses, and the shipping is immense.'

William Cobbett (1763–1835) came to Scotland in 1832 to see how the newly passed Reform Act had affected Glasgow, which he thought 'a city of the greatest beauty, a commercial town and a place of manufacture. Manchester and Liverpool in one.' Thomas de Quincy (1785–1850), the opium eater, spent his later years in Edinburgh, but between 1841 and 1843 stayed in Glasgow with two of the university professors, and again in 1847, to escape his Edinburgh creditors.

Charles Dickens (1812–70) paid several visits to Glasgow. He came in 1847, invited to be the principal speaker at the opening of the old Athenaeum, in Ingram Street. Subsequently, he was guest of honour at a 'grand soirée', held in the City Hall. He was delighted with the dinner provided by the Corporation, declaring that: 'Unbounded hospitality and enthoosymoozy was the order of the day.' Sir Archibald Alison, the Sheriff of Lanarkshire, proposed a toast in the novelist's honour. Dickens replied: 'I am no stranger to the warmth of Scottish hands and hearts; but the warmth with which you have responded to the proposal just made deprives me of the power of expressing my gratitude.'

He returned the following year in the role of actor, the leading player in his Company of London Amateurs, then touring several major cities to raise money for the purchase of Shakespeare's house in Stratford. Dickens appeared twice on the boards of the old Theatre Royal in Dunlop Street, as Slender in *The Merry Wives of Windsor*. They drew £681.17s.8d., the highest box-office return of the tour. Dickens donated some of the profits for the relief of Glasgow's unemployed.

He first appeared in the city as a reader of his own works in 1858, an occasion which netted him £600. 'I wish you could have seen them,' he declared in a letter to a friend,

> after Lilian died in 'The Chimes', or when Scrooge woke in the 'Carol' and talked to the boy outside the window. At the end of 'Dombey' yesterday in the cold light of day, they all got up, after a short pause, gentle and simple, and thundered and waved their hats with such astonishing heartiness and fondness that, for the first time in my public career, they took me completely off my legs, and I saw the whole eighteen hundred of them reel to one side as if a shock had taken the hall.

In the same year he was nominated by the students of the university as lord rector, but did not accept, as 'the trouble with his wife' – daughter of George Thomson of Edinburgh, for some of whose *Select Scottish Airs* Burns had provided the words – was beginning to be talked about, gossip which later thinned the audiences for his Scottish readings.

By December 1861, however, he had come to dislike Glasgow's weather, as he told Mrs Fields, the wife of his American publisher. 'The atmosphere of this place, confounded mists from the Highlands and smoke from the factories, is crushing my eye-brows as I write, and it rains as it never does rain anywhere else and always does rain here. It is a dreadful place, though much improved and possessing a deal of public spirit.'

He made his final Glasgow appearance in 1869.

William Makepeace Thackeray (1811–63) came to Glasgow in 1852 to deliver a series of four lectures. He left a fairly full account of his views, not only on Glasgow, but also upon the place of literature in the affairs of life. Working on his novel *Henry Esmond* at the time, he recorded his views in a letter to his friend Dr John Brown.

Thackeray did not like 'the number of Irishmen [sic] and women' in the city, finding that their faces repelled him and made him 'uncomfortable' – an aversion, it seems, that also affected him when he was in Dublin, and which he was not 'able to account for . . . philosophically'.

Turning to Glasgow itself, he went on:

What a hideous smoking Babel it is, after the clear London atmosphere quite unbearable . . . I look forward with some terror to a stay of 15 days here. But I won't move unless I find the place intolerable, and tolerable I confess it is not.

I am well into Vol III (of *Esmond*) and did my 6 sides of paper before sallying out like a man. Stirling of Keir gave me a letter to a large merchant, who was indeed just going out to see a sick relative, told me to call again at one o'clock tomorrow. He thinks I'm a sort of actor and he's quite right too. I shall go and be very respectable and humble. It'll be good fun. What a fine state madam would be in to see the great and illustrious Titmarsh cap in hand to a fat cotton or rum spinner, MOI! Well, I think it's good fun, and am laughing, I think, quite sincerely at the joke. We all think too strong beer of ourselves, or our friends for us; Que diable! Cotton and rum are as good for a man as novels; shirts and punch first, and then the luxuries of literature.

In a later letter he announced:

I am going to dine with the fat merchant – a very kind and worthy old gentleman. He was anxious about a sick brother when I went to him, and never having heard of me from Adam, why should he do anything but beg me to call next day? However, he came himself next day, and read Stirling's introductory letter, and even talked about going to my lecture; but I said for God's Sake don't, my dear Sir; a good bottle of claret and an arm-chair are worth all the lectures in the world – and so, Madam, they are.

Five years after Thackeray's visit, the Kilmarnock-born poet Alexander Smith (1829–67), who began life as a lace pattern-maker, ending up as secretary to Edinburgh University after some years as a struggling man of letters, published 'A Boy's Poem'. These stanzas on Glasgow, extracted from the work, catch the feel of the industrial city surging towards its productive zenith better than most.

Sing, Poet, 'tis a merry world;
That cottage smoke is rolled and curled
    In sport, that every moss
Is happy, every inch of soil; –
Before *me* runs a road of toil
    With my grave out across.
Sing, trailing showers and breezy downs,
I knew the tragic heart of towns.

City! I am true son of thine;
Ne'er dwelt I where great mornings shine
    Around the bleating pens;
Ne'er by the rivulets I strayed,
And ne'er upon my childhood weighed
    The silence of the glens.
Instead of shores where ocean beats,
I hear the ebb and flow of streets.

Black Labour draws his weary waves
Into their secret-moaning caves;
    But with the morning light,
The sea again will overflow
With a long weary sound of soe,
    Again to faint in night.
Wave am I in that sea of woes;
Which, night and morning, ebbs and flows.

I dwelt within a gloomy court
Wherein did never sunbeam sport;
    Yet there my heart was stirr'd –
My very blood did dance and thrill,
When on my narrow window-sill,
    Spring lighted like a bird,
Poor flowers – I watched them pine for weeks,
With leaves as pale as human cheeks.

Afar, one summer, I was borne,
Through golden vapours of the morn,
        I heard the hills of sheep:
I trod with a wild ecstasy
The bright fringe of the living sea:
        And on a ruined keep
I sat, and watched an endless plain
Blacken beneath the gloom of rain.

O fair the lightly sprinkled waste,
O'er which a laughing shower has raced!
        O fair the April shoots!
O fair the woods on summer days,
While a blue hyacinthine haze
        Is dreaming round the roots!
In these, O City, I discern
Another beauty, sad and stern.

Draw thy fierce streams of blinding ore,
Smite on a thousand anvils, roar
        Down to the harbour-bars;
Smoulder in smoky sunsets, flare
On rainy nights, when street and square
        Lie empty to the stars.
From terrace proud to alley base
I know thee as my mother's face.

When sunset bathes thee in his gold,
In wreathes of bronze thy sides are rolled,
        Thy smoke is dusty fire;
And, from the glory round thee poured
A sunbeam like an angel's sword
        Shivers upon a spire.
Thus have I watched thee, Terror! Dream!
While the blue night crept up the stream.

The wild train plunges in the hills,
He shrieks across the midnight rills;
        Streams through the shifting glare,
The roar and flap of foundry fires,
That shake with light the sleeping shires;
        And on the moorlands bare,

He sees afar a crown of light
Hang o'er thee in the hollow night.

At midnight, when thy suburbs lie
As silent as a noonday sky,
    When larks with heat are mute,
    I love to linger on thy bridge,
    All lonely as a mountain ridge,
        Disturbed but by my foot;
While the black lazy stream beneath,
Steals from its far-off wilds of heath.

And through my heart, as through a dream,
Flows on that black disdainful stream;
    All scornfully it flows,
Between the huddled gloom of masts
Silent as pines unvexed by blasts –
'Tween lamps in streaming rows.
O wondrous sight! O stream of dread!
O long dark river of the dead!

Frédéric Chopin (1810–49) came to Britain from Paris in 1848. In London, where he found the fog 'depressing', he stayed in Piccadilly. He gave two recitals, 'which were evidently enjoyed', he recorded. The journey from London to Edinburgh took him twelve hours. After a day's rest in the Scottish capital, he moved to Calver House, the home of Lord Torpichen, whose wife was a sister of Jane Stirling, Chopin's pupil (to whom he dedicated one of his nocturnes) and who made all the travel arrangements.

The Stirlings of Keir had owned their property since the fifteenth century. The laird was at that time William Stirling-Maxwell, who had succeeded to the title and estates of his uncle, Sir John Maxwell of Pollok, then just outside Glasgow and now housing the Burrell Gallery.

Chopin gave his 'Matinée Musicale' in Glasgow's Merchants' House at 2.30 p.m. on Wednesday, 27 September. Dr James Hedderwick, owner of the *Evening Citizen* saw him thus:

A fragile-looking man in pale-grey frock coat suit, moving about the company, conversing with different groups, and occasionally consulting his watch, which seemed no bigger than an agate stone on the forefinger of an alderman. Beardless, fair of hair, thin and pale of face, his appearance was interesting and distinguished: and when, after a final glance at his miniature horloge, he ascended the platform and placed himself at the instrument, he at once commanded attention. It was a drawing-room recital, more *piano* than *forte*, though not without episodes of grandeur.

The author of *Uncle Tom's Cabin*, Harriet Beecher Stowe (1811–96) arrived in the city in 1852, but she felt unwell during much of her stay, especially inside the cathedral, where she complained of the 'strain upon the head and eyes', possibly caused by staring upwards at the shadowy beams of the roof.

Garibaldi (1807–82) came to Glasgow in 1864, recruiting volunteers to fight for the cause of a united Italy against the Papal States. Apparently he recruited not only men who were members of the Glasgow Italian community, but also quite a number of Irishmen.

D.L. Moody (1837–99) and I.A. Sankey (1840–1908), the evangelists, who specialized in tub-thumping hymn-tunes, descended upon Glasgow in 1874, invited by one Pastor D.I. Finlay, returning again in 1881 and 1882. After the first visit, lasting almost six months, when they held their services in a tent on Glasgow Green and occasionally in the City Hall, one correspondent to the *Glasgow Herald* declared that he had 'lived in salvation ever since' – whatever that may mean – claiming also that his 'head still thrills at the vivid memory of these colourful days'.

Joseph Conrad (1854–1924) came to Glasgow in 1898. A former master of several Scottish-owned ships, he suffered the curious disease known as 'writer's block' after publishing his early novels and so planned to return to sea. However, the command he hoped for did not materialize and his creative powers returned, enabling him to write the masterpieces by which he is best-known today.

A correspondent in the *Glasgow Herald* of 1903, noting the adverse account which many visitors left of the city, complained:

There was a period during which the comments of the furthest-come visitors were friendly – nay, flattering; thereafter, as Glasgow waxed fat and kicked herself clear of the mud of the Molendinar she rose from and strode east and west, our visitors became colder in their eulogies, till at last the 'Second City of the Empire' rarely finds a visitor to pay her the sort of compliment she hungers for. They admit her enterprise, her commercial importance, the worth of her example to all other municipalities; but when it comes to saying that she is beautiful and, as it were, kissing her, they beg to be excused, and recall an important engagement in Edinburgh. Whether we like it or not, all the world except the West of Scotland is apt to look on Glasgow as the Cinderella of cities . . . Our city is in the position of the 'homely' looking girl, who has plenty of praises for her baking of scones or her literary acuteness, but knows that these things, very difficult of acquirement, never in this world attract lovers as a pretty face will do that is the gift of nature. Whatever you, who are a citizen of Glasgow, may think in your heart of her on a dirty, foggy November day, when St Rollox stock is more mephite than usual, it is a different sentiment that stirs you when abroad, and the foreigner, polite in all else, flicks you on the raw with the offending remark – 'Glasgow, oh! Glasgow! A big city, very smoky and dirty, n'est-ce pas?' Politeness, indeed! A man might just as well criticise your mother.

It may have struck that anonymous writer that he was summing up a recent trend; but as long ago as 1842, Henry Cockburn (1779–1853), the judge Lord Cockburn (whose *Circuit Journeys* is one of the delights of reminiscent Scottish literature), while on the North Circuit, wrote:

> We must have manufacturing towns. But there is no necessity for their being made out of the ruins of natural beauty or of retreats of academic learning. Who can doubt that it would have been better for Scotland, and even for Glasgow, if trade and the loom had been encouraged to fasten their black claws on any other part of the Clyde, and had left Glasgow with its College, its Cathedral, its river, and its Green, alone.

Sarah Murray had been the first of the many travellers who have visited Scotland solely with the idea of writing about it. One of the most industrious and most widely read of such 'travellers with a purpose' was the Birmingham journalist Henry Vallam Morton (1892–1979), whose series of 'In Search Of' books were designed to evoke the atmosphere of the places he visited rather than provide mere statistical details.

How vivid, for instance, is his picture of Glasgow in a foggy November night, when the air was an acrid yellow before the belated passing of the 1993 Clean Air Act:

> The fog which has tickled the throat all day relents a little and hangs thinly over the city, so that each lamp casts an inverted V of light

downward on the pavement. The streets are full of light and life. Pavements are packed to the edge with men and women released from a day's work, anxious to squeeze a little laughter from the dark as they move against a hazy blur of lit windows in which lie cakes, watches, rings, motor-cars, silk gowns, and everything that is supposed to be worth buying.

The sound of Glasgow is a human chatter punctuated by tramcars – coloured in broad bands like Neapolitan ices – grating round a bend to Renfield Street. There is a sharp clamour of bells, the asthmatic cough of an express engine clearing its throat on the road to London, and most characteristic of all, the sudden yelp of a tug in a Clyde fog – the yelp of a terrier whose tail has been stepped on – as she noses her way down the narrow stream.

And the Glasgow crowds in perpetual and puzzling flux go, some home to flats in Pollokshaws and – wonderful name! – Crossmyloof, where the Queen of Scots once sat on a palfrey; some to take the astonishing meal of high tea which Glasgow's cafés and restaurants have elevated to the apex of the world's pyramid of indigestibility (for I still cannot believe that tea agrees with the fillet steak); some to dance for 3s. in surroundings for which we pay 30s. in London; some to the theatre; but most drift up and down the golden avenues until the last Neapolitan ice takes them home to Camlachie or Maryhill.

He was impressed, too, with the size of Glasgow and the endless contrasts it contained:

I am amazed by the apparent size of Glasgow. Her million and a quarter people are squeezed into a lesser space than that occupied by several other great cities, and this compression gives a feeling of immensity. You do not suddenly leave the main streets to plunge into dark and trackless valleys of the dead as you do in Birmingham, Manchester, and Liverpool. Here are miles of main streets, all wide, all marked by a certain grim and solid quality – shops as fine as any in Bond Street; clubs as reserved and Georgian as any in Pall Mall – and in a few yards you leave a street, in which you could spend £1,000 on something for a woman's throat, to enter a street, equally broad and as well lit, in which perhaps the most expensive thing is a cut from the sheep whose corpse hangs head down, its horns in blood and sawdust . . .

This meeting of extremes is characteristic of Glasgow. The splendour of riches and the abjectness of poverty, seen so close together, appear sharper than in most great cities. East and west ends run into one another in the most grotesque way. In London, for instance, crowds are local. You know exactly the kind of people you will see in Piccadilly or Oxford Street. You know that the Aldgate Pump to Strand crowd at night will never go the extra yard to Cockspur Street; just as the Piccadilly-Leicester Square crowd will never cross the invisible frontier of Charing Cross. In Glasgow there are no frontiers.

This gives a rich and exciting variety to the crowds. My eyes are held by the passing faces. Sooner or later in the Bond Streets of this city, with their business heads under the biggest assembly of bowler hats in Great Britain and their crowds of perfectly lovely, fresh young girls, I shall see the stooped shoulders of some ancient wreck, the insolent swing of a youth with a cap over his eyes, the slow walk of a hatless woman from a neighbouring tenement bearing, much as the kangaroo bears its young, a tiny face in the fold of a thick tartan shawl.

This close-togetherness of Glasgow is one of its most important features. It means that a million and a quarter people live nearer the heart of their city than in any other social phenomenon of this size. This, I believe, explains Glasgow's clean-cut individuality. There is nothing half-hearted about Glasgow. It could not be any other city.

Iain Hamilton (1920–86), one-time editor of the *Spectator*, began his journalistic career on the Glasgow staff of the *Daily Record* just after the end of World War II. In his book *Scotland the Brave* (1957) he recalls fondly the Glasgow of his youth:

Golden Glasgow: misty, clanging, flaring, tumultuous city, its deep streets overhung by red and grey cliffs pierced by thousands of gas-lit windows, strings of coolies shuffling through the litter on the pavements, drunks in the gutters, luxury in the shop-windows, hills at the end of every street, the smell of the sea coming up from the tideway between ranks of cranes and rotting tenements and bringing a breath of life to the dullest air in the meanest alley. It would have been impossible for me then to imagine a city more splendid than Glasgow, and I still count it today the most romantic city I have seen.

Cicely Hamilton (1872–1952) recorded the impressions of many European countries 'as seen by an Englishwoman'. In the *Modern Scotland* volume in her series (1937), she wrote at length of the city and its slum dwellers, yet maintained a curious semi-disapproval of attempts to relieve their condition:

By courtesy of the officials of the Public Health Department I was guided to one of Glasgow's notoriously insanitary streets and introduced into several of their typical dwellings. All the tenants, when questioned, confessed cheerfully to bugs and, judging by the state of some of the woodwork, rats were no strangers to their domiciles. Needless to say, these prize specimens of Glasgow slumdom had been condemned by the sanitary authority; their occupants, so soon as a clearance scheme was ready to receive them, would move to decent surroundings in the suburbs, and the evil-smelling tenements, left to their vermin, would fall to the pick of the housebreaker. In one domicile we visited, the pick of the housebreaker was already at work farther down the block that contained it; and the occupying family, packed and ready to depart, were only awaiting the arrival of the barrow which would convey their household goods to a new and more sanitary dwelling. Some of their household goods – their bedding – had already been removed by a sanitary inspector; it would be restored, at the new and clean abode, after due disinfection for vermin; they can be conveyed from house to house in other articles of furniture as well as in wearing apparel; hence it is the business of local health visitors to keep an eye on migrating families and urge them to special efforts in the way of watchfulness and cleanliness. The office of health visitor in slum and slum clearance districts must be anything but a sinecure; it stands to reason that men and women who have dwelt for years, perhaps all their lives, in the squalid surroundings of a Glasgow rookery are likely to need persevering instruction in the arts of domestic cleanliness; and it says much for the health visitor, as well as for the average ex-slum family, that the authors of a report, issued on completion of Glasgow's forty thousandth new house, are able to state that 'the response to the improved environment and better accommodation has been phenomenal, fully ninety per cent of the re-housed tenants in slum areas showing in every way a decided improvement.' The ten per cent residium, one concludes, must be borne with and, so far as possible, prevented from becoming a nuisance to their cleaner-living neighbours.

One little woman whom we called on in her slum would, I suspect, need a good deal of attention from the health visitor before she discarded the sluttish habits acquired in her years of squalor. She was a friendly little soul, with a sloping forehead and unwashed face, who, like most of her fellow slum-dwellers, seemed quite pleased to be called on; the mother of three grubby infants under school-age – one of them in arms, one old enough to stand and stare at us, one crawling on the unmade family bed where, in the unrestrained manner of infancy, it had recently obeyed a call of nature. There were two more absent at school, the mother told us; these latter presumably, being better clad and washed than their younger brethren – the education authority would see to that, providing at least the necessary footwear. A query with regard to the husband and father brought the all too frequent reply that he was out of work; the income that he and his family obtained from the public purse being thirty-nine shillings a week. Whereby, as in other like-situated households, one glimpsed a problem affecting more than Glasgow and Glasgow's slums; the problem of the man with no particular skill who may find himself, when at length he gets a job, little, if at all, better off as to money than when he draws his dole in idleness.

In that respect at least, things seem to have changed little.

It is almost as if she foresaw, a decade and a half before Drumchapel and Easterhouse, the problems of housing schemes built without a social infrastructure:

In all departments of modern urban life planning is an urgent necessity; urban life to-day is on too vast a scale to be left haphazard to its own unhindered growth, its own experimental devices. Like all human activities, however, planning, large-scale planning, has its drawbacks, whereof perhaps the chief is its tendency to monotony; municipal estates, by whatever city they may be erected – and along with their advantages of cubic space and modern convenience – are apt to suggest an atmosphere charged with dullness. It is not only the regimented look of the houses, set down neatly, according to plan; with no trace of individual taste or guidance, or adaptation to the varied needs of their owners. To the making of a beautiful city goes an element of growth, and there is no suggestion of growth about a housing scheme; it is a ready-made article, turned out of the municipal factory, and as such – in its beginnings at any rate – lacking in many of the daily interest and small excitements that diversify the day in the older quarters of a town. These older quarters may be shabby and insanitary, but in and around them are the interests and excitements of a life more varied than that of the regimented suburb; as a rule they are nearer than the regimented suburb to streets with a traffic or crowd and vehicle. Nearer also to shop windows, where variety of content is an antidote to street monotony and to another and valued variety of cheap places of amusement. In the new and sanitary estate, on the other hand, shops will be comparatively few and sometimes almost lacking – and as for a vista of lit window and display of fashion, that may mean a journey by bus. Then, in all likelihood, there will be small choice with regard to entertainment; one accessible cinema in lieu of half a dozen. And the streets themselves, being purely residential, will afford little interest in the way of passing traffic.

Women, it is obvious, will suffer more than men from the tedium of life on new suburban estates; stay-at-home women, that is to say, whose duties to their families confine them to their own neighbourhood. Men who leave home in the morning and return to it only when the day's work is over will be less irked by the blankness of their dormitory suburb. A friend of my own – a woman who was formerly a trade-union organizer – and with whom I once discussed this aspect of suburban housing schemes agreed and more than agreed with my views on the depressing effect of their monotony. She went so far as to designate one of the newest and tidiest of our London housing schemes as a set of little prisons for women! Well-appointed little prisons where a woman's sphere was indeed the home, since there was nothing to interest her outside it! While a woman doctor I met in Glasgow, whose acquaintance with slums and their tenants is extensive, also knew of cases where the occupants of well-found municipal dwellings regretted their insanitary streets. She told me of women who had been moved from that slummiest of Glasgow districts, Anderston, into subsidised dwellings, fitted with modern conveniences; but who, to her knowledge, were bent on deserting their clean spacious quarters and returning to Anderston's familiar squalor, so soon as they could find vacant room. What those who are seeking to do good to their fellows sometimes forget is that one man's meat is another man's poison, and the hardships of one type of mind, the pleasurable comforts of another; it is probably no more than a minority of our countrymen who object to noise as a daily accompaniment of life, and although to some of us privacy is an absolute need, others delight in close-huddling and find privacy hard to endure.

John R. Allan (1907–86), author of that Aberdeenshire classic *Farmer's Boy*, described another aspect of pre-war Glasgow just a year after Cecily Hamilton was writing. Allan was sketching a Glasgow portrait for *Scotland – 1938*:

Once on a November afternoon I was walking along Buchanan Street about half past four o'clock. It was a busy day; hundreds of fashionable women were trafficking among the shops and the business men were returning from or going to the coffee-rooms. There was an atmosphere of money and well-being, the sort of thing that makes you feel pleased with yourself as long as you have a few shillings in your own pocket. Then a procession came up the street, with blood-red banners, that swayed menacingly under the misty lights. These should have driven the women screaming into the basements of the shops for they bore legends in praise of Moscow, warnings about the wrath to come. 'Communists', the word flew along the pavements. But no one screamed. The men that carried the flags were broken beyond violence by the prolonged misery of unemployment and could not sustain the menace of the legends. The ladies in the fur coats could look without fear on the procession, for it was not the first stroke of revolt but another triumph of law and order. A dozen constables were shepherding the marchers, and they were such fine big men and stepped along with such manly dignity that they themselves were the procession. The unemployed seemed to have no community with such banners, such splendid constables, and they may have known it, for they walked without any spirit, as if they realised they had no place in society, not even in their demonstration against it. The procession turned into George Square. The unemployed dismissed and went home wearily to their bread and margarine. The constables eased their uniform pants and went off to the station with property and privilege resting securely on their broad shoulders. It was just another Glasgow afternoon.

Then some months later I was looking out from the window of a coffee-house in Argyle Street about seven o'clock of a Saturday evening. I heard fife music; then a procession came out from St Enoch's Square. It was a company of Orangemen, or some such Protestants, in full uniform, back from an excursion in the country. They passed, an army terrible with banners, and comic, as men that have a good excuse for dressing up. They had just gone by when a new music came up to us and a new procession appeared, coming from Queen Street Station. They were Hibernians, or some other Catholic order, also returning from a day in the country; terrible and comic also, after the fashion of their kind. Orangemen and Hibernians! We said to ourselves. What will happen if they forgather? Being wise youths and having some pleasure on hand, we did not follow to see. But we met a man sometime later that night who swore he had been present. The Hibernians, he said, discovered that the Orangemen were in front, so they quickened their pace. The Orangemen, hearing also, slackened theirs. Some resourceful and sport-

ing policemen diverted both parties into a side street and left them to
fight it out. After half an hour, when all the fighters had thoroughly dis-
organised each other, bodies of police arrived, sorted the wounded from
the winded and despatched them to their proper destinations in ambu-
lances and plain vans. That is the story as it was told to me and I cannot swear that it is true in every detail; but it might have happened in
Glasgow that way, and I doubt if it could have happened in any other
town. Such incidents give Glasgow afternoons and evenings their distinctive flavour.

Some years ago an *Observer* journalist, Edward Mace, noticed that:

Glasgow taxi-drivers help you with your luggage and you can hardly
believe that you are in a British Rail terminal at Central Station, the
absence of squalor being unnerving . . . A streamer on the City Chambers
alleges that its MILES BETTER IN GLASGOW, a dig, I take it, at Edinburgh,
now relegated to being no more than an old stick-in-the-mud . . . There's

George Square in 1870, before the erection of Young's City Chambers building and
when most of the buildings were still hotels

nothing to touch Edinburgh's Georgian glory, or, if there is, not obvious-ly, because Glasgow is an Industrial Revolution phoenix with appropriate architecture, overbearing at first sight, until much delectable detail, now revealed as the result of cleaning, suggests that the citizens, though out-wardly slow, may not have been just the tight-fisted, severe Covenanters it suited their purpose to make themselves out to be.

Furthermore, the city is perched dead centre of fine surroundings and sights, like a cock on a midden. Great estates and fine mansions are ten-a-penny. There's the sweet delight of Loch Lomond where you can hear what silence once sounded like. And a rich profusion of gardens . . . Culturally, Glasgow's a freak, having achieved the seemingly impossible and opened a new art gallery . . .

And how do I myself remember Glasgow? Going in winter to chil-dren's parties in horse-drawn cabs, with the cabbies, in black coats to which age seemed to have given a patina of faint green, flapping their arms across their chests to keep warm, while they waited for their fares to come down the stairs of the party home, their breath, like that of the horse, curling visibly as it thinned into the cold air. Ice blocks decanted into MacAndrew's Byres Road fish shop and Miss MacAndrew, hands blue with cold, soon after setting out the slippery fish on the broken-down ice scattered over the marble shop-front counter. The daily hilly walk up Great George Street, along Hillhead Street and down Glasgow Street to the Glasgow Academy. The squeal of tramcars round curves and the humiliation aboard one when my mother made me spit on my handkerchief to wipe a smut from my face. Going to Auchenshuggle and other less enticingly named places on the top deck of a tram on a Saturday afternoon with my Uncle John (called Doan because I had so christened him as a child when I could-n't say John). The clean smell of the Irish butter and egg shop, or the Maypole dairy, both in Byres Road, as the shop assistant slapped and shaped a small piece off a huge round into a lined oblong for wrapping up and handing over the counter. Mr and Mrs George Todd, both large, both immensely kind, the one running the fruit shop on one side of Byres Road, the other the flower shop across the way. Wilkie, the grocer, sharp-eyed and alert in his brown apron as he made up orders amidst the scent of nameless spices. Colquhoun, the baker, where half-penny morning rolls and twopenny mutton pies came from and with an upstairs tearoom where we occasionally ate twopenny French cakes as a special treat. Murray's by the subway, a little slot of a shop where

272

An aerial view of Park Circus, the centrepiece of one of Glasgow's outstanding
conservation areas

you pushed your money across piles of folded newspapers and got, in return, halfpenny bars of chocolate. Bell, the toyshop, visited inside only on special occasions but more frequently window-shopped. Patterson, the shoe shop, smelling of patent leather.

Comedian Billy Connolly, writing in the *Sunday Times* in October 1986, perhaps provides the right note on which to end this gallimaufry, this affectionate final tribute of an octogenarian Glasgow poet to his native city: 'The time for trumpet-blowing and naïve pleas for recognition has long gone. If you are lucky enough to have been born there, or smart enough to wish to be there, then the time has come to be quietly pleased.'

Bibliography

Anderson, J.R., *Provosts of Glasgow from 1609 to 1832* (1947)

Annan, T., *Old Closes and Streets of Glasgow* (photographic prints) new edn (1977)

Baynham, W., *Glasgow Stage* (Forrester, 1892)

Bell, J.J., *The Glory of Scotland* (Harrap, 1932)

Berry, S. & Whyte, H. (eds) *Glasgow Observed: A Documentary Anthology 1771–1986* (Donald, 1987)

Brogan, C., *The Glasgow Story* (1952)

Browning, A.S.F., *History of Clyde Shipbuilding* (Argyll, 1991)

Burgess, M., *The Glasgow Novel*, 3rd edn (2000)

Butt, John, *The Industrial Archaeology of Scotland* (David & Charles, 1967)

Cage, R.A., (ed.), *The Working Class in Glasgow, 1750–1914* (1987)

Cairncross, A.K., *The Scottish Economy* (CUP, 1954)

Campbell, Duncan, *Billy Connolly: The Authorized Version* (Pan, 1976)

Chalmers, A.K., *The Health of Glasgow* (1930)

Chambers, R., *The Picture of Scotland* (1827)

Checkland, S.G., *The Upas Tree* (University of Glasgow, 1976)

Cleland, J., *Annals of Glasgow*, 2 vols (Hedderwick, 1816)

——*Description of the City of Glasgow*, 2nd edn (1816)

——*Rise and Progress of the City of Glasgow* (1820)

Conn, Stewart, *New and Selected Poems* (1987)

Cowan, R.M.W., *The Newspaper in Scotland: 1815–1959* (1959)

Craig, C. (ed.), *History of Scottish Literature*, vol. 4 (Aberdeen University Press, 1988)

Cunnison, J., & Gilfillan, J.B.S., *Glasgow: Third Statistical Account* (1820)

Devine, T.H., *Tobacco Lords c. 1770–1790* (Donald, 1978)

Doak, A.M. and Young, A., *Glasgow at a Glance: An Architectural Handbook*, rev. edn (Hale, 1977)

Duckworth, C.L.D. & Languir, G.E., *Clyde, River and Other Steamers*, 3rd edn (Brown, Son & Ferguson, 1972)

Eyre-Todd, George, *Glasgow Poets*, 2nd edn (Hodge, 1903)

Fisher, Joe, *The Glasgow Encyclopedia* (Mainstream, 1994)

Gallagher, T., *The Uneasy Peace: Religious Tension in Modern Scotland* (1987)

Gibb, A., *Glasgow: The Making of a City* (1903)

Gibson, J., *The History of Glasgow* (Chapman & Duncan, 1777)

Glasgow Style, 1890–1920 (Glasgow District Council, 1984)

Gomme, A. & Walker, D., *Architecture of Glasgow*, rev. edn (Lund Humphries, 1987)

Hanley, Cliff, *Dancing in the Streets* (Hutchinson, 1958)

House, Jack, *Pavement in the Sun* (1967)

——*Music Hall Memories* (Drew, 1986)

Hume, John, *Industrial Archaeology of Glasgow* (Blackie, 1974)

Kellas, J., *The Scottish Political System* (Cambridge University Press, 1975)

Kellet, J.R., *Glasgow: A Concise History* (1967)

——*The Impact of Railways on Victorian Cities* (Routledge & Kegan Paul, 1969)

Kinchon, P., *Tea and Taste: The Glasgow Tea-rooms 1875–1975* (White Cockade, 1991)

Leisure in the Parks (Glasgow District Council, 1980)

Lindsay, M., *Clyde Waters* (1952)

——*Glasgow*, 3rd edn (Hale, 1989)

——*History of Scottish Literature*, rev. edn (Hale, 1992)

——*Collected Poems 1940–90* (Aberdeen University/Mercat, 1991)

Lockhart, J.G., *Peter's Letters to his Kinsfolk* (Blackwood, 1819)

MacGeorge, A., *Old Glasgow* (1880)

MacGregor, G., *History of Glasgow: From the Earliest Period to the Present Time* (1881)

MacKenzie, P., *Glasgow Characters: Memoirs and Portraits of One*

Hundred Glasgow Men, 2 vols (1857, 1881)

——*Old Reminiscences and Remarkable Characters of Glasgow* (Forrester, 1875)

MacLennan, D. & Gibb, A., *No Mean City to Miles Better* (housing study, undated)

M'Carra, K., *Scottish Football* (1984)

McKean, C. et al, *Central Glasgow* (1989)

McRorie, I., *Clyde Pleasure Steamers* (1985)

Morgan, Edwin, *Collected Poems* (Carcanet, 1990)

Muir, J.H. (James and Muirhead Bone) *Glasgow in 1901* (1901)

Oakley, C.A., *Our Illustrious Forebears* (Blackie, 1980)

——*The Second City*, 4th edn (Blackie, 1990)

——*The Last Tram* (Corporation of the City of Glasgow, 1962)

Phillips, A., *Glasgow Herald: Two Hundred Years of a Newspaper, 1783–1983* (Drew, 1983)

Power, William, *My Scotland* (1934)

Purser, John, *History of Scottish Music* (1992)

Rafferty, J., *One Hundred Years of Scottish Football* (Pan, 1973)

Reid, J.M., *History of the Merchants' House of Glasgow* (undated)

Reid, P., (ed.) *The Forming of the City* (1993)

Riddell, John F., *Clyde Navigation – A History of the Development and Deepening of the River Clyde* (Donald, 1979)

Royle, T., *Companion to Scottish Literature* (Mainstream, 1993)

Scottish Railway Locomotives (Glasgow Corporation, 1967)

Slaven, A., *The Development of the West of Scotland* (1975)

Smout, T.C., *A Century of the Scottish People, 1830–1950* (Collins, 1986)

Stamp, Gavin & McKinstry, Sam (eds), *'Greek' Thomson*, 2nd edn (1999)

Stewart, I.C., *Glasgow Tramcar* (1983)

Strang, J., *Glasgow and Its Clubs* (1864)

Swan, Joseph, *Select Views of Glasgow and the Environs* (1828)

University of Glasgow Through Five Centuries (Glasgow University, 1979)

Walker, F.M., *Song of the Clyde: A History of Clyde Shipbuilding* (1984)

Whyte, Hamish, *Mungo's Tongues: Glasgow Poems 1950–75* (Mainstream, 1993)

——*Noise and Smoky Breath: An Illustrated Anthology of Glasgow Poems 1900-1983* (Third Eye, 1986)

——(ed. with Simon Berry), *Glasgow Observed* (1987)

Worsdall, F., *The Tenement: A Way of Life* (Drew, 1979)

——*Victorian City* (Drew, 1982)

——*The City that Disappeared* (Drew, 1961)

Index

Numbers in italic type refer to illustrations in the text